The
Boys of
Benning

Stories From The Lives Of Fourteen Infantry OCS Class 2-62 Graduates

Co-editors:
Dan Telfair, Zia Telfair, Thomas B. Vaughn

authorHOUSE®

AuthorHouse™
1663 Liberty Drive
Bloomington, IN 47403
www.authorhouse.com
Phone: 1-800-839-8640

Published by AuthorHouse 2/28/2013

ISBN: 978-1-4817-1712-0 (sc)
ISBN: 978-1-4817-1710-6 (hc)
ISBN: 978-1-4817-1711-3 (e)

Cover photograph by Gary Love of ProPhoto, Fort Benning, GA

Library of Congress Control Number: 2013902817

As you read the chapters of *The Boys of Benning*, you will find the book could well be titled "The Best of Benning." These stories show what men of grit, determination, and loyalty to this country can do. From all walks of life they came together; and OCS was the crucible of stress and competition that helped forge the steel that made these men. They personify what their families, friends, the U.S. Army, and the USA can look to with pride.

As the First Platoon Tactical Officer, it was an honor to serve with these true patriots.

DOUG FINGLES
LTC, U.S. ARMY, RETIRED.

The Boys of Benning touches me in a profound way because it reminds me of my growing-up years having my father's WW II buddies and their families visit us, and traveling around the country visiting several of them. It highlights a group of men brought together from various backgrounds who served and sacrificed for our country during some of its most difficult times. The bond created among them can never be broken, and they have gone on to serve our nation and our communities with distinction and honor long after their military service.

ANDREA LAWRENCE
PRESIDENT, TENNESSEE FISHER HOUSE FOUNDATION

The Boys of Benning highlights the lives of fourteen graduates of a 1962 Infantry Officer Candidate School Class. And what remarkable lives they have been-and continue to be! For them, the arduous OCS experience was a defining, life-changing experience. It forged their values, by which they have conducted themselves with distinction and honor ever since.

These "Boys of Benning" went on to become outstanding leaders-in and out of the military. They personify the high ideals of Duty-Honor-Country. We would all do well to emulate them in our professional and personal lives. We would all do well to share this book-this insightful story-with our children and grandchildren!

JANICE BOWLING
STATE SENATOR, TENNESSEE GENERAL ASSEMBLY

I consider *The Boys of Benning* an important book for current and coming generations as both an inspirational and historic document. True heroes have a built-in reticence when it comes to expressing and sharing their experiences of valor and bravery.

These soldiers will leave behind battleground tales untold. However, this book will give you a true insight into the kind of person who serves our country and who is in turn molded and influenced for the rest of a meaningful life. I heartily recommend *The Boys of Benning*.

JACK WHITE, CHAIRMAN, BOB WHITE MUSIC, INC.
DIRECTOR OF CHAPLAINS FOR LEGACY HOSPICE, INC.

Table of Contents

Dedication

This book, *The Boys of Benning*, is dedicated to four of our Officer Candidate School classmates lost in battle. All served our country in the Republic of Vietnam, and all died in combat there.

Rest in Peace:
Captain Bob Hoop, KIA, RVN, May 13, 1968
Major Jerry Laird, KIA, RVN, January 22, 1969
Captain Ron Van Regenmorter, KIA, RVN, March 17, 1967
Captain Barry Zavislan, KIA, RVN, March 6, 1967

Preface

These are the stories of graduates of Infantry Officer Candidate School Class 2-62, a class that graduated on March 30, 1962 at Fort Benning, Georgia, just as Vietnam was about to become a household word across the United States. Of the 238 aspiring officers who reported to the 52nd Company in early October 1961, only 119 endured and survived the trials and tribulations of OCS and graduated as second lieutenants. Of those, fourteen have chosen to share their stories.

Upon graduation from the "Fort Benning School for Boys," the somewhat pejorative nickname for Infantry OCS, "The Boys of Benning" would go on to make their respective marks, on the military, and on society, far beyond the military milieu.

The stories told here are remarkable in their diversity, from those who remained "with the colors" for full and fulfilling careers, to those who served for a time, then left the Army for civilian careers. Despite that diversity, we all share a common bond, forged in the crucible of Infantry OCS Class 2-62. That experience molded us into a "band of brothers," whose friendship, loyalty, respect, and trust transcend time, distance and circumstance.

Just how transcendent our common bond has become was on full display on March 30, 2012, when twenty-one alumni gathered at the National Infantry Museum in Columbus, Georgia for our 50th Anniversary Reunion. In that fitting place, the years melted away as "soldiers once and young," now old and gray, renewed and strengthened our common bond.

The idea for this book grew out of that historic reunion, and a collective desire to document our stories, not for fame and fortune, but for families and friends. If this book gains a wider audience, we will all be pleasantly surprised.

Although *The Boys of Benning* chronicles the lives and times of our writers, before, during, and way after OCS, we make no claim for a definitive history of the seven-plus decades our stories encompass. Instead, we will settle for reflective reminiscences, military and civilian, that each of us has found worthy of sharing.

That said, "No man is an island," and each of our lives was touched indelibly by foreign and domestic events and issues far beyond our ken. From the Bay of Pigs fiasco and the Cuban missile crisis to the Berlin Wall, Vietnam War, and the assassination of President John F. Kennedy, his brother Bobby, and Martin Luther King Jr., we lived through tumultuous times, most of them against the backdrop of the Cold War. We saw the Berlin Wall go up in 1961, and come crashing down in 1989. We also witnessed the rise and demise of our principal Cold War foe, the Soviet Union. We learned way too late that Vietnam was more about nationalism than communism, and that China has become communist in the abstract, but with a penchant for capitalism in practice, to include investing in and lending to the good old USA.

In short, the recollections shared within these pages are gifts from the head and the heart, from men who have led lives of distinction and honor. They deserve sharing and preserving.

THOMAS B. VAUGHN
COLONEL, US ARMY, (RETIRED)
CO-EDITOR

Acknowledgements

The fourteen authors of the chapters that follow, each story covering over seventy years of their lives, have debts of gratitude to far too many people to possibly acknowledge. However, each owes a tremendous debt to one man, Colonel (retired) Bill Hadly. Then Captain Hadly was the 52nd OCS Company Commander who led us through one of the most challenging periods of our lives, and prepared us for all that followed. It is fitting that his story should lead into the chapters that follow.

Captain (later Colonel) Bill Hadly, Plain of Reeds,
Vinh Long Province, Vietnam, 1963.

Prior to Commanding 52nd OCS Company, Class 2-62

After graduating from West Point in June 1955, I was assigned to the Basic Infantry Officer's Course (BIOC) at Fort Benning. I stayed at Fort Benning after BIOC and completed the Airborne and Ranger courses before being assigned to the 38th Infantry Regiment, 2nd Division at Fort Lewis, Washington. I arrived there in the spring of 1956 and was assigned as Platoon Leader of the 105 Recoilless Rifle Platoon and later as a Battalion Communications Officer. I was married to Jane Grassman in July of 1957.

That summer, I received orders to Berlin, Germany with a stopover at Fort Benning for Communications School. In Berlin I was assigned to Company D, 6th Infantry Regiment as Mortar Platoon Leader. Eventually the Regiment was reorganized into the 2nd and 3rd Battle

Groups and I remained in the 2nd BG. I became the Honor Guard Platoon Leader and an Assistant S-3. One of my duties was to command the guard at Spandau where Rudolf Hess and Baldur von Schirach were imprisoned after the Nuremberg trials following WWII. (We rotated between the Russians and British.) While with the 2nd BG, I earned the Expert Infantryman's Badge.

To OCS

In the summer of 1960, I received orders to the Advanced Infantry Course at Fort Benning. After graduation I was assigned to the Officer Candidate School Battalion; first to 51st Company as XO and then as Commander of 52nd Company.

This assignment was an awesome responsibility. We were molding the future backbone of the leadership of the Infantry. War was looming in SE Asia and the life and death of these future officers and their men rested in our hands. I have many memories of the training we went through, but I remember vividly a field exercise in the bitter cold winter. The previous OCS Company to undergo this exercise had suffered several cases of frostbite. This was preventable, but it required vigilance and knowing and caring for your troops. I had a death in my family, but because of the seriousness of assuring our OCS men did not suffer frostbite, I cancelled my emergency leave so I could go to the field with the troops. As it turned out we did not suffer any cases of frostbite. This, after all, was what we were trying to instill in our OCS candidates; leading soldiers in dangerous situations.

After 52nd Company

That spring (1962), I received orders to South Vietnam as part of the initial group of advisors sent there by President Kennedy. After training in a Materiel and Training Assistance (MATA) course at Fort Bragg, I was assigned to a short course in the Vietnamese language at the Presidio of Monterey, California.

When I arrived in Vietnam, I was assigned as a Vietnamese Ranger Trainer at Trung Lap (near Cu Chi). We trained small RVN units; first of squad size, then platoon. Our major training device was patrolling.

Five or six days a week, we would take these small units out on patrol; first in the daylight and then at night. We had enemy contact often during the day and almost every night. It turned out that Trung Lap sits on top of the vast tunnel system going through the Cu Chi District, which can be visited by tourists today.

In October of 1962, I received word that my father had died and I tried to return for his funeral, but I was too late. When I got back to Vietnam, an urgent requirement for an Airborne Advisor had just occurred, and I was asked if I wanted the assignment. I was due to go to Vung Tao, a resort-like area for Ranger Individual Training, since my assignment to Trung Lap was considered so dangerous. I immediately accepted the airborne assignment and began an intense airborne refresher training course that was completed just prior to Tet 1962. The 7th RVN Airborne Battalion was stationed at the airbase at Bien Hoa, for which they had a defense mission. However, since the Airborne Brigade was the Strategic National Force, we were seldom at our home base. I participated in two combat parachute jumps; one near Tay Ninh, where we routed a regiment of NVA, and the second in the Plain of Reeds.

I was wounded on that operation by stepping on an anti-personnel mine after contact with VC forces. I was evacuated by an ARVN helicopter in a coma to the Saigon morgue. There were several dead and wounded ARVN soldiers on the medevac helicopter, and I suppose the morgue was where they separated the dead from the wounded.

Eventually, I was hospitalized at the USAF dispensary at Tan Son Nhut Airbase. A few days later, I left the hospital without authorization, and with a cast from my toes to my hip. My driver took me to my battalion which was starting a defensive mission at a pacified village. A couple of weeks later, my chain of command caught up with me and returned me to a hospital in Saigon. From there, I was evacuated to Walter Reed.

I spent the next four years at West Point in the Admissions office rehabilitating my injured leg and foot. Since I was the first graduate returning from Vietnam, I was asked to give talks to the cadets and many civic organizations throughout New York State. I took up handball and racquetball and in the evenings after work, drove down to NYC to get a master's degree from Columbia University.

In 1966-67, after my assignment at West Point, I attended Command and General Staff College at Fort Leavenworth. Upon graduation, I volunteered for Vietnam. Initially I was assigned to the 2nd Field Force Vietnam (IIFFV) in Intelligence where I ran the ground reconnaissance effort. Just prior to Tet 1968, as I was promised, I was assigned as the S-3, 4th/47th Infantry, 9th Infantry Division, on the Riverine mission out of Dong Tam.

During this tour, I was awarded the Bronze Star for valor for saving several soldiers trapped by the VC at their river drop off point, by piloting a "Boston Whaler" under heavy enemy fire to rescue them and to recover a couple of bodies. On another occasion, I rescued some women and children from a burning building in no-man's land during a fire fight.

After my second Vietnam tour, I was assigned to the Pentagon, first to Deputy Chief of Staff for Personnel, and then to the Office of the Chief of Staff. Toward the end of this assignment, I volunteered again and was assigned to be a Battalion Commander in Vietnam, but the orders were cancelled as the war was winding down. Instead, I was assigned as Commander of the 2nd/16th, 1st Infantry Division, at Fort Riley. We deployed on Reforger exercises twice and my command was extended to two years. After that assignment, I attended the Naval War College in Newport, Rhode Island and was then assigned to the Southeast Asia Task Force (SEATAF) in Vicenza, Italy. My first job was as Deputy G2/G3 and then as G1. While there I was promoted to full colonel. Our area of operations covered Italy, Greece and Turkey, and included our US manned nuclear weapons sites in those 3 countries, a Logistical Command in Pisa, and an Airborne Battalion at Vicenza. While at SEATAF, I won the senior men's championship in handball, racquetball and badminton.

By the time I departed SEATAF, I had decided to retire, as my six children were starting college and I needed additional funds to support them. I was required to spend one year before I retired in 1979 at the Army War College at Carlisle Barracks, PA. I had served four years at West Point as a cadet and twenty-four years of active duty. My decorations included two Legion of Merits, five Bronze Stars (one for valor), two Meritorious Service Medals, one Air Medal, five Army Commendation Medals (one for valor), and the Purple Heart.

Retirement and Civilian Life

I took employment at SRI International in Menlo Park, CA. It is the largest not-for-profit research company in the world. My job was to take SRI's innovative research to military and commercial customers and integrate it into their field operations. As an adjunct, I would bring technical problems from customers to be solved by SRI researchers. I established an organization called Center for Technology Transfer and Integration (CTTI), and over the years had small organizations at many military bases and commercial sites. As examples, we transitioned computers into tactical operations at Fort Bragg and assisted Sprint at their site in Kansas City. After almost twenty years, I retired again. Meanwhile, all of my six children had graduated from college. Five of the six have master's degrees and one, who is a professor at Stanford, has a Ph.D.

Following my second retirement, we moved to Montana and built a large home on ten acres fronting the Flathead River. I enjoyed fly fishing and hikes in the magnificent Glacier area as well as golf at several local courses. Our children and eleven grandchildren came to visit to enjoy the two ski areas in the winter and boating on the Flathead River in the summer. It was simply beautiful in the summer and fall but was cold and overcast in the winters much of the time.

Colonel (Retired) Bill Hadly and Jane, his wife of 55 years, at their home in Tucson, 2012.

In 2005, we sold our house and moved to our present home in

Tucson. Soon after moving here, in June of 2006, our oldest son died of a heart attack in Dallas. All of our other children and grandchildren are healthy and getting on with their lives. Jane and I enjoy visiting them. We spend a lot of time traveling to Texas, California, and Washington. We have also traveled quite a bit outside of the Continental United States, visiting Ireland and Israel and cruising to Alaska and the Antarctic. For some time, I have been volunteering at a homeless shelter, taking meals to shut-ins and taking disabled people to appointments and shopping. This is somewhat dependent on my health. I also golf and take daily walks when I can.

The Graduates

Colonel Rudy Baker, XVIII Airborne Corps, COSCOM
Chief of Staff, Fort Bragg, NC, 1984.

The Early Days

I was born on March 26, 1936 in Johnston County, North Carolina, east of the small town of Four Oaks. We lived on a dirt road in a one-room house. The house had no glass windows, only wooden shutters. The day I was born it had snowed so much the doctor could not get to the house. I was delivered by a midwife. When the doctor arrived the next day, all was well. However, my mom and dad could not agree on a name, so the doctor left and recorded my birth as "Baby Baker." That would become an issue years later when I applied for OCS. Mom and Dad finally agreed to name me Rudolph, with no middle name. I finally learned to stop all the questions about the middle name by telling folks we were so poor we could not afford a middle name. It must have been true, because my next brother also had only one name.

We were like most tenant farmer families (share croppers) in that part of eastern North Carolina. Our family worked long, hard hours, but managed to survive. I was the oldest of five boys born to Jay G.

and Lizzie C. Baker. I have always been fond of saying I was the oldest, meanest and ugliest, so no one should mess with me. It was a hard life, but we always had plenty to eat, mostly raised on the farm. It is difficult for some to believe today that our family did not have running water in the house. We used an outhouse and drew our wash water from a well. Mom did the family wash in a tub and hung the clothes on a line to dry. The first real shower I ever had was when I joined the Army.

I was actually working in the tobacco field, pulling bottom suckers, before I started school. There were no kindergarten classes, just grades one through twelve in a single building. When I started to school, we walked about a mile up a path to the school bus stop located on a dirt road. Then it was a fifteen-mile ride to the school. My elementary grades were in Four Oaks School.

School was a lot of fun, just to get away from work at the farm. I always did well academically. However, I was small and often got in fights at school or on the school bus. By the time I reached high school I had learned that I was too little to fight and too short-winded to run, so I needed to try to get along with most folks.

My nature was to have a quick temper and my dad and I were never close, so at the age of fourteen, I left home. My Uncle Henry let me live with him and help on the farm he tended. His one stipulation was that I must continue to go to school if I lived with him. I attended Wilson Mills High School during that time. I have been accused of having a little wild streak back then. My cousin and I borrowed his older brother's 1940 Mercury Coupe and hauled a load of moonshine whiskey to Maryland one weekend. Of course I could not drive, but I could help load, and I needed to make some poolroom money.

After a year of that, my mother came to me and asked me to come back home. I moved back and stayed until I graduated from high school. One valuable lesson our dad taught all of us boys was that when the crops were harvested, the first thing you did was pay all bills, and if there was any money left, you bought shoes and clothes. If no money was left, then you got a second job to buy what was needed. I have known my dad to work the "green end" of a saw mill all winter to make ends meet until he could put in the next crop.

As a share cropper, my dad would never live at one location more than three years, and most of the time it was only one year. The moves were always within Johnston County though, so I only attended three different schools: Four Oaks, Wilson Mills and Selma. I graduated from Selma High School on May 24, 1954.

Following high school, I was accepted to attend North Carolina State University in Raleigh. As the summer progressed, it became obvious that the conditions of the crops would not provide any money for college. On a Friday afternoon in July 1954, after cropping tobacco all week, I stopped at the end of a row, threw my straw hat on the ground, put my foot on it, turned to my dad and said, "I quit." Dad looked at me and said, "You can't quit; you own three acres of this tobacco." My response was something to the effect that he could have the three acres and whatever it would bring.

How I Ended Up in the Army

A cousin of mine lived in High Point, North Carolina and worked in a furniture factory. He was home that weekend and told me he could get me a job there if I wanted to go home with him. That sounded better than the tobacco patch, so off I went. True to his word, on Monday he took me to work with him, and a few hours later I was working in the factory. Friday evening when we left work, I had sawdust in my hair, nose, ears, and eyes. I looked at my cousin and told him, "Pick up my check on payday because I am not going back."

The next week, I looked for a job, but couldn't find one. On July 20, 1954, I visited the recruiting offices in High Point. I stopped at the Navy recruiting office and there was a sign on the door, "Be back in one hour." I waited patiently on a bench outside the office for one hour. The Navy recruiter didn't show up, so I did the next logical thing (at least to me at the time). I went across the hall and joined the Army.

Rude Awakening

It was a long bus ride from Raleigh, North Carolina to Fort Jackson, South Carolina. After being served a "breakfast" at about 1:00AM (I know the roll would have dented the wall if it had been thrown at it), we were allowed to sleep until 5:00AM. Then the rat race began; new clothes, boots, haircuts, etc. I threw the old shirt and slacks away because I could not afford to ship them home and civilian clothes were prohibited. Little did I realize that seven years later I would return to the Reception Center as the NCOIC of the night shift.

Three days later, while doing pushups in the sand on Tank Hill, I thought, "Son, what have you gotten yourself into this time?" However there was no quitting. Basic Training proceeded as it always has and always will, and at the end of the eight weeks, I had gone from weighing 117 pounds, soaking wet, to 135. Then it was time for orders to Advanced Individual Training (AIT). I thought I had enlisted to go to a diesel mechanics school. This was the first time a naïve eighteen-year-old country boy learned that "If you ain't got it in writing, you ain't got it." My next assignment was to Fort Leonard Wood, Missouri, better known as "Little Korea." There was only one brick building on the entire installation. After another eight weeks of training in the Combat Engineers, I was awarded a 117 MOS (that is one pick, one shovel, seven days a week). I had also managed to gain up to 160 pounds and remained within 5 to 10 pounds of that weight for over 30 years, except when I returned from Vietnam at about 125.

Enlisted Assignments

As part of a "carrier company," 150 of us set sail from Camp Kilmer, NJ to Germany for assignment to the 299th Combat Engineer Battalion. I lost ten pounds in twelve days crossing the Atlantic. We arrived in the 299th Battalion area on Christmas Eve, 1954. I think everyone except the cadre designated to get us settled was drunk. I was fortunate in this assignment and went from private to staff sergeant (E-5) in 25 months from my date of enlistment. There were no buck sergeants at that time.

There were two incidents that I recall especially about this tour. The first happened when the Army came out with the Specialist grades. I was promoted to Sp3 (E-4). Specialists were not allowed to hold leadership positions, but corporals at grade E-4 were noncommissioned officers and held leadership positions. A good friend of mine (I thought) by the name of Marco, was promoted to corporal. After his promotion, he became a tough guy to deal with. I caught every dirty detail he could find for me. Unfortunately for him, a few months later I was promoted to SSG (E-5) and the detail business was reversed. When I left to come home in June 1957, Corporal Marco was still performing details.

The other incident that taught me to always do your job well occurred in the woods. Early in the morning an individual approached our perimeter and did not give the password. We put him in the front-leaning-rest position for several minutes until we could confirm he was in fact a major, the Battalion XO. His last comment to me was, "Sergeant, I will see you a corporal tomorrow." Needless to say, I got to my Company Commander as soon as possible. The CO told me not to worry. I never heard anything else, but I did see the former major in the battalion area a few weeks later wearing NCO stripes. A Reduction in Force (RIF) had caught up with him.

When I returned to the United States, I left the Army. I soon found though that available jobs were limited. I could go back to the tobacco patch or drive a dump truck for $40 a week. Neither appealed to me, so after seventy-six days, I reenlisted with my same rank. Assignment as the Admin NCO for the Raleigh Recruiting Main Station followed.

At about the end of two years at the Recruiting Station, the Army came out with proficiency pay of $30 per month for MOS 121 (Combat Engineer NCO). My MOS had not been changed, so off I went to the 70th Combat Engineer Battalion, Fort Campbell, Kentucky. During the remainder of my three-year enlistment, I served as an Engineer Squad Leader and the Company Training NCO. After that, I reenlisted to be the Aviation Safety NCO at Campbell Army Airfield. It was an opportunity to get away from the Combat Engineers.

Service as the Aviation Safety NCO was fun and allowed me to develop a love for flying. At that time the Army had a "blood stripe" policy. If an NCO in the company was reduced in rank, the stripe would remain in the company, but eligible NCOs had to appear before a board to compete. The board made the recommendation for or against promotion, and commanders normally followed the recommendation. We had a reduction in the company and a stripe for E-6 was available. I went before the board, but the guy promoted had a date of rank of 1949, whereas mine was 1956. I thought, "Rudy you are paddling a boat upstream." I completed my application for OCS the same day. I also completed an application for Helicopter Flight School, but that was denied due to depth perception issues.

I will always remember a question asked by the Colonel that headed the OCS board. He asked, "Sergeant, are you prejudiced?" It took me back for a moment, and then I answered, "Yes Sir, I guess I am to some extent, considering where I was raised, but it will never interfere in any military duties I have to perform."

In the summer of 1961, while I waited for word on the OCS application, I continued to be the Aviation Safety NCO. One Sunday morning, the phone rang, and dummy-like, I answered it. The Company First Sergeant was on the line and he said, "Sgt Baker, be in front of the orderly room at 0800 hours Monday morning with bag and baggage ready to go to Fort Jackson, SC for ninety days." Thus, my return to Fort Jackson as the NCOIC of the night shift at the Reception Center.

The buildup for the Berlin Crisis was taking place and the night shift was from 6PM to 6AM seven days per week. That got old fast, but there was nothing to do but drive on. After about sixty-plus days of that schedule, I received a welcome phone call from the First Sergeant to return to my unit. I had orders for OCS at Fort Benning, Georgia.

My Time at OCS

I started a process similar to what every OCS candidate has to go through. In my case it was to relocate a pregnant wife and two kids back to North Carolina and find enough money to buy new uniforms and boots. An uncle loaned me $300 for the purchases. I reported to OCS and hoped and prayed that I had the ability to finish the course.

I am not sure what I expected upon entry to OCS, but I soon learned to expect the unexpected. I made the mistake of reporting in with my NCO stripes (although I do not know what else I could have done). It cost me over 100 pushups just to get into the building. I was bombarded with comments and questions like: "Brace against the wall." "Who told you to move, Candidate?" "Did you shine those boots with a brick?" The Tac Officers had a way of saying "CANDIDATE" that made it sound like the lowest form of life on earth. As an NCO for over five years, I was not used to having officers in my face and yelling at me. At the end of the first three weeks, if I could have taken my stripes and returned to Fort Campbell as the Aviation Safety NCO, I probably would have. However, I could not face being called a quitter, and I knew if I left OCS, I would probably end up on orders to Korea or some other undesirable location. (So I completed OCS, and then I was assigned to Korea.)

The OCS program is designed to discipline and train individuals to become effective officers in the United States Army and to be prepared to lead soldiers in combat as infantrymen. The program is tough, and those who make it have been thoroughly tested. As I recall, our class had 238 on the initial roster, and was down to 207 at the end of the first week. We graduated 119 brand new second lieutenants. It was, without a doubt, the most mentally challenging course I have ever been through. However, as I look back, it was also the time when I grew up and learned to accept all of life's challenges and opportunities to excel.

OCS taught me self-discipline to a degree that I did not realize possible. It opened doors that would never have been there without the commission I received through the program. Later, I was able to attend the Degree Completion Program at the University of Nebraska at Omaha (UNO) to earn a BGS degree, and still later I was afforded the opportunity to attend Syracuse University and complete an MBA degree. Even my civilian employment after retirement would not have happened without OCS. Most importantly though, OCS provided me with the skills, discipline, and opportunity to lead troops in peace and war.

Nothing is more sacred than to be trusted to lead our troops in a way that ensures the mission is accomplished and casualties to our own troops are minimized. I will always be thankful for the opportunities provided to me during over 25 years of commissioned service. The values instilled in all of us during OCS still serve us as we continue to make a difference in the communities where we live.

Commissioned Service

After OCS, I attended Airborne school and a ten-week motor maintenance course. I had applied for Airborne, Ranger and Flight schools. The depth perception issue precluded Flight school and I was told that there were not enough Ranger slots for everyone. I had been selected for the Motor Maintenance course, the last thing I really wanted.

Following the schools, I was assigned to Korea to the 1st Cavalry

Division, 1st Battle Group, 12th Cavalry, Combat Support Company. The company was authorized thirteen officers, but we had only four second lieutenants assigned. The Company Commander was four months my senior. I served as Recon Platoon Leader. It was a very meaningful job. The platoon had four jeeps for recon, a mortar squad with an M113 armored personnel carrier (APC), and a motorized Infantry squad with another M113 APC. We had our own small combined arms team. After about six months of having fun, the 1st Battle Group had failed an IG inspection, with a rating of "VERY UNSATISFACTORY" in vehicle maintenance.

Colonel Allen came on board as the new Battle Group Commander. He screened the records for every officer in the battle group, and found the record of my attendance at the motor maintenance course at Fort Benning. (I thought I had hidden all reference to it.) Colonel Allen called an officer meeting, and announced that I was the new Battle Group Motor Officer. He also told all present to forget about the Motor Officer working for the S-4 (the usual arrangement); that I worked directly for him, and when I put out instructions or information on vehicle maintenance, I was speaking for him. Talk about pressure! However, it worked out fine and we passed the next IG with high marks, mainly because a new maintenance warrant officer came in just days before I took the job.

Following Korea, I returned to Fort Campbell, Kentucky for duty with the 1st Battle Group, 502nd Airborne Infantry. When I checked in at Division Headquarters, the G-1 Assignments Officer called the Commander of the 1st Battle Group, who said, "If he is like the one you sent me last week, I don't want him." It seemed that one of our OCS classmates had been assigned to the Battle Group, and immediately told them he was going to leave the Army a short time later. After confirming that I did not plan on getting out, I was accepted. Another surprise was when I learned that only two officers in the Battle Group were not Regular Army: the aforementioned OCS classmate and me. What a way to get welcomed!

My assignment was as the Assault Gun Platoon Leader, with six self-propelled anti-tank weapons (SPATS), five of which were down for maintenance. The Company Commander let me know that we had an Annual Training Test (ATT) in a few weeks and the Battle Group

Commander wanted all six SPATS to go on the exercise. Needless to say, my experience as the Battle Group Motor Officer in Korea came in handy. Short story: all SPATS went on the exercise.

Later, the Army restructured to the regimental system and the 1st Battle Group was split into the 1st and 2nd Battalions. The new Commander of the 2nd Battalion called for me one day and said, "Lieutenant Baker, welcome to the 2nd battalion, 502d Airborne Infantry. You are the second officer assigned. I am the Battalion Commander and you are the S-4. Tomorrow we start building this battalion."

We built the unit, and it was assigned to the 1st Brigade, 101st Airborne Division, along with the 1st and 2nd Battalions of the 327th Airborne Infantry. After the unit was built and trained, I got my first company command, CO of Charlie Company. I was in high cotton as a first lieutenant. However, my joy lasted only a few months.

MG Beverly Powell took command of the 101st Airborne Division. Shortly thereafter, he met with all battalion and brigade commanders in the division. He had made a decision to have captains in command of every company in the division and wanted it completed within the next week. Capt Rawls, the Battalion S-3, took command of Charlie Company, and I became the Battalion S-3 as a first lieutenant. The S-3 was a major position and I had difficulty understanding how I had enough rank to be the S-3, but not enough to command a company. My Battalion Commander just told me to be quiet when I asked him that question. Later, when a major was assigned to the Battalion as the S-3, I stayed as the assistant S-3 (a captain position). Eventually, I was assigned back to a rifle company as the Executive Officer for B Company, with the troops, and having fun again.

Deployment to Vietnam

In May 1965, the 1st Brigade, 101st Airborne Division with its three battalions, was alerted for deployment to Vietnam. The next day, Dave Johnson, the Battalion S-1, called me and said, "Rudy, message from the Battalion Commander. Tomorrow morning, you are the Battalion S-4. He does not want to see you, just high port and cross over. He will talk to you in a few days."

Every day for the next three days, I tried to see the Battalion Commander, without success. Then one morning I looked up as he came through the door to my office and closed the door. He did not allow me to say anything. He just looked at me and said, "Rudy, you know the officers in this battalion. If you were in command and had to move this unit to Vietnam, who would you make the S-4?" What can you say to a comment like that except, "Yes Sir"? It was another quick move for the family back home to North Carolina.

When I visited my mother, we were not allowed to discuss the deployment, but she was no dummy. My own mother said to me, "I know you are going to Vietnam. Why do you stay in the Army? You are just dumb to stay in and you are plain stupid to jump out of airplanes." Did your mother ever call you dumb and stupid in the same sentence?

In early July 1965, the troops and equipment were moved to San Francisco and put on a ship headed to Cam Ranh Bay, Vietnam. I was placed on the advance party, and we flew a C-124 from Travis AFB, California to Nha Trang, where we were attached to the 5th Special Forces Group until our unit arrived in country. Some of us were able to make two parachute jumps with the SF during that time. In late July, the troops arrived and we started operations. The history of that first year is well-documented in a book published by the 101st Airborne Division Association; *Vietnam Odyssey–The Story of the 1st Brigade, 101st Airborne Division in Vietnam*. I will limit my input here to a few incidents that will always be with me. Our battalion moved from Nha Trang by LST to Quin Nhon in August 1965, with the mission of helping secure Highway 19 from Quinn Nhon to An Khe, the new base for the 1st Cavalry Division. As part of the security mission we began to conduct search-and-destroy missions to the north of Highway 19.

On the evening of September 17th, 1965, we had a battalion briefing on the operation that would take place the following day. It was a helicopter assault into an area near the village of An Nihn. The Battalion S-3 stated that it was probably another walk in the woods. The operation started the next day, and after the first lift, helicopters were shot up so badly that the second lift could not be completed. The Commanders of A and B Companies never got on the ground. Both were wounded inside their helicopters as they attempted to land. At one point during the day, we heard the Battalion Commander on the ground reply to a question from the Brigade Commander in his helicopter, who had asked, "What do you need?" The response was, "troops and ammunition." We listened to the radio traffic all night as strikes from Air Force aircraft, helicopter gunships and artillery were called in for support.

When the relief force got into the area the next day, the Battalion S-3 and the Charlie Company Commander were both dead. Later, the A Company Commander was in the hospital in Camp Zama, Japan and the B Company Commander was in Walter Reed Hospital in Washington, DC. We lost thirteen killed in action (KIA) and numerous wounded. The next day I was a company commander again. I still go to panel 2E, row 86 at the Vietnam Memorial and have difficulty reading the thirteen names on the wall.

Late in the day on September 18th, while the battle was still in progress, I had a medevac helicopter land at our site to pick up medical supplies. He was instructed to fly low over the battle site and kick out the supplies behind our troops who were deployed in the tree line. While they were loading the medical supplies, I had our men load some ammunition on the chopper. The pilot stated that as a medevac pilot, he could not carry the ammunition. I "explained" to him that if the troops did not get the ammunition they might not need the medical supplies, and that he was the only bird flying. I asked him to kick out the ammo at the same time he kicked out the other supplies. He finally agreed and the mission went well.

A few days later, the Battalion Commander called me and asked me to meet him at Brigade Headquarters. The Brigade Commander wanted to see both of us. When we met with the Brigade CO, he told me that he had a complaint against me from the helicopter pilot. The pilot said I had threatened to shoot him if he did not carry the ammunition. I informed the Brigade Commander that I did not threaten to shoot him. What I said was that if he did not fly the ammo, I would jerk him out of the cockpit and beat hell out of him with my .45. The Brigade Commander said, "In the future just be careful how you explain things." I said, "Yes Sir" and got out of there.

During my tour as the Battalion S-4, I learned a lot about moving units, ensuring that troops were taken care of, and how critical it is for the logistics support of any operation to be fully planned and reviewed. One case in point: Our units deployed to Vietnam with our jump boots and they were worthless for the terrain in Vietnam. After a few weeks, most of the boots were rotten and coming apart. At one point I had six soldiers sitting with me at the S-4 supply point because their boots were not adequate to go on patrol. Efforts were made to get boots shipped up from Saigon, but they were slow coming. It just happened that LTG Throckmorten, Deputy CG for MACV, came for a visit at my location that day. He wanted to know why they were with me and not out on patrol, and I asked him to look at their boots. He told me that there were plenty of boots in Saigon. Needless to say he made some calls, and the next morning we had boots come in by helicopters. The Brigade S-4 called and asked me what I had told the general. I said I had just told him the truth.

Later, we had a change of battalion commanders. The new guy, Lieutenant Colonel (later Lieutenant General) Hank Emerson, went by the call sign "Gun Fighter," and believed in the checkerboard concept of operations. The tempo of our operations picked up, and time passed fast. We were fortunate and managed to hold casualties to a minimum in our company. Gunfighter had a policy that when you had less than sixty days left in country he would remove you from command of a company. He said you would either get too cautious or too foolhardy, thinking you had it made.

In late May 1966, when we completed our operation briefing for the next morning, the Battalion Commander turned to me and said, "Rudy, meet Captain Johnson. He is taking command of your company for this operation. You will be the S-4 again until you rotate." I said, "Like Hell! I am going with my troops." His response was, "Captain, you are now the Battalion S-4." That is where I spent the last days of my first tour. I was listening to the radio the night before I left the Battalion area near Dak To when I heard Company Commander Bill Carpenter call napalm in on his own position.

Two Years Stateside

The next assignment was to the Infantry Officers Advanced Course at Fort Benning, Georgia and from there to the 82nd Airborne Division, where I served as the Assistant G-4 for Supply and Budget. I was promised that I would get down to the street with the troops later. However, orders came for attendance at the Military Advisors Training and Assistance (MATA) course with the Special Forces School and then Vietnamese language course at Biggs Army Airfield, Fort Bliss, Texas. While I was in the MATA course, the 3rd Brigade of the 82nd Airborne Division was alerted to deploy to Vietnam. I went to the Division Chief of Staff and he pleaded my case to Infantry Branch for a reassignment to the 3rd Brigade. NO GO! So I finished the MATA course and language school and departed for my second tour in Vietnam.

Second Vietnam Tour—Advisory Duty

I had studied the Saigon dialect in Vietnamese, but when I arrived in country I was assigned to be an advisor to the 23rd Army of Viet Nam (ARVN) Division in Ban-me-Thout, where they spoke Radia. Most of the Vietnamese officers spoke English though, so we could communicate.

The 23rd ARVN Division had three regiments: the 45th, a good hard-fighting outfit; the 44th, a good unit, but not up to the standards of the 45th; and the 53rd Regiment, which was worthless. Their concept of operations was "search-and-avoid." The advisory duty was good at times and frustrating at others. I worked mostly in the Tactical Operations Center (TOC), an underground bunker. Our main worry was the 122mm rockets. It was refreshing to get out in the field at times.

Since I was promoted to captain on my first tour, I guess it was logical that I would be promoted to major during my second tour. I was fortunate for it to be a below-the-zone promotion. When you work for good people, they take care of you when you perform, and get three pounds of your butt when you don't. Later in the tour, our Senior Advisor (a Colonel) and the 23rd ARVN Division Commander were killed in a helicopter crash during a major battle at Duc Lop Special Forces Camp. The next day, my boss came into the TOC and said, "Rudy, I'm flying down to Duc Lop. Do you want to go with me?" My response was, "Sir, let me clarify what you said. If you are asking me to go Duc Lop with you, I have my helmet and gear here and I am ready to go. On the other hand, if you are simply asking if I want to fly to Duc Lop, my answer is, 'Hell No'. They are still shooting at folks down there." He went on his way and I returned to my duties.

Some weeks later a Special Forces detachment with about 100

Civilian Irregular Defense Group (CIDG) soldiers with them strayed into Cambodia and got into a firefight. The leader called for air support. Of course any airstrike had to be cleared through the 23rd ARVN Division. When I plotted the location, it was clearly inside Cambodia. I knew if I sent it in that way, the airstrike would be denied. I called for clearance using a location just inside Vietnam. I knew that when the fighters talked to the leader on the ground, they would put the strike where it was needed. The trick was to get the clearance. It worked and the team broke contact. All Special Forces troops survived and only a few of the CIDG troops were lost. The team returned to our compound. About two hours later, I got the worst chewing out from some Colonel in Saigon. He informed me that only General Westmoreland had the authority to clear a strike across an international border. I apologized and thought to myself, "What are you going to do to me, send me to Vietnam?" The Special Forces troops who survived couldn't care less about an international incident with Cambodia, and I felt the same way. The rules of engagement were the most frustrating part of the duty in Vietnam. Like all other assignments, this advisory duty finally ended and I returned home.

Stateside Duty Again

This time orders were for the Degree Completion Program at the University of Nebraska at Omaha (UNO). I had received a Regular Army commission and Infantry Branch told me I needed to have a degree. When I completed my Bachelor of General Studies (BGS) degree, follow-on orders were for Fort Bragg to the 1st Corps Support Command (COSCOM). I learned prior to leaving Omaha that the COSCOM Commander, none other than Gunfighter, had asked for me by name to be assigned as his G-3 (Operations Officer).

In the meantime, he had been promoted to brigadier general and assigned as the Assistant Division Commander of the 82nd Airborne Division. I did something I had never done before. I called the general at his home a few nights before I was to come to Fort Bragg, and told him my situation. His instructions were that when I arrived at Fort Bragg, I should not sign in, but come to his office instead. That is exactly what I did. The general called for the G-1 Assignments Officer, a major, and told him to find me a job in the Division. I was holding orders for Command and General Staff College with a reporting date in August though, and no one wanted a new major for less than six months.

The Assignments Officer told me to go home and call him the next day. I called every day for a week. The response was the same, "Call me tomorrow." After a week of this, I showed up in his office and told him I was going to sit on the end of his couch until I had a job. He sent me to do my jump refresher training and told me to come back when that was complete. Some four hours later I was in his office again. He said, "Rudy, you are going to be the Deputy G-2 until you leave for C&GSC." I said, "Good," and he went upstairs with me to meet the Division G-2. As I was being briefed by the G-2 that afternoon, I was called to Gunfighter's office. He looked at me and said, "Tomorrow morning you report to the 3rd Battalion, 325th Infantry as the S-3. I want you to straighten out that outfit." I replied, "Sir, I am going to be the S-3, not the Commander." He pointed to the door without further comment.

The next day, I joined the battalion. The XO and I made a great team. Within a few weeks, we had planned the training for the battalion through the summer, and felt good about what we were going to accomplish. It was too good to last.

One afternoon, the Battalion Commander came in from Brigade Headquarters and called me to his office. He told me the Brigade Commander wanted to see me the following morning. Based on previous experiences, I asked, "What did I do now?" He answered that the Brigade Commander wanted me to be the Brigade Executive Officer until I left for C&GS. He also said there was no point in fighting it because he had lost that battle already.

The next morning I went to see the Brigade Commander to plead my case to stay with the battalion. I started by saying, "Sir, I would prefer to stay with the battalion and finish the training plans we have developed. He quickly let me know that my preference did not mean anything to him. Then I tried another approach. I told him that two of his staff officers, the S-1 and the S-3 were senior to me. His answer to that was, "They will not give you any trouble. I have already talked to them." I knew there was a lieutenant colonel coming in about the time I was scheduled to report to CGSC, so without further discussion, I became the XO of the 2nd Brigade. It turned out to be a fun job, and I could make a parachute jump about whenever I wanted.

Command and General Staff College came next and it was a time for some real professional development. During the year, when we were required to submit our "dream sheet" to branch requesting our next job, I listed my three top choices as Fort Bragg. Down in the remarks section, I stated that I would like to go for a master's degree sometime in the future. At that time the Comptroller of the Army had temporarily closed the Comptroller field to Finance officers. He wanted some muddy boots in that field. This all came together at the right time, because Infantry Branch called and told me they had an MBA slot for me at Syracuse University if I wanted it. Never one to turn down a chance for something better, I asked if I could go to the University of Alabama instead. The response from the other end was, "Listen, I am offering you a chance to go to Syracuse. If you want Alabama, put your application in and take your chances." I answered quickly that I would take Syracuse, and asked where it was located.

The MBA program at Syracuse was through the Army's Comptrollership program. It was fifteen months long and tough. I was released from C&GSC a week early so I could report to Syracuse in time for the first summer session. At the end of fifteen months, we graduated and were given our assignments. I went to Fort Benning to the Leadership Department of the Infantry School. We taught leadership, management and decision making to the career courses. It was a great assignment, but after about twenty months, when I made a comment and the captain in the right corner of the room raised his hand, and I knew exactly what he was going to ask, it was time for a change. I ended up as the Assistant Director of the School Management and Budget Office. That was another good assignment. Challenges were numerous because of strength reductions in process at the time.

After I had been at Fort Benning less than three years, I received a call from Infantry Branch saying they needed a major for a comptroller assignment in Iran. It was a Technical Assistance Field Team position providing financial advice to the Iranian Ground Forces Logistical Command. It was a two-year assignment with family. I took it and we left for Iran.

Three weeks after I accepted the assignment, terrorists ambushed three US Air Force lieutenant colonels and escaped. It was a classic ambush. They cut off the car, machine-gunned all passengers, and escaped in a third car. Oddly enough, the Iranian driver was not hurt. This same type of ambush happened during our second year in Iran, except the victims were three Rockwell employees. Again the Iranian driver was not injured. Despite these issues, it was a very rewarding job. We soon learned that the Iranians did not want any financial advice. They wanted someone to run the Military Sales Program for them between the Iranian and US governments. We had an office for that specific purpose. I was the senior major and had three majors and four sergeants major working for me. My guidance from the Chief of the Military Assistance Advisory Group (MAAG) was to keep us out of trouble.

By the time I departed two years later, we had automated the system and it worked very well. As we closed out contracts, we paid off some past-due bills, but also found millions of dollars left over that were just sitting there not drawing any interest. The US banks that held the money loved it. Another case involved publications. We discovered that the US had shipped over eleven million dollars worth of publications to Iran, but had never billed for them. When I returned to the US to update the two-star USAF general in charge of the Military Sales Program and briefed him on this situation, he looked at me and said, "Major, you are crazy." My boss, an Army brigadier general, asked him to get someone to take our data and check it out. Before we left for lunch, the guys returned and told the USAF general that they had already been able to find four of the eleven million, and it appeared that our data were correct. That led to a major effort to automate the system.

Although the Shah was in power, the security situation was stressful. We had to go to work in civilian clothes and then change to our uniforms on the Iranian military compound. We had an armed Iranian guard in our vehicle to and from work, but I could never feel secure. We were not allowed to carry weapons outside our homes. However, I had one major who carried a pistol in his briefcase at all times. When we rode to work and back he had the briefcase open with his hand on the weapon. I cautioned him once and his response made sense to me, so I never said anything else. He said, "Rudy, I would much rather explain to someone why I shot a terrorist than to explain why I am dead."

There were some excellent things that did happen during this tour. Our oldest son ran track around the pyramids and the youngest got to play basketball in the University of Kuwait. Our daughter graduated from the Tehran American High School, and worked for the US Government in Iran until we returned to the United States.

One funny situation occurred when the high school basketball season began (funny now, not funny then). As we prepared to play the University of Kuwait at the Tehran American High School, both teams ran out on the floor. My oldest son pointed at a fat guy on the Kuwait team and yelled, "I got fat boy." The "fat boy" turned out to be the Crown Prince of Kuwait. I kept a low profile and thought that it might be a short tour. However, we never heard anything from the incident. I did counsel my son that despite his team spirit, he should not call people fat. His response was, "Well, Dad, he was fat." There were numerous stories that could be told, but I do not want to waste the time of folks who have been in similar situations.

My first call concerning a stateside assignment was to offer me a recruiting district in New York City. My response was, "I am not going there." After a moment of silence, I was asked what I meant. (It is generally unacceptable to tell someone you are not going to follow orders.) I told the fellow on the other end of the line that I had over twenty years of active duty, and would retire before accepting an assignment in New York City. He said he would call back. The second offer was to serve on the DA IG traveling road show as a comptroller inspector. Since I had never been assigned to the Pentagon, I did not fight this one. Fortunately, two things happened. I came out on the lieutenant colonel promotion list, below the zone, and then came out on the battalion command list. Since there were no battalions in the Pentagon, I avoided Washington.

When the battalion command slate came out, I had been selected to command the 3rd Battalion, 325th Infantry, in the 82nd Airborne Division. It was another dream come true. The timing of the battalion command change caused me to serve as the Division Comptroller for about eleven months before the command became available. It was a great opportunity to become familiar with the current operations of the 82nd Division again.

Battalion Command

The best job in the Army is, without a doubt, the command of an Airborne Infantry battalion in the 82nd Airborne Division. I had commanded two Airborne companies and served as the S-3 of the Battalion I was now going to command. When I took command of the Battalion, I was extremely honored and humbled at the same time. I recognized what an opportunity I had been given, but I also recognized the awesome responsibility I had before me to ensure the unit was ready to deploy within eighteen hours, and fight and win upon arrival in a combat zone.

We did all the things any battalion does to maintain its readiness such as normal training exercises, Emergency Deployment Readiness Exercises (EDREs), etc. During my tour of command we did some special things. One was a thirty-day cold weather training exercise in Alaska. We jumped a 700-man task force into Fort Wainwright, Alaska with only one jump injury. The temperature at Pope AFB in North Carolina was about 60 degrees when we departed. When we jumped, it was minus nine degrees at jump altitude and zero on the ground. Everyone had to learn to ski, and I did, though not very gracefully. Upon returning to Fort Bragg, I informed the Division Commander that it took the Army twenty-four years to get me on a set of skis and it would take twenty-four more to get me on them again. I did learn that the easiest way to cross country ski is to tie a rope to a jeep and hold on. Overall, it was a very meaningful exercise and the unit benefited from the environmental training.

When the Iranian revolution took place, our battalion was the Division Ready Force (DRF). We were alerted to prepare to deploy to rescue the US Embassy hostages in Iran. We reorganized the battalion into four rifle companies because we were not going to take any heavy weapons beyond the M-60 machine guns. When we started to develop battle plans, it turned out the Corps G-3, (who had served in Iran with me), and I had better maps than the US Army. We had the ESSO oil maps which showed all the little streets and alleys around the Embassy area. In fact both of us had driven these same streets making our weekly trip to the commissary. After a few days, the National Command Authority decided that we were not going to deploy, so we stood down. We did learn some valuable lessons though which were useful years later in contingency planning.

My battalion command tour ended all too quickly. I was again on orders to Washington to serve on the DA Inspector General world-wide Inspection Team with duty as a comptroller inspector. As I finished my last exercise with the Battalion, I was still in the field when I got a call from the XVIII Airborne Corps Chief of Staff. The General asked, "Rudy, if we can get your orders changed to stay at Fort Bragg and head a new program called the Battalion Training Management System (BTMS), are you willing to head the program?" You know my answer: "YES SIR!" He soon called back and said, "We have your orders suspended for one year so you can launch this program, but then you will have to go to Washington." That was OK by me.

The Battalion Training Management System

A major from Special Forces Command was selected as my deputy and we went to Fort Eustis, Virginia for two weeks to a "train-the-trainer" course. Upon completion of the course, we returned to Fort Bragg and recruited and trained a thirteen-man team to teach BTMS to all battalion commanders and their staffs. It went so well the Corps Commander directed us to develop a day-and-a-half course for brigade commanders and their staffs. The course was to be taught on Friday and Saturday until noon, and was not welcomed by all of the brigade commanders, considering all else they had to do. However, things continued to go well. After about eight months, I started to plan to move to Washington.

A new lieutenant colonel had been assigned to the 82nd Airborne Division as the Division Inspector General (IG). For some reason, the DA IG called the 82nd Division Commander and told him this guy would not be suitable as the Division IG, and it would be some time before they could assign a new one. The Division Commander told the DA IG that he had a former battalion commander (me) at Fort Bragg who was scheduled to go to the DA IG office in Washington in a few weeks, and asked why they couldn't make me the Division IG. A brief call later I was reassigned as the 82nd Airborne Division IG.

Division Inspector General

The Inspector General School in the Pentagon was a new experience for me. I learned all the do's and don'ts of the role of an IG. It was really an eye opener. I had always heard that the IG is "here to help you," but never believed it. My fellow battalion commanders in the division did not believe it either. Guys that only months before would have a beer and shoot the breeze with me now avoided me. It seemed that they would only do one of two things; either try to avoid me completely, or drop a "hot rock" on me, i.e., pass something on to me in which they did not want to be involved. They knew that as the IG, I would have to do something about it. It took more than six months of constantly walking the division streets and stopping at battalion headquarters before folks quit saying, "The IG is here. What does he want?" It was a challenging but rewarding job.

The first day I went on an inspection of a battalion, the major who headed the inspection team and I went to the unit motor pool. Most motor pools had two dumpsters at the entrance. As we approached the motor pool, the major asked me which dumpster I wanted to take. I gave him a strange look and asked, "What are you talking about?" He explained that he and the old IG always went into the dumpsters to see what good stuff had been thrown away as the unit got ready for our inspection. I said, "Major, I am not going into a dumpster and neither are you. If you want to find out what was done as the unit prepared, just ask the troops. They will tell you." I told him to ask soldiers as he went around, "Tell me what unusual things you did to get ready for this inspection?" He was amazed at what he learned without getting into a dumpster.

At the IG course, I learned that the DA policy was for the Commanding General to be the rating officer for the Inspector General. When I returned to Fort Bragg, I learned that in the 82nd Airborne Division, the IG was rated by the Chief of Staff and senior rated by the Division Commanding General. I mentioned this to the G-1, but he said, "Rudy, that is the way it has always been done in this Division." I accepted that, continued to do my job, and did not think anything else about it. (I have always thought that any officer who worried about his efficiency report probably had a reason to worry.)

Months went by and I was really enjoying the job. One Friday afternoon, we had a situation develop that I felt needed to be brought to the Division Commander's attention. I knew he was getting ready to leave town for the weekend, so I hurried to see the Chief of Staff. I explained the situation to the Chief and he said, "Rudy, let's not bother the CG now. He is trying to get out of here." I emphasized the urgency of the situation again and got the same response. Finally, I said, "Sir, if we both do not go through that door to the CG's office, I am going to the side door and see him." He gave me a hard look, but said, "You are prepared to do that, aren't you?" I said, "Yes sir." He told me to come with him, and we went in to see the CG. The Chief said, "Sir, I wanted to wait and give you some information on Monday, but Rudy insisted that we come in." Then he asked me to brief the CG.

After I briefed him, the CG said, "Rudy, go down and see the Division Command Sergeant Major (CSM) and tell him I said to get on top of this, and it had better be stopped before close of business today." I left and went to see the CSM. When I returned to see the Chief of Staff, I told him that appropriate action was being taken. He replied, "Thank you, and by the way, you no longer work for me; you report directly to the CG. However, you will always keep me informed, just as before." I said, "Yes sir, I will." As my two years as the IG ended, I was selected to attend the Army War College and left the Division.

War College

The Army War College was another great professional year. Our perspectives there shifted from our tactical world to national and international affairs. The entire experience was something I had never been exposed to before. It broadened my outlook, and the comradeship and friendships established went with us for the remainder of our military careers, and into our second careers in many cases. Again, when the team of assignments officers came to visit the class, the first assignment choice I was offered was to the DA IG office. I told the Assignments Officer that the Commander of the 1st Corps Support

Command (COSCOM) at Fort Bragg had asked that I return to be his Chief of Staff, and I would like to do just that. His response was that the only way I would get back to Fort Bragg was if a General Officer asked for me to fill a specific position. I immediately called the COSCOM Commander and explained the situation. A few hours later I got a call from the Corps G-1, an old friend of mine, asking me what he should tell the Corps Commander that I could do at Fort Bragg. I gave a flip answer and said, "Tell the CG I can do any job on Fort Bragg, including his." I ended up at Fort Bragg as the Chief of Staff for the 1st COSCOM.

1st COSCOM Chief of Staff

The job at COSCOM was extremely rewarding. I learned more about what makes the Army function in that position than at any other job I ever had. The COSCOM had sixty-one company-size units, with no two of them exactly alike. They ranged from transportation units, maintenance units, well drilling units, laundry and bath units, and postal units, to graves registration units. Sometime after I went into the position, the Corps Commander came down for an update briefing. I introduced myself and started to introduce the briefing officers. The CG stopped me and said, "Rudy, I understand that you can do any job at Fort Bragg." Embarrassed, I responded, "Yes sir, I will try any of them." He laughed and the briefing continued. Another lesson learned: Be careful how you give flip answers, even to old friends.

On a Saturday in October, I was in the COSCOM Headquarters finishing some Warrant Officer packets that had to be couriered to Washington. The phone rang and it was the Corps Duty Officer wanting to know where the COSCOM Commander was located. The Corps Commander needed to talk to him. I told him the Commander was in San Francisco supporting the Army Reserves on an exercise. He asked for the Deputy Commander, but he was in New Orleans, doing the same thing. Then he wanted to know who the senior officer was and I responded that I was the senior officer at that time. He said, "Get up to the Corps War room ASAP."

The operation for Grenada had just kicked off. I did not get back home until after the Rangers jumped on Tuesday morning. I was the only colonel in the command that did not deploy to Grenada. The Commander told me to stay at the headquarters and see that everything went smoothly. He said he would take care of the other end and left me behind. The operation had some issues, but we managed to handle them. One situation caused me to have to go to Green Ramp where troops were boarding aircraft because a brigadier general had removed our Graves Registration Team from a flight to put on, as he phrased it, "more fighters." After a discussion about needs and priorities, our team caught the next plane.

Following Grenada, the COSCOM Commander had a series of after-action meetings to discuss what went right and what went wrong from the logistical aspects of the operation. Needless to say, we found plenty to do. The next several months were dedicated to planning to support a five-division force in the Middle East. Our focus was on Iran, but it was designed to work in other places as well. We did loading plans for troops and equipment in all types of situations. We did it to the point of identifying specific loads of each type of equipment and supplies that would be needed to support the force. We would run computerized load plans and backup plans. We did this, in many cases, at least six days per week and sometimes seven. At one point I approached the Commander and told him that our troops needed to get home to their families for the weekend. He agreed. However, on Monday we were right back at it. Only when the COSCOM Commander was completely satisfied that if the call came, we could provide the support required, did we slow down. Later, when Desert Shield/Desert Storm took place, I could see that all the planning was well worth it. As we watched the operation unfold, we could see that our basic plans were being followed. I was retired at that time, but still on Fort Bragg, with the First Citizens Bank as the City Executive, and I had enough friends to stay updated.

When I had served as the Chief of Staff at COSCOM for about two years, I got a call from the Corps Commander one day. He said, "Rudy, the Corps G-1 tells me you would make a good Corps G-4 (Logistics Officer)." Our discussion went something like this, "Sir, I do not want to be the G-4. Why can't I stay here as the Chief? Am I not doing a good job?" His response, "You are doing fine, but you have been there for two years and it is time to move. If you do not want to be the G-4, what do you want to do?" I said, "If I cannot stay at COSCOM, let me be your comptroller. I understand he is leaving. The Commander was silent for a moment and then said, "You are a comptroller, aren't you? Ok, the job is yours. Please tell the G-1."

Then I had to call the G-1, and I actually felt good about it since he had not had the courtesy to tell me he had recommended me for the G-4 position. At any rate, in a few months I became the Comptroller for XVIII Airborne Corps and Fort Bragg.

XVIII Airborne Corps Comptroller

That was for me another of those dream jobs. I soon learned the ropes and found that I had some of the best military and civilians I could possibly ask for to accomplish the missions. My Sergeant Major (SGM) and I are still best friends, and we are now both members of the Vietnam Veterans of America (VVA) Chapter 990 in Smithfield, NC. I recall one day hearing the SGM saying something like this to an NCO, "Sergeant, you do not want to bother the Colonel with this. Let's you and I go have cup of coffee." I never asked any questions, and to this day do not know what it was all about. When you have personnel like that working for you, you cannot go wrong.

When I was nearing two years in this job and almost four years at Fort Bragg, I got a call that the Army Comptroller (Lieutenant General) was coming to Fort Bragg and wanted to meet with me. I knew the General had a son assigned to an Engineer unit on post, and figured this was just a chance for him to visit, and my part in it was a way to make it an official visit. Little did I know. When we met, the General said, "Rudy, I need you to come to Washington to work in my office as the Chief of the Management Division." Once I recovered, I responded like this, "Sir, I really prefer to stay in the field. Can I not stay at Fort Bragg?" He said that I had been at Fort Bragg for four years, and it was time to move. I said, "OK, but send me to Fort Hood or any other field installation." At the end of our discussion he promised to look around and get back to me. A few days later the General's secretary called me with a message, "Rudy, the General told me to tell you that he needs you in Washington, and nothing else is available." I said, "Tell the general, I will get back to him."

What I was really waiting on was the Brigade Command list. I knew that if I was not selected, it would be my last opportunity. The board had adjourned, but the list had not been released. I knew an individual who had served on the board and tried to find out something, because I was stalling on my decision to retire. Of course he could not tell me anything official. The next day, he called me back and said, "Rudy, let's take a hypothetical situation. If an officer's record went before a board with three panels of five people, each with instructions that all selections had to be unanimous, and the record cleared two boards, but the third board had one 'No', what would you think?" I said, "I would think that officer should consider retirement." I submitted my retirement papers the next day. I made the request for May 1, 1987, because I had promised the Corps Commander that I would not do anything until the new budget had been submitted.

Second Career

My retirement was at 9:30AM at Fort Bragg, and I was processing in to my new job at First Citizens Bank Headquarters in Raleigh at 3:00PM the same day. The bank sent me through training for almost five months. I spent at least a week in every department in the bank, and went to all the appropriate schools. I was placed under the eye of the City Executive at Camp LeJeune Marine Corps Base for all my training. My first week was as a courier and coin roller. The next week I went to teller school in Raleigh, and then was assigned to the Commissary Branch of the bank at Camp LeJeune. A lady from the commissary came through the door with several money bags in her hands. I was sitting between two good looking young ladies. She stopped half way across the lobby and stared. Then pointed at me and said, "A rose between two thorns!" Then she proceeded to drop all those bags in my window for me to work. The ladies could not stop laughing. However, I finished the week and balanced every day. Then it was on to all the other types of work in the bank. At the end of the training, I was not an expert in any field, but I had experienced it all, even commercial loans, which I never saw after training.

When I returned to Fort Bragg, I shadowed the current City Executive for a month and watched all his decisions. The second month, he shadowed me and let me make all decisions, but he provided advice when appropriate. Then he retired. Soon after he left, I held my first employee meeting with all associates. I had already visited all six branches on Fort Bragg and the one on Pope AFB. After introductions, I laid out two expectations for all: Do your best at all times. Do not say "No" to a customer. You all have the authority to say "Yes" within your area of responsibility, but only I will say "No". Later, I gave that authority to branch managers, but it set the tone.

I stated a new policy. If an employee was assigned to a branch and wanted to be reassigned to a different branch at the same job level, he or she should let the Personnel Officer know. When an opening came up, he or she would be transferred, and we would post the vacancy at the losing branch. That was of course subject to the gaining branch manager's approval. My Operations Officer said that I could not do that. When I asked why not, he said that Raleigh would not allow it. I told him I was not going to ask them. It worked. Initially we had three or four names, and after that, none. I also put out a memo to folks in the main office not to park in the first five spaces in the first four rows in front of the bank. I had observed that the workers took up the first spaces and customers had to park beyond them.

I really enjoyed the job and things went well. When the troops deployed for Desert Shield/Desert Storm, the bank did not have an automated bill paying service. We coordinated with the command and had customer service representatives at the deployment areas to take accounts to be paid. During the deployment we paid bills each month by hand. Troops loved the support. We also took Powers of Attorney (POA) and kept them at Fort Bragg. Corporate did not want them. I recall one POA written on the top of a C-ration box, and we still took it. One day I heard a ruckus at the Head Teller's location and went to see what was going on. It turned out that a young soldier had given a POA to both his girlfriend and his wife. Both had shown up for his pay at the same time. We froze the account until the soldier called to cancel the POA for his girlfriend, and asked us to honor the one to this wife.

When the troops returned from deployment, many had accumulated a considerable amount of money in their accounts. Some of them wanted it all in cash. We had a young soldier come into one of the branches and walk out with $10,000 in cash stuffed into his pockets. It was so bad that the Deputy Corps Commander called me and asked if I could put a limit on how much cash a soldier could withdraw. We discussed the implications and agreed that the bank would limit the amount of cash to $3,000, and provide the remainder in travelers' checks or bank checks at no cost to the soldier.

We always provided special amounts of cash in requested denominations for Special Operations Forces, and Corporate Headquarters was aware of this. However, one day early in Desert Shield, I was asked to wire five million dollars to an overseas location. Since it was paid for by US Government check, I proceeded to send the wire. It was only a few minutes before I got a call from our security folks at Corporate Headquarters wanting to know what was going on. I explained that I had a US Government check from the Finance Officer that covered the transaction, and everything was fine. In addition to our Fort Bragg operation and our banks on Camp LeJeune and Cherry Point, we also managed all the Treasury General Accounts in the area for the US Treasury. Corporate Headquarters did not understand the operations, and did not want to get involved, so we pretty much ran our own banks. In fact, when we would go to a meeting at Headquarters, most of the time we were told that we military banks were different, so we should not be concerned with much of the information. One day, a new executive said to me, "Rudy, you guys are no different than any other First Citizens Branch." I replied that we might not be different, but we sure were unique. A lot of laughter followed.

One day, after eighteen years with First Citizens Bank, I was driving to work and thought to myself, "Rudy, almost thirty-three years of active duty and eighteen years with the bank totals fifty-one years. What about retirement?" I went to the office and sent my boss an e-mail telling him I was retiring in six months. I received a return reply that suggested we talk. We did, and I stayed on one more year in a part-time position. I had no management responsibilities for branches or bottom lines. I spent the year doing public relations work with the Fort Bragg and XVIII Corps Command and the local community. I also chaired the Military Affairs Council for the Fayetteville Chamber of Commerce during that year. That was a lot of fun.

During my years with the bank I served on the Board of Directors of the Association of Military Banks of America (AMBA), a trade association for military banks. We held two board meetings each year. The first one, in the spring, was always in Washington, DC, and we visited all Financial Managers (Comptrollers) at DOD and all the military services. Again it was fun, and kept us current on the needs of the military when it came to banking. I was President of the Association in 1996-1998. We always had a second Board meeting someplace nice in September. I was also fortunate to serve on the Board of Directors for the Armed Forces Financial Network (AFFN). In that organization, we had four board meetings each year. I was Chairman for two years.

That is probably more than anyone ever wanted to know about my second career. I will just say that I am one of the luckiest men in the world. I had two great careers and loved both. My wife told me one day and I quote, "You never did retire; you see soldiers, help soldiers and smell soldiers every day." I replied, "Thank God for that." I still love soldiers and always will. The 82nd Airborne Division Chorus performed at my retirement function at the bank, and yes, I cried.

After Retirement

What do you do after retiring twice? One day, not long after I had retired from the bank, I was putting out sod in the yard to cover some bare spots. Within three hours, I received three different telephone calls with job offers. All three were contractors wanting me to go overseas. I told them I was not going overseas, that I had been there, done that, and got the T-shirt, end of discussion. Late that afternoon one of the guys called me back and said they were going to do some pre-deployment exercises with the 10th Mountain Division in Fort Drum, New York, and they needed an operations officer. I told them I had not been an operations officer in over eighteen years. Their response was that I had not forgotten how. They asked if I would fly up with them the following week to discuss what they would be doing, and see if I would be part of the team. They would pay for my time and all expenses. Enough said. I flew up to Fort Drum with them.

The owner of the small company we were to work for had been looking for a general officer to be the Team Leader. All of those guys were off making the big bucks. About 4:00PM, he turned to me and asked if I would be the Team Leader. I told him that if the pay was right I could. To make a long story short, we did four exercises over the next year, two at division level and two at brigade level. The last one we did ended at noon on a Friday, and the Brigade Commander, his battalion commanders, and their staffs left for Iraq the next morning. The small company I worked for was bought out by a larger firm who wanted to move all the exercises to Fort Polk, and wanted us to go for ninety days at a time. I said, "I am out of here."

During the 2010 census I was employed as a team leader for one phase of the census, and the next phase I was the Field Operations Supervisor (FOS) for the northern half of Johnston County, NC. We had eight team leaders with a total of 152 people. It was almost like commanding a company again. Later in 2011, I was hired by the Census Bureau to conduct current population surveys in Johnston County. That lasted for fifteen months, until May 2012. I am currently unemployed.

Unemployed does not mean not working. I am a member of the Airborne and Special Operations Museum Foundation Board of Directors, where I serve on the Executive Committee and the Personnel Committee and chair the Finance Committee. Additionally, I chair the Johnston County Veteran Services Advisory Board. Since that is not enough to keep me busy, I have served on the Johnston County Emergency Medical Services Advisory Committee for the last twelve years, and I currently chair that committee.

The Veterans Affairs Office for the Vietnam Veterans of America (VVA) for Johnston County is also my responsibility, and I am one of seventeen people on the VVA Honor Guard. My wife Pat and I were selected to be grand marshals for the most recent July 4th community parade.

This is much longer than I anticipated when I started, but to highlight seventy-six years from birth to the present takes some time. Since this project started from OCS Class 2-62, it is appropriate that I conclude the summary from that perspective. Without a doubt, all the success I have enjoyed and all the fun I have had over these past fifty plus years can be traced to those six months at OCS. The self-discipline I learned and the high standards set during that course stayed with me to this day. The support of our cadre and classmates was the glue that held us together then, and led to our successes throughout our military and civilian careers.

Colonel (Retired) Rudy Baker and wife Pat, Grand Marshals, July Fourth Parade, with grandchildren John Ross and Megan Peedin, Clayton, NC, July 4, 2012.

Whether we made the Army our career, or chose to go into other fields for our lives, the building blocks for all of us started with OCS Class 2-62. When Thomas Vaughn called and left me a message in early 2012, I looked at the name and said, "I do not remember a Thomas Vaughn." However, when I returned the call, much of it came flashing back. The night that my wife Pat and I entered the room for the meet and greet at our fiftieth class reunion, the only person I recognized was Bill Hunter. It is hard to believe that I had not met or served with any of the other reunion participates. Pat and I thoroughly enjoyed our time at the reunion, and I hope we will have another. May God continue to bless all of us, and all present and future members of Infantry Officer Candidate School; "The Fort Benning School for Boys."

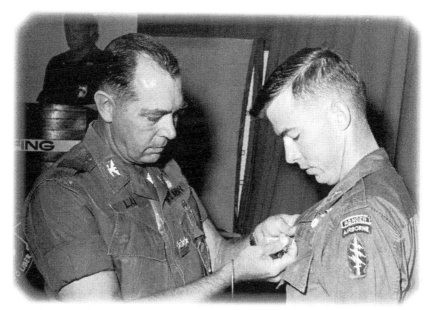

Captain (Later Colonel) Ed Burke on right receiving the Bronze Star from Colonel Ladd, CO, 5th SFGA, Vietnam, 1968.

Prelude

Officer Candidate School was a stepping stone that helped me get through the minefield of life. By the time I arrived at Fort Benning to join class 2-62 I had already committed to the Army as a career. As I point out later in my discussion of the early years, my philosophy before the Army was at best to deal with today and see what happens tomorrow.

The Early Days

My recollection of life growing up in Olyphant is not vivid. We often talk about that small town in Northeastern Pennsylvania where I was born, baptized a Catholic and registered as a Democrat, and where every day is pretty much like the day before. To this day we remark that the hard core residents are afraid they will lose what they never had. The old timers joke about leaving town to get a decent job and returning to be buried where they can stay active in politics.

My father was a bookkeeper in a coal breaker. Sometime in my early years he was appointed as a Justice of the Peace, now referred to as District Justice. Later he was elected Town "Burgess," now called Mayor. He was also on the county payroll as an assessor. Life was good. Coal was king. The union ran the coal business, the Democrat machine ran the town, and everybody was peaceful.

We had Catholic school for most of the ethnic groups that worked the mines. I attended St. Patrick's school and stayed with the same school until high school graduation. Nobody in town seemed to have been impacted by the Korean War. The Pennsylvania National Guard (28th Infantry Division) was activated for the duration of the Korean War and was sent to Germany to backfill active Army units that were sent to Korea. After the war the 28th Division returned to Pennsylvania, and a lot of the guys got out. The Division was actively recruiting and I was convinced by the recruiters to sign up and share the excitement. Needless to say small town Northeastern Pennsylvania was not a hotbed of excitement. At that time I was fifteen. When I graduated high school I was a staff sergeant, Infantry squad leader in the 109th Infantry, 28th Division, Pennsylvania National Guard.

Some of my school buddies had dreams of medical school. I followed them to the University of Scranton. The University is a Jesuit school and it was rapidly expanding. Soldiers returning from Korea brought money and increased the size of the student body. It also helped that the Catholic schools fed the University. Graduation from high school was an entry ticket. A freshman at the University of Scranton was required to register for ROTC. That introduced me to Army officer possibilities, providing an opening that expanded on my enlisted experience. Prior to ROTC exposure my future career aspiration was to be a first sergeant in an Infantry division.

By the end of the first semester in college I recognized my academic limitations. I volunteered for six months of active duty for Army training. With basic training as a private at Fort Knox, followed immediately by advanced Infantry training at Fort Dix, I was ready to return to the National Guard, prepared to be a highly trained squad leader with an Expert Infantry Badge. My earlier exposure to experienced soldiers prepared me for the Expert Infantryman test given to all graduates at Fort Dix. Nobody was more surprised than I was when I nearly maxed the test. Soon after returning to my unit I was promoted to sergeant first class.

Shortly thereafter, I again volunteered for active duty. The maximum enlisted rank for a National Guard NCO going on active duty was staff sergeant. That resulted in a one-grade reduction, but master sergeant was the top enlisted grade and I was young. I was sent back to Fort Dix as a basic training platoon sergeant. That assignment lasted less than a year when the Army began stripping training units to fill the 2nd Infantry Brigade at Fort Devens. The Brigade was prepared to back the Marines' entry into Lebanon in 1956. The Marines entered Lebanon without resistance and the 2nd Brigade settled down to a quiet training cycle.

The Deputy Brigade Commander suggested that I apply for the United States Military Academy Prep School (USMAPS). Again to my surprise, and to the surprise of my family and my fellow soldiers, I was accepted to USMAPS at Fort Belvoir, VA in 1959. Before I completed USMAPS my two-year National Guard commitment ran out, and I reenlisted Regular Army. After completing USMAPS I received an appointment to West Point, Class of 1964, and reported there in July 1960.

The plan was working until I failed to pass academic requirements at the end of the first semester at West Point. Since I had reenlisted Regular Army I was returned to the Regular Army as a staff sergeant assigned to the 24th Infantry Division in Augsburg, Germany. As soon as I settled into my unit, I started working an application for Officer Candidate School. The timing was perfect and I was ordered to Fort Benning in June of 1961 to Infantry OCS Class 2-62.

I want to point out that I have refused previous attempts to have me provide input to a *Band of Brothers* kind of story. In my opinion, a soldier's story related to non-veterans is either unbelievable, a made-up war story, or both. For that reason it is best for combat veterans to keep their stories to themselves unless they are sharing them with someone who has also been in combat. Additionally, I believe that very few combat veterans expect thanks or praise for what they saw as doing their job. Without trying to fully explain my decision, I want to let readers know the two reasons I elected to participate in this project. First, I know where OCS Class 2-62 came from. For most of the last fifty years, we walked a path that caused me to have great respect for those who recently met at Fort Benning to mark our fiftieth anniversary. Second, those who met at Fort Benning left with a belief that we may influence some that come after us by sharing how we made our commitments to Duty, Honor and Country.

My Time at OCS

The bus ride from Pennsylvania to Fort Benning, GA was an education. It was my first experience with "separate but equal" as practiced in the South. My experience in the Army, including Basic Training, AIT, USMAPS, West Point, and as a soldier in Germany were without experience of racial segregation. Soldiers were not politically correct; we just never gave a thought to the issue. On the bus ride and later in Columbus, Georgia I saw white-only restrooms, white-only water fountains, and white-only lunch rooms. I welcomed arrival at Fort Benning and the protected life of a soldier. I am proud to say that I never saw anything that could be referred to as unfair treatment because of race, gender or religion in my following thirty years of commissioned service.

The OCS program did not cause me any anxiety since I had completed Infantry Basic Training and AIT, 1st Army NCO Academy, USMAPS and Plebe Year at West Point, one almost immediately following the other. I was fortunate to be assigned to the First Platoon in my OCS Company. The First Platoon Tac Officer was a captain and a graduate of ROTC. As I recall, the other Platoon Tacs were recent OCS graduates and they were more prepared to train OCS Candidates than future officers. The First Platoon did well under the guidance of a more mature and balanced model, and that made a big difference in my overall attitude. The major thing that impacted me during OCS was the friendships I formed, some lasting to this day, more than fifty years later. Our reunion at Fort Benning for our fifty-year celebration was as is often the case with soldiers. We had not had any contact since graduation with most of the reunion participants, but we picked up conversations that were interrupted many years ago, and continued where we left off.

Airborne and Ranger Schools

We had positive attitudes as OCS Candidates. When the volunteer applications were circulated most of us signed up for Ranger, Airborne, Flight School, and whatever other volunteer assignments were available. The eye test eliminated me from Flight School but I made the list for Ranger and Airborne training. Never in my dreams had I believed I would be allowed to attend Ranger training, and I thought I only had a small chance for Airborne training. As luck would have it, we graduated in March and neither the West Point nor ROTC classes would be ready for post-commission training until sometime after July. That provided training opportunities for us that otherwise may not have been available.

After a short leave I reported to Airborne training at Fort Benning. The course turned out to be a gut check with a lot of running and physical training. Since we were just out of OCS the Airborne training was a snap and for the most part fun.

We had about a two-week break between Airborne and the start of Ranger School, so Millard Burke, a first platoon OCS classmate, decided to take a few days to visit his home in Pensacola, Florida, and I joined him. Three days of water skiing resulted in major sunburn for this Northeastern Pennsylvania, never-use-sunscreen, seldom-in-the-sun-for-more-than-an-hour guy. I spent the next week moaning and getting sprayed with sunburn lotion. We were of the opinion that a visit to the medics would result in a court martial for stupidity, if for no other reason. I started Ranger school with silver dollar size blisters. Later, I concluded that the reason I made it through Ranger school was that I was delirious for most of the Fort Benning phase. Major Lesson Learned: I was a brand new Airborne, Ranger, Infantry Lieutenant; a leader of men, but not smart enough to stay out of the sun. I realized that I still had a lot to learn.

First Assignment as a New Lieutenant

The Deputy Commander of the 2nd Infantry Brigade tracked my success and failure. He had been my advisor when I was assigned to the Brigade at Fort Devens. When I graduated from OCS he managed to have me assigned to 2nd Army Headquarters. Later, it seemed to be a bad idea, and he asked if I would be interested in assignment to the Big Red One (1st Infantry Division) at Fort Riley, Kansas. The 1st Division was preparing for Reforger, an exercise to reinforce Berlin. That seemed like the perfect assignment for a new Infantry second lieutenant. OCS classmates Thomas Vaughn and Jim Hamilton and I were assigned to the same Battle Group.

Following about a year of training at Fort Riley, we launched for Germany. As I recall we launched out of an Air Force base in Missouri aboard a double deck prop driven aircraft. The bird hauled a huge load, but in my opinion it did best converting avgas to noise. After a loud and noisy flight we were convinced that we were about to land at Frankfurt. However, our aircraft was diverted to McGuire AFB. As the senior officer on the aircraft, I was told to unload the troops and baggage on what seemed to be the biggest concrete patch I had ever seen. While we off-loaded, the aircraft refueled and before anyone could tell me what was happening it cranked up and departed heading south. An Air Force colonel arrived in a sedan and asked me what a pile of Army troops was doing on his runway. I told him I was the Troop Commander for this lift. We were heading for Frankfurt, Germany when the Air Force dropped us there. I had no idea where I was and what I was doing, but it seemed to be his problem. About an hour later a flatbed arrived for the equipment, and buses for the troops. We were transported to Fort Dix where we hung out for three days. We were later informed that the aircraft was diverted to haul 82nd Airborne Division troops to Selma, Alabama to help settle a problem between the Alabama Governor and the President.

The Alabama crisis passed and our unit was finally picked up and transported to Frankfurt. We joined with prepositioned equipment, and the Battle Group convoyed to Wildflecken. After three months of training we convoyed to Berlin. The tactical road march to Berlin crossing the Russian sector of East Germany was interesting. Our mission was to exercise the United States right to access the US Sector in Berlin. The Germans were glad to see us and we were glad to be there. Berlin was still considered occupied, and in the early '60s, West Berlin was great duty. For the first month I was detailed as Officer in Charge at Check Point Charlie five nights a week. Berlin Brigade Military Police did the work. I was there as an officer because the Russians and East Germans would only talk to an officer; not that they wanted to talk to me on the night shift anyway. For the next two months I was detailed to drive around in a military sedan in East Berlin. The purpose was to show the flag and exercise access. At the end of our tour we passed the baton to another battle group from the 1st Infantry Division and we flew back to Fort Riley. It was very quiet at Fort Riley after Berlin.

Goodbye Big Army, Hello Special Forces

Excitement at Fort Riley was limited to taking college courses at Kansas State University. I was still working on a degree. Some of the guys were looking for opportunities for the future, and Special Forces appeared to be an attractive alternative. My Company Commander and a group of the officers that hung around the Officers Club were Special Forces qualified. They got us involved in the Fort Riley Sport Parachute Club. It was only a matter of time until I had my volunteer papers working at Infantry Branch. Vietnam was starting to heat up and Special Forces had a recruiting priority. That can be translated to say that anyone who could pass the physical, was airborne-qualified or willing to go to jump school, and indicated interest in Special Forces could expect orders in the mail.

The Special Forces qualification course at Fort Bragg was another gut check. After OCS, Airborne, and Ranger training we had no surprises, but the course was tough. After completion I was on orders to 10th Special Forces Group, Bad Tolz, Germany.

I returned to Olyphant, Pennsylvania and married Anne Louise (Nancy) O'Malley on February 13, 1965 before heading to Germany. Life was good in Bavaria in 1965. Ed Junior was born at the US Army Hospital in Munich, Germany in February 1966. In April Nancy was medically evacuated to Walter Reed for major eye surgery. I received orders for Vietnam and the good life got complicated. The only thing that saved me was help from Dallas Cox, my OCS First Platoon classmate, and his family. Dallas, Betty, Rene, and Lisa helped me pack and gave me a crash course on baby care in hopes that I could get Ed back to the United States safely. The Army assigned me to Fort George Meade, delaying my Vietnam orders for about six months. About a week after Nancy's last appointment at Walter Reed my orders to Vietnam hit the wire, and off I went.

Vietnam seemed to be the place to be for soldiers. Given that the Army mission is to go to foreign countries and fight the enemies of the United States, we were not doing that in Germany. In 1967 the Special Forces mission in Vietnam was to win the hearts and minds of the people, but fighting the VC was the means to that end. Shortly after arrival at 5th Special Forces Headquarters in Nha Trang, a group of us were told we were going to the Command and Control Detachment located at Dha Nang. On arrival I was given a briefing on the Studies and Observation Group (SOG) mission and further assigned to Forward Operating Base (FOB) #2 in Kontum.

For the most part FOB 2 was the support base for reconnaissance teams that operated in Laos. At that time the public position was that the United States did not have boots on the ground in Laos. Thus, we were operating in "black" mode. As a junior captain, I was given command of a Civilian Irregular Defense Group (CIDG) "Nung" battalion. We were responsible for the defense of the SFOB, and when required, we provided a 100-man "hatchet" force to exploit targets found by the recon teams.

After a couple of training missions in the Kontum area, the hatchet force was assigned to destroy a bunker complex. The complex was found by one of our recon teams. It was reported to be a Command and Control (C&C) site for the lower end of the Ho Chi Minh Trail. We were expecting a fight, but the site was abandoned when we arrived. The complex was also used as an aid station. We scattered white phosphorous (WP) grenades, and destroyed everything we could. Since we had gone to a lot of trouble to get there, we searched the heavily-used trails for two nights and three days. We started to feel like we were bait in "Indian Country." Our luck held on this mission though and we were extracted without a fight. That was unusual, as we later discovered that VC trail watchers usually directed response teams to take the bait.

A later mission was launched out of Kham Duc. One of the recon teams was ambushed while running a trail in daylight. Two of the Nungs were able to escape and were picked up by supporting helicopters. We were launched on an urgent mission to execute a body-recover and/ or prisoner-rescue. The reader can appreciate how uptight the rescue mission team was, knowing they were heading to an ambush site in

"Indian Country." The good news was that as the Ground Commander, I had top priority for anything that flew. The two Nungs who escaped from the ambush were volunteer guides to get us to the ambush site, but whose side they were really on was questionable. The site was secured without incident and it seemed to me that it would be prudent to drop 500 and 1000 pound bombs and napalm on any site that threatened our mission. Helicopter gunship and USAF ground support aircraft did more than a few attacks for good measure. As it turned out, the team members we went in to help were all dead, and were discovered in shallow graves. Assuming the worst, our guys carefully cleared the site and recovered the bodies. The remains of the team that was ambushed were identified, accounted for and prepared for evacuation. While we waited for extraction it again seemed prudent to expend available ordnance on possible enemy positions. The possibility existed that we could target the people that ambushed our guys. At least we tried.

The last mission I will discuss was a follow-up after another American was lost. Captain Dick LeGate was killed when he came upon an NVA unit while leading a recon mission. His body was recovered, and our leadership believed we should exploit the target he encountered before he was killed. He had been operating in a really hot area, and we bit off more than we were ready to chew. We took fire as we landed. After we broke contact, we had a quiet day and night. We set up an ambush on the trail and we were alert the first night. On night two we were probed and both sides took casualties. An NVA soldier we killed inside our perimeter was well-equipped and armed with an almost new CHICOM AK-47. After my team received a lot of casualties, we were replaced by a fresh team from Phu Bai. The new team had a mission to break contact and prepare for extraction. We later determined that we got hit by NVA troops that were on the way to execute Tet-68 operations. Soon after our encounter, the 173rd got hit hard in and around Kontum and Pleiku. By the time Tet-68 kicked off I was back at 5th Group HQ in Nha Trang preparing for return to the 'States. I left after the Tet offensive and was surprised when I got back to the USA to find out from Cronkite that we lost. I can assure all that we hammered the VC and NVA, giving better than we got. I was also surprised to hear that we did not have boots on the ground in Laos and Cambodia. The Secretary of Defense and Walter Cronkite said it was true, so it must have been true.

Between Vietnam Tours

Early arrival for the Infantry Career Course at Fort Benning meant an assignment doing something useful. Some of the early-bird assignments were just busy work. However, I found a job as Commander of a Non-Commissioned Officer Academy (NCOA) Company. That turned out to be a great job. The students knew they were preparing for Infantry combat in Vietnam and the cadre knew the mission was serious. The students were selected because they had displayed leadership qualities. The NCOA program was designed to give combat-essential skills to small-unit leaders, in order to give them the best chance to do their jobs in combat. Small unit leaders were scarce, and they were badly needed. The program was up to Fort Benning standards, and the candidates I observed and rated excelled at every turn. When my Career Course class started, I was pulled out of command and sent to school. Our next family member, Kathleen, was born at the Fort Benning hospital.

After Career Course, Infantry Branch decided that I needed to go to degree completion somewhere. Did I mention that I had a mixed bag of college credits when I finished OCS, and the Army wanted all officers to have a college degree? The University of Nebraska at Omaha accepted all my credits and my application for Bootstrap. Omaha was family time, but I got orders for a second tour in Vietnam as soon as I graduated.

Back to Vietnam

This time, Infantry Branch agreed to assign me to a US Army division. I figured I had paid my dues as a Special Forces target for the NVA on my first tour. When I arrived in Vietnam the second time, I did not even bring a green beret in my rucksack. However, as we all understand, the needs of the Army have priority. Colonel Mike Healy, Commander of 5th Special Forces Group, needed combat-experienced Special Forces majors and that was the end of my assignment to the "Big Army." When I arrived at Nha Trang I was assigned to the Group S-3 as the Operations Officer. In about a month I moved to Plans and began working on the plan to redeploy Special Forces Group back to Fort Bragg. The border Special Forces camps were first converted to Region Ranger and a new command was created to run cross-border operations. A big job that consumed most of the year was the transfer of Special Forces logistical operations to more conventional Army units. By April 1970 all we had left were the remains of 5th Special Forces Group Headquarters that were about at end-of-tour. We loaded on a special-mission aircraft at Nha Trang and landed back at Fort Bragg shortly thereafter. After the Unit Colors were passed, I was assigned as an instructor at the Engineer School, Fort Belvoir, VA.

Fort Belvoir

Teaching command, staff and leadership to Engineer captains was a welcome change of pace. Fort Belvoir was kind of an old home as I had spent a year there when I attended the Military Academy Prep School. I bought a townhouse ten minutes from Fort Belvoir and life was good. Nancy, Ed and Kathleen seemed to like the assignment and I assumed it was just a matter of time to get orders for tour number three in Vietnam. One of the Engineer officers I knew from Germany commanded the Personnel Control Facility (PCF), responsible for processing return-to-military-control soldiers that had been absent without official leave (AWOL). As you may guess, Engineer officers were not fighting for the job. I saw it as command, and I volunteered. It was a lieutenant colonel command position and the incumbent reported to the Fort Belvoir Chief of Staff and to the Engineer Center and Fort Belvoir Commander, a major general.

During my eighteen months in command of PCF, Fort Belvoir, I had the opportunity and duty to interview over 1,800 soldiers to determine disposition of their cases. As a Special Courts-Martial Officer, I referred about 300 cases for court martial, with 150 to Special Courts and about 25 to General Courts. The rest were disposed of by Summary Courts or Field Grade Article 15s. Everyone except a few hard cores had the opportunity to get charged for bad time and shipped to Fort Riley to the Retraining Brigade. Successful completion of retraining would lead to an honorable discharge upon completion of enlistment obligation. The command was a challenge. At any given time 300 of the soldiers on my morning report were in the post stockade either in pretrial confinement or serving court martial sentences. Most senior commanders were of the opinion that the return-to-military-from-AWOL soldiers were draftees absent to avoid Vietnam service. In fact, most had enlisted and almost none were avoiding Vietnam service. The majority were just plain losers.

It came as no surprise when my tour at Belvoir was cut short to attend Command and General Staff College (C&GSC).

Fort Leavenworth

Life as a student at Fort Leavenworth had more pluses than minuses. I connected with many great friends who are still good friends to this day. Warren, the third and last member of our family, was born at Fort Leavenworth. (Twenty-eight years later Warren left the Army as a Captain, Infantry, 10th Mountain Division. In 2010 he became a Special Agent of the FBI, stationed at Las Vegas. Some would say that is a more dangerous environment than Afghanistan.) We all assumed we would be back in Vietnam after we graduated. As it turned out the politicians saw we were winning and threw in the towel. I was assigned to stay at Combined Arms Combat Development Activity. I stayed at Fort Leavenworth, but the family had to move from student quarters to permanent party quarters. As an action officer in Infantry Systems Branch I had the opportunity to have an impact on future systems. For example, we were working on the Ranger reorganization. The budget folks changed allocation of night vision devices to one per squad. Every chance I got I changed it back to one per Ranger. It was well worth whatever it cost, as we found out later.

My desk also worked small arms and military canines. We tried to keep the dog program funded to a level that would ensure viability. I was fortunate in that I was able to add college credits to the credits gained as a C&GSC student, and was able to leave Fort Leavenworth with a master's degree from Kansas State University and a commercial pilot license. When the Army decided that I was starting to enjoy my time at Fort Leavenworth, orders arrived to move to the Army Staff.

Army Staff and Joint Staff

Much to my surprise and probably to the surprise of most of my friends, my assignment was to War Plans, Office of the Deputy Chief of Staff for Operations (ODCSOPS). The assumption was that only fast burners were assigned to ODCSOPS. I could only assume they needed a Special Forces grunt to serve as "Napoleon's Lieutenant." While assigned to ODCSOPS

I managed to get a multi-engine pilot license and was well on the way to a flight instructor license. After two years of working Joint Actions I was assigned to the NATO Fire Support Requirements Study. I could discuss the study as a separate paper. However, it is enough said that nothing was changed as a result of the study and the Air Force retained the Close Air Support mission without any changes. As we could see the end of the study approaching we all started looking for a new job. I was able to successfully compete for a position in the Office of the Joint Chiefs of Staff (OJCS) National Military Command Center (NMCC).

The NMCC is for all purposes the Duty Officer for the National Command Authority. We were on Team 5, led by the Navy. During my tour we had three Admirals. Needless to say I learned a lot about Navy language and customs. We were on duty when the hostage rescue attempt was launched. This made for an exciting day. We were also on duty when a nuclear missile exploded (non-nuclear explosion) in Arkansas. Imagine my surprise when I saw a four-star sitting at the desk in the front office. When I looked at the conference table the junior was a three-star. It was another exciting day.

To keep this short I will relate one more operation. I was detailed from my team to a Crisis Team assembled when the United States deployed the AWACS to Saudi Arabia. The regular NMCC Team works eight hours and rotates every week. The Crisis Team worked twelve hours for three months. There was no break until the crisis was over.

At the end of my two-year NMCC assignment, I was selected for a one-year assignment to Saudi Arabia. The good news is that I was able to complete a master's degree in International Relations at Georgetown University. Then I was off to Saudi Arabia and the start of a new learning experience.

Saudi Arabia

I was assigned to United States Military Training Mission (USMTM), Khamis Mushayt, Saudi Arabia. When I got my orders I went to the NMCC Intelligence Center for a briefing on the mission and location. I could not find anyone that could tell me anything about Khamis Mushayt. When I got to USMTM Headquarters they asked me why I came alone. They said the Saudi's preferred family and they would pay for transport if I would agree. It is a long story, but I'll keep it short. I went home, packed up my family and came back to Saudi Arabia.

Again to keep an ugly experience short, I will only relate the summary. One of my majors was ordered home by the Saudi Minister of Defense. I checked every source for a reason and could find nothing beyond Saudi arbitrariness. The Army Chief located in Riyadh blamed me and got the USMTM Commander, an Air Force major general, to send me home early. It took me two years to expunge the unsupported record that was made by USMTM to justify the early termination.

Back to the Washington DC Area

Concepts Analysis (Bethesda)

When I arrived back in the US, I was assigned to the Concepts Analysis Agency. I was again working on the war games and studies that I worked on while assigned to DCSOPS. I am not an Operations Research System Analysis (ORSA) kind of guy, so I looked for available jobs back on the Army Staff. Having a current Top Secret Special Background Investigation (TSSBI) clearance from the NMCC and DCSOPS as a force development staff officer, I managed to make a contact that had a high priority ability to grab anyone needed for a hot project. I was told by the Concepts and Analysis (CAA) Chief of Staff that the CAA Director would not honor a request for reassignment. All were surprised when I got immediate orders to DCSOPS.

DCSOPS (Special Project)

When I reported to an office in the Pentagon I joined a group of about twelve headed by a Signal Corps colonel. I could not be briefed on the job until my clearance was validated. I had three things that concerned me. First, it was interesting that my NMCC clearance needed to be validated before I could start the job. Second, I was glad to be free from CAA, but I wondered what I was doing in a group that was Signal Corps and technology-focused. Third, I was back in DCSOPS which was a good thing, but I had no idea what I had wished for and had apparently received. Things started to happen fast. My clearance was validated and we had a brigadier general assigned. A big change occurred when our office was cut loose from DCSOPS and became an ever-growing agency located at Arlington Hall. Our new name, Command Systems Integration Agency (CSIA), was quietly hung on our door.

CSIA

CSIA represented Army support to a national program. The program was fully-funded and supported at every level. I was promoted to Colonel and assumed the Deputy for Operations and Security, and a Signal Corps Engineer was Deputy for Technical (I say "geek") Matters. I transferred from the program to become Commander of Special Projects Support Activity (SPSA) in late 1989. I assume the names were changed to protect the program and to this day I tell everyone I erased the tape when I walked out the door.

SPSA

As Commander of SPSA, Fort Belvoir, I was dual-hatted as Assistant Deputy Chief of Staff for Research, Development and Engineering (Special Operations Forces) Army Material Command. Army support for classified Special Forces projects was accomplished by SPSA. Additional support for Special Warfare required by Special Operations Command and Army Special Warfare at Fort Bragg was coordinated by the DCS Office at Army Material Command Headquarters. SPSA also procured and modified non-standard aircraft for Special Operations Aviation and non-standard weapons for classified missions. March 1992 marked the end of thirty-seven years of Army service, seven years enlisted and thirty years commissioned. As we say in Special Forces, "When you can't hump the rucksack, out you go."

Civilian Life

After mandatory retirement I toyed with various job opportunities in the Washington area. It hit me one day that nobody would pay me what I would want to make me endure the Washington traffic. I also realized that as a result of extensive command time I would probably not do well as a paper-pusher. A partner and I started a construction company in Florida after Hurricane Andrew. That was a learning experience. Attempts to start an employee-owned company were not accepted by the workers. In addition, it was impossible to compete in Dade County (Miami) as an English-speaking contractor. After Hurricane Andrew, media and politicians complained that the building code was inadequate. I said that the code was not only adequate, it was overkill. Of course, nobody else observed the code requirements. We did follow the code requirements, and as a result we could not compete. After two years I resigned from the company and took a job as the Plans Officer working nuclear planning at the Pennsylvania Emergency Management Agency (PEMA). Pennsylvania has five nuclear generation sites. I took the job as the Plans Officer for the Beaver Valley Site on the Ohio River, north of Pittsburg. Two years later I was promoted to Central Pennsylvania Area Director, responsible for coordination with the central twenty-six counties of Pennsylvania. After ten years with PEMA, I retired.

Retirement

Somebody told me once that a former DCSOPS guy could be dropped on a desert island and he would be working twelve hours a day and taking work home by weekends. I try to deny the accusation, but shortly after retirement, I started a Ph.D. program. I completed all course requirements and was an All-But-Dissertation (ABD) when I experienced a health issue. Time ran out and I accepted a third master's degree from Capella University in Business. In addition I am on the Executive Committee at the Tobyhanna Army Depot AUSA Chapter. I am also an executive member of the Northeastern Pennsylvania Retiree Council.

Conclusion

As I tried to write this story I wanted to encourage people beginning their journeys to "just keep on keeping on." No excuses. I learned early that you only fail when you quit. Nobody can make you feel inadequate without your concurrence. OCS served as a stepping stone to success. Friends I met at Fort Benning are still friends. My career had many twists and turns, but all things considered, life was good and still is. Nancy and I married soon after OCS and she still puts up with me after

46 years. She completed her degree when I was in Vietnam. I earned my bachelor's degree using the Bootstrap program at the University of Nebraska at Omaha, and two of my three master's degrees while still on active duty. Our two sons and our daughter were born at Army bases and they all went to college on Army ROTC scholarships. Ed was promoted to colonel in February 2012. He will attend Senior Service School this year and assume brigade command in 2013. Kathleen was a captain in a reserve unit and a deputy program manager working Star Wars when she took a sabbatical to care for her two girls. Warren completed his Army obligation as a captain in the 10th Mountain Division. Ed, Kathleen, and Warren all managed to get master's degrees. Warren served as a Municipal police officer, and is currently a Special Agent, FBI, in Las Vegas.

I can't wait to see what happens next.

Left to Right, Lieutenant (Later Captain) Kathleen Burke, Colonel (Retired) Ed Burke, His Wife of Forty-Six Years Nancy, Lieutenant (Later Captain) Warren Burke, and Captain (Later Colonel) Ed Burke Jr. University of Scranton ROTC Commissioning Ceremony, Scranton, PA, May 28, 1995.

Captain (Later Colonel) Dallas Cox, CO, D Company, 27th Infantry, with his Artillery Forward Observer (Lieutenant Ford), Vietnam, 1968

The Early Days

I was born the second of seven children and raised on a hillside farm near the New River in the community of Hiwassee, Virginia. The area was marked by both poverty and tranquility. My first seventeen years gave me the best of all preparations for a successful life. I had a Christian mother and father who taught their children the value of hard work, discipline, obedience and the Golden Rule. The other two important elements in my life came to me later; luck and timing. I walked a mile to a two-room school for seven years and later rode a bus fifteen miles to the high school in Dublin, Virginia, where I graduated in June 1954. I was then seventeen years old, with my life ahead of me. High school graduates were usually given a dinner bucket or a ticket out of town. College was not even considered an option.

The Korean War was over and men were returning to what few jobs were available. My ticket out of town was the military. My older brother was already in the Air Force, and most people advised me to do the same. I did not realize there were limits on how far I could advance in the Air Force, and the blue uniform and the opportunities that were available were heady stuff. I left home at seventeen. At that age, I thought I was sick of home, but it did not take long for me to be very homesick.

At the time I joined the Air Force, had I been given the opportunity to write down everything I wanted out of my thirty-five years of military service, I could not have imagined the magnitude of the opportunities before me. I did not know it, but my guardian angel had hitched me to a star that tested me, but did not exceed my grasp.

My first train ride took me from Pulaski to Sampson Air Force Base in New York for basic training. Most people seem to think that basic training is difficult, but I found it easy compared to living on a hillside farm. What I enjoyed the most was the hot showers. We did not have indoor plumbing on the farm.

Most of the time was spent in classrooms. The marching, guard duty, and a week of bivouac were easy and enjoyable compared to what I would later encounter in the Army. The fact that the guy who slept on the top bunk above me was a black man from New York was a new experience. We became very good friends and talked at length about the relationship of the races in the South. There were few blacks where I grew up, and I only saw them in passing. Schools were segregated.

The weather in the Finger Lake area of New York is nice in the summer, but by the time I left it was getting colder. When I arrived at Warren Air Force Base at Cheyenne, Wyoming, it was really cold. The wind would blow snow through the windows. The only warm place was in bed.

I trained at Warren Air Force Base to be an engine mechanic. We learned on everything from small two-cycle engines to large diesels. I figured I could always work as a mechanic. Like most farm boys, I was already a fair jack-leg mechanic. The training lasted about six months, and when I left I believed I could work on most any engine.

I was sent to Great Falls Air Force Base to work on the ground power equipment for the B-52s stationed there. It was really cold in Great Falls. The rumor was true; only one strand of barbed wire protected us from the winds of the North Pole. You knew it was cold when the APs asked to see the blankets in your car as well as your pass when leaving the base. Unlike today, you had to have a pass to leave the base back then.

In July of 1955, I received orders for Korea. I was then eighteen years old and heading across the Pacific. I hitch-hiked from Montana to Virginia to see my family. I had not seen Mom and Dad in over a year, and had to see them before I left.

After my visit home, Dad put me on a Greyhound bus in Pulaski and said to me, "I hate to see you go son, but you have to go before you can come back." The trip to California took seven days and nights. We boarded the USS A. E. Anderson at Fort Mason, CA, and sailed for thirty days to Yokohama, Japan. We had a twelve-hour shore leave there and I spent all the money I had. We continued on to Inchon the following morning. We disembarked about two miles out at sea, and continued in small landing craft. I arrived in Korea without a dime, but was given a small advance pay. It had been an amazing 10,000 mile, 38-day trip for an eighteen-year-old boy from the mountains of Virginia.

I was stationed across the Han River from Seoul at K-16. I was part of the team that provided all the power for the installation and the ground power units to assist with starting aircraft. The airplane of the President of Korea was stationed there, and I saw him come and go many times. I remember most the time when a young Billy Graham made his visit to Korea. I still have a picture of him as he came off the airplane.

In addition to providing the power for the airfield, I was also on rotation to the adjacent radio homing sites. This meant that two of us would live on top of a mountain in a Quonset hut. I would keep the generators operational and the other guy would operate the radios. Officers would visit the sites to hunt pheasants. I still have pictures of some of those beautiful pheasants. We would give them to the locals to eat.

I had been in Korea for about three months when I was sent to Japan to a special school. It seemed to me I would be traveling a lot. I could not believe I would have the good fortune to see Tokyo and other parts of Japan.

My tour in Korea was a very good one. The war had done much damage, but the country was beginning to rebuild. I had excellent people with whom to work and live, and we had most everything we needed. The thirteen months went very fast. At the end of my Korean tour, I was reassigned to Langley Field, Virginia, near my home. How is that assignment for luck? The ship voyage home was very slow. By that time, I had enough travel money to buy an aircraft ticket from California to Roanoke, Virginia. It was good to be home.

At Langley, I was assigned to the 509th Fighter Bomber Squadron. We had just been equipped with the new F-100Ds with nuclear capability. It was new for all of us, but the training was intense and enjoyable. However, the long hours got in the way of my love life. I met and fell in love with Betty Huddleston, who was a nurse at the Medical College of Virginia in Richmond. She worked the 4-12 PM shift. I would pick her up at midnight, have something to eat, drop her off, and get back to Langley just in time for duty formation. It was killing me. I either had to marry her or go AWOL. To my good fortune, she agreed to marry me.

We had been married for about three months when the squadron was ordered to Ramstein, Germany. We did not have air refueling, so we had to stage the aircraft across. We had ground crews in Newfoundland, the Azores, and Tripoli. It took over thirty days to get everything to Ramstein.

When I told Betty I would be away on TDY for six months, she asked, "What is TDY?" That was the first of many separations over thirty-five years. She often remarks that she should have left me then.

The pilots with whom I worked encouraged me to start taking college courses at night. I followed their advice, and enjoyed the classes. They gave me something to occupy my free time in Germany. That was the first of several years to follow in Germany. I have very fond memories of my first tour there, and the teachers in the education center. I would go to Heidelberg at every opportunity.

When I was discharged as a Staff Sergeant in 1958 at Langley Field, I applied for and was accepted at William and Mary College in Williamsburg. Betty was working as a nurse in the local hospital and I was working part time as an automobile mechanic. It was not long until Betty was pregnant with our first child. She worked until ten days before the birth of Renee. I was taking an exam at the time. She just went to the hospital and called me to tell me we had a baby girl.

I decided I could not go to school, work, and raise a family. Looking back, I realize I was just not willing to put forth the effort. By that time, I had about 40 hours of college credit. I dropped out of college and joined the Air Force Reserves to complete my six-year obligation. I jumped from job to job and never made much money. In three months we had another baby on the way.

With a wife and two children, I knew I would have to find something with security and a future. I remembered the good days in the Air Force, and applied to re-enlist. However, they would not take me with three dependents. My only choice was the Army, so in July 1960, I started my second military career. My mind was made up to complete twenty years. That was one of the happiest and best days of my life.

I was sent to Fort Jackson, SC for Infantry Basic Training. It was certainly different from Air Force basic, but I did not care what it took. I was in for the duration and gave it my all. I had an advantage because, unlike most of the young men there, I had seen major areas of Asia, and parts of North Africa and Europe. I just wanted to finish, get my family, and get on with life. I was promoted to E-3 when I graduated.

My first assignment was to Fort Bliss, TX as an automobile mechanic. I went to Virginia and picked up the family. We put everything we owned into a 1958 Plymouth and drove to El Paso.

We were able to find a decent place to live within walking distance of the post. Betty immediately went to work as a nurse on the 3-11 PM shift. My neighbor kept the girls until I got home about 4 PM. We were paying off debts and were happy. We both had work.

I had worked in the motor pool for about three or four months when I was called to the Personnel Office. CWO Bennet, the Personnel Officer, told me he needed a finance clerk. He had reviewed my records and seen that I had prior service and good scores on my tests. He also noticed I had taken several accounting courses in college. He asked me if I would like the job, and I told him I would. At that point, he said I would be promoted to E-4 the next day. I nearly fainted. That was the highest pay jump for a junior enlisted man with prior service. Back then, there was something called a "blood stripe." When a member of a unit was reduced in rank, that rank could be given to another member of the same unit. As the saying goes, it is an ill wind that doesn't blow someone good.

That was an excellent assignment. I enjoyed the service to the soldiers, and CWO Bennet was a real gentleman. One day, he called me into his office and asked, "Why are you here?" When I asked what he meant, he said, "You should be in OCS." I told him I would love to, but didn't know how to go about it. He gave me a form to fill out, and within a week I was before an OCS selection board. In another week my family was on their way to Betty's parents' house, and I was on the way to Fort Benning. That was a major milestone in my military career.

My Time at OCS

I was then in a position to have the career I wanted. The door had been opened and I had to produce like never before. OCS teaches many things, but two things remain with me. I took away a new respect for the Officer Corps, and an appreciation for the fellowship and respect of people I knew I could always trust. I also learned to take care of the problems of today. Tomorrow will always have enough problems. These two traits have never failed me. I made two promises to myself; I would prepare myself so that when called I would be ready, and I would never allow myself to be numbered with those cold and timid souls who know neither victory nor defeat.

I was in a league with many people who had much more worldly experience, education and social graces than I ever thought possible. I doubt that I would have made it without my roommate, Ed Burke. He was a great mentor, and if the truth be known, he probably felt sorry for me. He remains one of my three true friends. It has been said that if you have five friends you are wealthy. I have three, and I know I am wealthy.

After six months of physical agony and fear of failure and humiliation, OCS was over. The proudest day of my life was when I pinned on those second lieutenant bars. My family always served in the military, but I was the first officer.

My Commissioned Career

I think it was the next day that most of the class started Airborne training. After my five jumps were completed and I pinned on my parachute wings, I attended the Motor Officer course at Fort Benning. Instead of turning wrenches, I would be scheduling and supervising maintenance.

Once again, we headed west in the 1958 Plymouth. We drove to Fort Lewis, WA where I was to be the brand new Motor Officer for the 1st Battalion of the 22nd Battle Group. We had nice quarters on post, but not much furniture. Betty went to work at Madigan Army Hospital. We were set to enjoy living together for a while.

I had been at Fort Lewis for about six months or so when my commander, Colonel Brown, called me in and said, "I have to fill a quota for Ranger School. You are a new lieutenant and need the training." I saluted, packed up the family, and headed to Betty's parents once again. I graduated from Ranger Class 2-64 approximately three months later.

While in Ranger School the talk was all about Special Forces. Special Forces sounded like a good deal. Jump pay for an officer was $110 and that was a lot of money. However, I had to pass the language aptitude test. In the interim, I picked up the family in Virginia and headed back to Fort Lewis. While on a maneuver in Yakima, Washington, I took the language test and passed. I applied for Special Forces and was soon on my way to Monterey, CA to take Spanish for six months. That was unbelievable and exciting. At that point, I barely had a working knowledge of English. The drive down the coast was breathtaking.

We were given quarters on Fort Ord, and I reported in at the Presidio of Monterey. It was a beautiful place, but quickly turned into a nightmare for me. I was told I would not be taking Spanish. They had enough Spanish students, but only two for the Serbo-Croatian course. What is a second lieutenant to do but say, "Yes Sir"?

I did not know what Serbo-Croatian was. I had to look it up in the dictionary. Things went downhill from there. The course lasted a year, and there were three guys in the class: one Italian speaker, one Polish speaker and one hillbilly from Virginia. There was also the problem of rank. I was the only officer, and felt that I should set the example. That was not to be. The only things that kept me going were my pride and my determination to never quit. I think I learned more English than I did Serbo-Croatian, and graduated third out of three in my class. Never in my life have I had such a hard year. Serbo-Croatian is the hardest language taught at the Defense Language Institute. However, it was worth it. I was able to use my new language to great advantage during my military career and in civilian life after retirement.

Following language school, we arrived in Fort Bragg in July for the Special Forces School. We rented a trailer with no air conditioning. Lucky for me, I was in the field most of the time. The girls had to suffer with it. The course went quickly, and in the fall we were on our way to the 10th Special Forces Group in Bad Tolz, Germany. It was a beautiful place and a choice assignment. I had the Yugoslav Team. My OCS roommate Ed Burke was also there.

In the spring, I attended the German Mountain School. It was very good winter training, and would have been useful if I were headed to Eastern Europe. I did not know it then, but my combat time was to be in the jungles of Vietnam. The thing I remember most during the mountain training is that the Germans were always borrowing my sleeping bag. Their sleeping bags were just blankets sewn together with arms attached. I understood why the Germans suffered so much from the cold in Russia.

Along with most of the members of 10th Special Forces, I received orders for Vietnam around May 1965. Betty and the girls went to Dublin, VA, where Betty went to work while I was gone.

I arrived in Nha Trang, and reported to Headquarters, 5th Special Forces Group. I was briefed and sent on to the C Team at Da Nang. I stayed there about three weeks, and helped move the team headquarters from the airfield to the new camp around Monkey Mountain near the surrounding beautiful beaches.

One day LTC Facey saw me come in with a load of material. He said, "Pack your bags. You are going to Gia Vuc." The captain there had been killed. I loaded my gear and was airborne in a short time. Gia Vuc is the southernmost camp in I Corps. I had a fine team, and soon we were all familiar with each other and what each did around the camp. By that, I am referring to "housekeeping" chores. Unlike other Army units, Special Forces teams do their own cooking and housekeeping. I always cooked breakfast when I was in camp, and shared this chore with the Team XO, Lieutenant Virgil Carter, when I was on patrol or out of camp. He was an excellent officer and a fine artist. Much of his work can be seen in the Special Forces Museum.

We patrolled the area to gather intelligence and interdict the movement of the Viet Cong. Our duties were to train and work with the ARVN Special Forces. They had a force of Montagnards from the surrounding villages. Small enemy units routinely attacked the camp.

My Team Sergeant, MSGT Billy Greenwood, ran a tight team, and it was a pleasure to lead these men. We all rotated patrol and other duties. It was not unusual to be out of the camp from ten days to two weeks at a time. This long period away from camp was hard during the monsoon season. The nights were cold when we were wet to the bone. It was especially hard on the Montagnards, because many of them suffered from TB.

I was rotated back to the C Team after about six months. Normally, that would have meant a job with the evenings free to enjoy the club and the beaches. The beaches there are among the most beautiful in the world. That was not to be. In about two weeks the camp at Lang Vei was hit hard and the Commander was killed. LTC Facey again told me to pack up.

I went to Lang Vei and found it in a real mess. The recent attack had been an inside job. One of the Montagnards was a Viet Cong (VC). He let the attackers in by blowing the corner bunker. We had the same problems faced by the forces in Afghanistan today. VC inside the camp, whom we had trained, joined forces with the other VC once they penetrated the camp. The communication bunker, the team house, the command bunker and the two team vehicles were destroyed. The American and Vietnamese Special Forces were able to retake the camp, but the US Team Captain plus many Vietnamese and Montagnards were killed.

My job was to stabilize the situation, restore the integrity of the camp, and build up the morale of the forces. We were not hit hard again until we had rebuilt most of the defensive positions. We were located on Route 9 about ten miles from Khe San and about five hundred yards from the Laotian border. The camp was a very old French outpost and very vulnerable. The 5th Group decided to build a new camp about five hundred yards from the old one.

We started clearing an old French minefield so the Sea Bees could come in and construct a new fighting camp. We were successful in clearing the minefield, but did lose one Vietnamese soldier in the process. After the minefield was cleared, the Sea Bees came in and started construction on the new camp. They were about half-finished when my time was up. Captain Frank Willoughby replaced me. He would finish the camp, and a few months later he would fight the only VC tank unit faced by Americans during the war. The camp was finally overrun. An excellent book, *The Night of the Silver Stars*, describes this fight. Several Americans were killed and others captured. The camp is now a Vietnamese museum.

I returned to Fort Benning for the Officer's Advanced Course. Within weeks, all but a few of us were told we were to be sent back to Vietnam when we finished the course. I think we consumed more alcohol than usual from then on. Betty and the girls moved to Battle Park where other wives were waiting for their husbands to return. (Note: As part of our OCS Class 50th reunion, we revisited these quarters. They are still in use but undergoing renovation.)

When I next arrived in Vietnam, in the summer of 1968, I was assigned to the 1st Battalion, 27th Infantry, in the 25th Infantry Division. That is a very famous division from the Pacific Theater during WW II. The 27th Infantry (Wolfhounds) was already known to me. As a young man, one of my neighbors in Virginia had served with the 27th during WW I in Siberia. He told us many tales from Russia and about communism. He also told me of the military cemetery he worked on while there. The 27th was the first American unit to fight communism. I thought this was a grand tradition to carry on, and an honor to serve in the unit.

Regular US Army Infantry units like Company D, 1/27th Infantry are a totally different experience from Special Forces. I knew who was on my side, and I could depend on them. It was a pleasure to lead those men. I spent most of the time teaching them battle drill as we moved about. It served us well. Those young men had little training, but learned quickly. We had contact with the VC nearly every day. Sometimes it was just snipers, but other times it was company-size units and larger.

The 25th Division Commander was quoted in the book *Some Even Volunteered*, by Alfred Bradford, as saying that Company D was the best company in the Division. When something was critical, Delta Company seemed to get it.

We moved from the Hoch Mon Bridge near Saigon to Tay Ninh, back to the graveyard near the Vietnam Airborne drop zone. Every time something was moving toward Saigon we moved to block it. After building several fire support bases, all named Mahone after a Civil War general, we established FSB Mahone about thirty miles north of Saigon and about four miles south of Dau Tieng.

I commanded Delta Company until I was promoted to major. Giving up the command was not easy, but I just moved up and became the Battalion Executive Officer. I had developed a close bond with the company, and held a great feeling of responsibility for the men. There is a real warrior code of honor. The Internet allows me to still stay in touch with many of them.

The Battalion Headquarters was at Dau Tieng, near the 3rd Brigade Headquarters, in an old French rubber plantation house. It was very nice. It took several direct hits, but we just patched it up. Our job was to help protect the 3rd Brigade and the airfield at Dau Thieng. The base was hit very hard during Tet '69. We had one Distinguished Service Cross winner that night, and many other acts of heroism.

The best and worst day of my life took place on an air assault to develop a new fire support base. The helicopter I was in was shot down. I made a pact with God that, if he would let me come home to my family, I would serve him the rest of my life. I can still feel His hands today as he caught that helicopter and put it softly on the ground. Praise His Holy Name!!! He kept his part of the bargain, and I am making progress on my part.

Just before I rotated back to the 'States we moved the Battalion to Chu Chi. The 1st Infantry Division replaced us at FSB Mahone.

General Williams recommended me to General Westmoreland to represent the 25th Division on a six-month speaking tour when I returned to the 'States. I was assigned to Fort Hood, and worked out of the 1st Armored Division's Public Affairs Office. I spoke three or four times every day in front of every kind of audience. Texas is a big place, and I drove over 35,000 miles in the process of speaking to thousands of people. I only had two hostile audiences. One was a talk show in Dallas, and the other was a library club in Huntsville. Texans, unlike a lot Americans, were not so critical of our role in Vietnam. They certainly did not blame me. It was a great experience and an honor to represent so many fine soldiers.

When I came off the speaking tour, I was assigned to Project MAASTERS. That was a program to evaluate the use of sensors to monitor movement across the DMZ between North and South Vietnam. Since I was Special Forces, they assumed I knew nothing, and sent me to the Basic Intel Officers School at Dundock, Maryland. I finished, came back to Fort Hood, and remained there until the summer of 1971. Once, during a staff meeting in the field where we stayed most of the time on Project

MAASTERS, the Brigade Commander told me to take his helicopter and go back to the Education Office to see the recruiter from William Carey College. He thought they might take me to finish my degree. In about a month, Betty, the girls, and I were on the way to Mississippi.

I spent a year at William Carey and received my BA. Infantry Branch representatives called and said, "Now you have a degree, you need to be educated." After a short refresher language course in Monterey, the family and I were on our way to Belgrade, Yugoslavia. I studied at the University of Belgrade. That was the start of my training to be a Foreign Area Officer. My areas of interest were Greece, Turkey, Cyprus and Yugoslavia. In addition to my studies at the University, I traveled all over Yugoslavia and made side trips to Greece, Bulgaria, Romania and Italy. That was the opportunity of a lifetime. While at the University, I received what the Yugoslavs called a master's degree.

On some of my travels, my family went with me. When they couldn't go, it was not easy on them. I would be gone on trips, and they would have no idea where I was. That assignment certainly prepared me for the possibility that the Soviets might attack Western Europe from the South, as the thinking went at the time. I would have been prepared to parachute behind Soviet lines. I went back to Yugoslavia several times during the five years I taught in the Foreign Area Course at Fort Bragg from 1974 to 1979.

After my year in Belgrade, I wrote for my next assignment. I was told the "Communist University" was probably not the best I could do, so they sent me to the University of Indiana. By that time, I had about all the education I could stand. However, as a good soldier, I thought of the assignment as just another mission I had been given. The problem of these one-year education assignments was that they were all-or-nothing missions. Unlike the first time I went to college, and gave up when things got difficult, I did not have the option of taking a course over or failing a course. I was given a year and had to produce, or I would probably be out of the Army. Heavy reductions in the military were being made, and failure had no place. I spent many long hours in the library and at home to complete the MA at the University of Indiana. However, my education was not over.

My next assignment was to the Command and General Staff College. It was not as difficult as my MA program, but I did have to devote more time to it than I wanted. After leaving Leavenworth, I was ready for some normal family life. My children were teenagers. They thought all I did was study.

After C&GSC, I was assigned to the School of International Studies at Fort Bragg. I taught in the European Seminar and soon made lieutenant colonel. It was a great school. The entire globe was covered, and each area had men well versed in their areas. They had studied and traveled in their areas as I had. We were all kept abreast of the world on a daily basis. Some of my fondest memories were made there. I even learned to play bridge during the students' lunch period. By then, my children had entered college. Betty and I had purchased our first house, and assumed we would retire in it. It seemed things could not get better. However, they did.

In 1979 I received orders for the 21st Support Command in Germany. I was not sure what a Foreign Area Officer would do in a logistics command. I was assigned to the Security Plans and Operations Department working for another Special Forces guy, Colonel Jim Zachary. I was given the task of developing the concept and writing the plans for host nation support for American troops in case of war with the Soviet Union. I had excellent officers working for me, although none were logistics specialists. I had never heard of it before, but the Army had a list called a TPFDL (tip-fiddle), Time Phased Force Deployment List. This list had every unit of the Army and even some notional units. Our job was to plan for their deployments and locations in Europe, should it come to war with the Soviets.

The concept was simple. We called it the "can top theory," similar to the practice of putting a can top on a parade ground to denote the locations of parading units. We indicated the location for each unit to occupy as it deployed. We coordinated with the host nation to provide a plan to move them from the ports to that location. The plans were simple in concept, but presented a very complex job of coordination. I looked at every schoolhouse, garage, and parking lot in most of Western Europe. I made many friends and drove many miles. It was a great experience for a European Foreign Area Officer. I also had a truly professional group of officers with whom to work. Betty had a great job at the hospital in Landstuhl. The time went very fast. Our daughter Lisa went to the University of Maryland in Munich. Daughter Renee was at the University of North Carolina at Wilmington, and visited us in Germany. We all enjoyed that tour very much.

I returned to Fort Bragg to pick up where I left off; teaching in the European Seminar for the FAO program. We bought our retirement home and were prepared to stay in Fayetteville, NC.

To the complete surprise of all of Fort Bragg, two of our number were promoted to colonel. No one was more surprised than I was. Betty was working at the VA Hospital in Fayetteville. We decided not to retire. With three more years to serve, I was on my way to Washington. It took us two years to sell the house. Betty again had to remain behind, because we could not afford to live in Washington and make a high mortgage payment in Fayetteville at the same time. For two years, I lived in a rooming house during the week and drove to Fort Bragg on the weekends. That was not a pleasant time for either of us.

My assignment was as the Director of Low Intensity Conflict in the Joint Special Operations Agency. I had a great Marine general as my boss. That was a time of great transition and there was much turmoil between the more conventional forces and Special Operations. It was rewarding to see the concepts we developed being used in Afghanistan twenty years later. I served my two years on the Joint Staff, and when I was offered a job and quarters at Fort Belvoir, I jumped at it.

I remained the Senior Army Advisor to the 310th Theater Army Area Command (TAACOM) until I retired in July 1989. It was a very fine last assignment. I was able to see the Reserve side of the Army, and came to appreciate the concept of "Twice the Citizen."

Retirement

I have a large family and could share my mother's care with my brothers and sisters. Betty is an only child though, so our first responsibility was to help her mother. Both of our fathers had been dead for some time. The old saying is true. You can go back, but you cannot go home. Everyone changes.

I had spent my entire productive life in the military service, and did not know how it would be in civilian life. We did not know if we could live on retirement income without working. We bought an old house and spent five years restoring it, working on one room at a time and just buying what we could pay for each month. It was a labor of love. When we finished, it was ours.

Each day of my twenty-three years of retirement has been filled with joy. I have had the pleasure of heading up a committee to build a Veterans Memorial in Pulaski, VA. I served on the Base Closure and Realignment Commission (BRAC) committee to reduce, rearrange and dispose of much of the Department of Defense property. While working to save the Redford Army Ammunition Depot, I discovered there were many surplus acres around Dublin, VA. I persuaded Congressman Rick Boucher to obtain eighty acres for a military cemetery. We dedicated it in May 2011. It is amazing what the powers-that-be will do if someone is willing to do the work, but give them the credit. I went back three times to post-war Yugoslavia to help with elections. My language training served me well. My Yugoslav driver and his family followed me home. They stayed five years in America before returning to Croatia. I currently serve on the town council of Dublin, VA.

As I try to sum up my thirty-five years in the military and twenty-three years in retirement, my thoughts keep coming back to a young man who lost his life in Vietnam. He wrote in his diary, "How frustrating life is! To whom should I unburden myself? In whom should I confide? Who can understand my pent-up feelings? No one could possibly, except us, the soldiers!"

These words were written by a man I never met. His name was Mai Van Hung. He was my enemy, yet we were closer in feelings than most soldiers are with their own countrymen. He understood the warrior code of honor. I am afraid our young men returning from the Middle East might feel the same frustrations experienced by Mai Van Hung, and by their fathers after Vietnam.

Rudyard Kipling wrote about the returning soldiers' problem:

"Oh it's Tommy this an' Tommy that an' Tommy go away,
But it's Thank You Mr. Adkins, when the band begins to play.
For it's Tommy this an' Tommy that an' chuck him out, the brute,
But it's, Savior of 'is Country when the guns begin to shoot."

My frustration comes from the US citizenry not seeing the personal success enjoyed by the soldier, and what an asset he is to our country.

The soldier's uniform levels his standing in the service. Every member of the service, like civilians, wants to be successful. Success is measured differently in the service. It is not measured by the amount of money one makes, or how many friends one has, or how nice one's house and car are. Success for the soldier is measured by how loyal he is to his fellow soldier and his country; how well he carries out his mission; and the pride he feels in a job well done. In the parade of life, he can march with his head held high. That is the success I would like to see for all Americans.

The flag bearers in my life have been my wife Betty and my daughters Renee and Lisa. They did not wear the uniform, but they carried the burdens of giving unfailing support to our country and to me.

Front row left to right: Colonel (Retired) Dallas Cox and Betty, wife of 55 years, daughters Lisa, Renee and son-in-law Dr. Markus Jucker. Second row left to right: granddaughter Katherine Jucker and grandson Joseph Jucker, Dublin, VA, 2009.

*Captain Roy Douglass (Left) and OCS Classmate Jerry Laird,
Hau Nia Province, Vietnam, 1966. (Note: Jerry Laird, by then a
major, was killed in action January 22, 1969, Vietnam, RIP).*

Prelude

There had to be something better than serving as an enlisted soldier,
living on $78 a month, with a wife and child in Alaska! Since I wanted
to be a career soldier, OCS was the only answer I could realistically see
at the time.

The Early Days

I literally came from the "wrong side of the tracks." (I believe fellow
OCS classmate Joe Jellison lived on the other side of the tracks in a
cemetery. His father was a caretaker or something like that. Joe enlisted
before me, though.) My parents only had eighth-grade educations.
Consequently, they were unable or unwilling to assist me in setting any
life-goals, and they generally did not know how to mentor me. However,

they did support me in the Boy Scout program, and I achieved Eagle in 1957.

Fortunately, Ball State Teacher's College tuition was only $50 per quarter, and I had a relatively good stash from my paper route, so I went to college on a whim. I didn't have any specific goals, or even a good idea of what I wanted my major to be. While at Ball State, I worked as a bank messenger for the College Bursar. I managed to keep my grades at bare minimums long enough to make it to the first quarter of my junior year before I exhausted my money. While in college, I was in AFROTC, became a member of the drill team, and attained the grade of cadet second lieutenant. I also pledged and became a member of the Phi Sigma Epsilon social fraternity and the Alpha Phi Omega service fraternity. However, I was not a good student, grade-wise, and I was rapidly depleting my funds, strictly for books and classes. I had a sparse social life because I lived at home and rode a bicycle to college until I acquired a 1948 Plymouth coupe late in my sophomore year. Also in the latter part of my sophomore year, hoping to become a USAF pilot, I went to Wright-Patterson AFB for my upper division/pilot physical. I was informed that I was partially color-blind, and could not be admitted to pilot training.

At that point I decided to quit college and join the US Marines, but when I went to the recruiting station in the Post Office, all of the recruiting offices were closed for lunch. The Marine recruiter told me so through the transom of his office door. However, the US Army recruiter, sandwich in hand, opened his door and said, "Come here boy. I have a deal for you!" That's how I came to join the US Army.

The Decision to Apply for OCS

I enlisted on September 15, 1959, and reported to Fort Knox, KY, but my entire training company was transferred to Fort Hood, TX two weeks later. Basic Training was accomplished in C Company, 50th Armored Rifle Battalion, and I was selected to be the Trainee Platoon Sergeant. Following Basic, I attended Advanced Individual Training (AIT) in A Company, 50th Armored Rifle Battalion. I was selected to be the Trainee Platoon Sergeant again, and was surprised at the end of the training to be selected as the Honor Graduate. With that honor, I was supposed to be retained at Fort Hood to serve on cadre for the next cycle. However, at midnight the day I graduated, the Charge of Quarters woke me to tell me that I was due to be on an airplane to Fort Wainwright, Alaska in two hours. I made the airplane with no time to spare, and discovered that my final destination was to be Fort Richardson, Alaska. We arrived at Elmendorf AFB on February 12, 1960, and snow was piled higher than the empennage of our aircraft. That was my first PCS, to the 2nd Battle Group, 23rd Infantry Regiment, US Army Alaska (USARAL), in Anchorage, AK.

My assignment surprised me because I was a Senior Rifleman with a smattering of sniper training. Nevertheless, I was assigned as a Fire Direction Computer, Weapons Platoon, C Company. During my tenure in Alaska, I was selected to attend the USARAL NCO Academy, as an E-2. I graduated fourth in my class comprised of E-2 through E-6 grades. As was the custom, the top five graduates were promoted to the next higher grade, so I made PFC early. Since we were mountain and ski troops, I learned to cross-country ski and how to rock climb and rappel. The latter came in pretty handy in Ranger School. A short time later, I was promoted to SP4, and given additional duties as Company Training NCO and Company Information NCO. I was relatively happy with my Army life, but my wife and new-born were coming up to Anchorage in November, and living on the economy with my family was going to be very expensive.

I decided that being an officer would be a better way to support my family, so I began to study for the officer candidate test (OCT). After some delay, I was invited to appear before the OCS Board, and was one of two soldiers out of seven applicants who passed the board. Shortly after the board, I was promoted to E-5 via a "blood stripe," and even passed my first and only "Pro-Pay" test before OCS. Then came my second PCS, and it was to 52nd OCS Company, Fort Benning, GA.

Time at OCS

I honestly didn't consider OCS a "survival" process. I only knew that I wanted to be an officer more than anything else I could think of, and that I had a second son on the way (born in February 1962), which would require more money than I was making as a sergeant E-5. After fraternity hazing and then NCO Academy, I didn't find OCS particularly difficult, except for the "scholastic" part and the public speaking, but I got over those. While I can still see almost every classmate's face as they were in our six months together in 52nd Company, I only recall having a few close friends: Rick DeGennaro (his wife and mine shared a house together), Bob Fish, Dave Davis and ole' Herbert Greene, who taught me how to spit shine using a sponge.

Assignments Immediately after Commissioning

In our latter weeks in OCS, we were all given the opportunity to sign up for Flight School, Airborne and Ranger Schools as well as other training, so I requested Airborne and Ranger Schools. My next PCS was to the 1st Battle Group (BG), 9th Infantry (MANCHU), 2nd Infantry Division at Sand Hill, Fort Benning, GA. My request for Airborne School was denied because of my color vision, so Infantry Officer Communications School was substituted (unbeknown to me until I received orders to go). I dutifully completed the training before reporting into the Battle Group. Two of my classmates in the communications training were Lieutenants Buck Deaton and Joseph Stillwell III.

When I did report in to the Battle Group Commander, Colonel Clifford Pershing Hannum, he asked me what I wanted to do and I replied, "I want to be an Infantry Platoon Leader, Sir!" Colonel Hannum thought that was admirable, but wanted me to "cement" my communications knowledge in my head first, so I was assigned as the Communications Platoon Leader in HHQ Company. What a letdown!

As the Battle Group began preparations for Swift Strike, a road march up to the Carolinas to maneuver against the 82nd Airborne Division, I received orders for Ranger School, also unbeknown to me until the orders arrived. What a surprise! The Battle Group made the road march and maneuvered against the 82nd, while I wallowed in the mud at Fort Benning, roped and patrolled the Appalachian Trail at Dahlonega, GA and waded around the swamps of Eglin, Florida. I was so mad that I got orders to go to Ranger School yet couldn't go to Airborne School that I didn't sew on a Ranger tab until I was assigned to Germany in 1974, but that is another story.

After a short stint as Communications Platoon Leader, I was made Communications Officer because my predecessor was relieved over a SNAFU related to the PA set being used by the Division CG. Fortunately, boredom as a commo officer ended when I was reassigned as the 4.2 Mortar Platoon Leader in the Combat Support Company. Shortly thereafter, we all went TDY on a new concept called "ROTAPLAN" to Baumholder and Mannheim, FRG. While we conducted an FTX to Hohenfels, we converted from battle group configuration to battalion configuration. While the others were at Hohenfels, I was recalled back to Baumholder after a week into the FTX and assigned as an Escort Officer. My assignment was to escort a busload of high-ranking German civilians and officers to Fliegerhorst Kaserne for President Kennedy's visit. I was able to see President Kennedy when he toured the kaserne.

Back to the 'States

Upon my return to the 'States, I was assigned more TDY, this time to Norfolk, VA for three weeks of duty with the Navy as one of the Division's Brigade Embarkation Officers. As fall of 1963 neared, our newly reorganized battalion began preparations for participation in Exercise Swamp Fox at Fort Stewart, GA. I was ready to go show my stuff as a rifle platoon leader, but the Battalion Commo Officer fell off a track and broke his leg. Guess who they called to sub for him.

While we participated in Exercise Swamp Fox at Fort Stewart, GA, President Kennedy was assassinated in Dallas, Texas. We spent two days at Fort Stewart drawing war stocks and anticipating deployment somewhere. After we stood down, we returned to Fort Benning. I couldn't get away from the Commo Officer assignment any other way, so as a new first lieutenant, I asked for and was assigned as Executive Officer, A Company, 1st Battalion. Captain Font, the CO, didn't have me long though, because in the spring of 1964, I went TDY again for three weeks to Norfolk, VA as one of the Division's Brigade Embarkation Officers. It was great duty!

Upon returning to Fort Benning, I was informed that the old color vision test for Airborne School was replaced with a red-green lens test. I took the new test and passed, reapplied for parachute training, and in April 1964 I finally received orders to go to Airborne School.

Other than an Air Force Forward Air Controller assigned to the 101st Airborne Division landing on top of my parachute on our first jump, nothing really extraordinary happened during my quest for the silver wings. After getting my wings, the Expert Infantryman's Badge (EIB) was next in my sights, and the timing was great. The 2nd Infantry Division was going into the EIB training cycle. After testing, I was one of the fortunate few who received the beautiful blue badge with the musket on it that so many tried for. No matter, my destiny was to once again become the Battalion Commo Officer. This was a case of doing my job too well, too often.

One week we were visited by some guys in green berets who just came back from some place in Indochina. They told us about punji stakes and traps, spider holes, ambushes, how to (and how not to) react to an ambush, and showed us how to sandbag our vehicles. Awesome stuff! When the strange soldiers left, I was still the Commo Officer, but not for long. Fortunately, I was selected to go TDY once again; this time to Needles, California in the Mohave Desert, as an umpire on Exercise Desert Strike. My assistant umpire/driver was an E-7 from the 82nd Airborne. He and I jumped in with the 101st, and followed them all over the desert, with a cooler of beer wedged between the radios in the back of our jeep.

During the waning days of Desert Strike, I received PCS orders to be an instructor at the US Army Infantry School at Fort Benning. Wow! I was going to be a tactics instructor at the Infantry School! Not!

Subsequent Assignments

In May 1964, I drove to Main Post at Fort Benning to the US Army Infantry School, and reported to Captain (later Lieutenant Colonel) Clarence Schlaffer, my boss for the next year-and-a-half during my tenure with the Communications-Electronics Department. Captain Schlaffer and I had earlier worked together in Alaska. He was the Battle Group Training Officer and I was one of the six company training NCOs. I was assigned to his department as an Instructor in Applied Communications. First, however, I had to go to the five-week Instructor Training Course, also known as the "Charm School" where I was lucky enough to present a fifty-minute class on radio-telephone procedures for my graduation and certification as an Infantry School Instructor.

As a certified instructor, I taught many, many classes, but also became a master at bridge (one and a half master points) during many fast and furiously played hands at lunch. I also served as escort officer for an influential Signal Corps officer, Lieutenant Colonel Thomas Matthew Rienzi, in 1964, and again in 1965. I was one of only two Infantry officers in the heavily-Signal Corps Communications-Electronic Department. Colonel Beyer, the Department Director, tried to persuade me to change my crossed rifles for crossed flags, and Colonel Rienzi was the catalyst. It didn't work, though. In 1965, I went TDY again, this time to Fort Eustis, VA and Aberdeen Proving Grounds, MD to field test an Aerodynamically Stabilized Balloon with antennae that flew up to 500 feet for the purpose of extending the rated ranges of Infantry radios. I brought the balloon back to Fort Benning, and we used it for many requirements. I flew it at many activities, until I handed it over to another officer. He promptly lost the balloon when he forgot to tether it, and it flew away.

In April of 1965, newly promoted Lieutenant Colonel Schlaffer asked me if I wanted to go to Pathfinder School, since I was teaching all the Pathfinder-related courses. Naturally I jumped at the opportunity. I made eight jumps out of the CV-7A Caribou, including one strictly illegal "daisy-chain" jump and two jumps with the T-10 Experimental; the new parachute with the moveable risers, and a six-foot elliptical orifice for a six-knot forward or lateral rush. Once I had my Pathfinder Wing, I was sent TDY to the 11th Air Assault Division to temporarily fill in as the Pathfinder Detachment Commander. The regular Detachment Commander was attending school somewhere else at the time. I did not make any jumps with the Pathfinders, but I did meet then Lieutenant Colonel Hal Moore, and I qualified for my Sky Soldier Badge. When the regularly assigned Pathfinder Detachment Commander assumed command from me, I went back to being an instructor of Applied Communications in the Communications-Electronics Department. Although I enjoyed the prestige and showmanship all instructors experienced, I was becoming bored, and so I applied for Vietnam. I was quickly turned down, so I bought a new house. Two months later I received PCS orders to Military Assistance Command Vietnam

(MACV) with a delay en route at Fort Bragg, NC to attend the Military Advisor Training Assistance (MATA) course. The heat and humidity, and the "MATA Mile" were not adequate preparation for what was to come at my destination on the other side of the world.

In May 1966, I reported to the Senior Regimental Advisor, Major Looney, who advised me to learn how to use chopsticks since lunch was soon to be served. After much fumbling with the chopsticks and a .45 caliber bullet, I managed to barely master the art of using chopsticks and consumed lunch. Shortly after lunch, Major Looney told me I was assigned as the Senior Advisor, Team 43, in Advisory Team 99, III Corps, MACV. There were four US soldiers in my team: XO, Lieutenant Wickens; Heavy Weapons Advisor, SFC (later promoted to E-8) Raymond; Light Weapons Advisor, Staff Sergeant Lackey; and RTO, PFC Pohl. Pohl was killed one night while we were pinned down by heavy weapons fire, and couldn't get the ARVN to provide fire support. We couldn't get US support because of priority of fire to another unit. Our unit, 1/49 Battalion (ARVN), was in a compound in Cu Chi at the corner of Highway 1 and a dusty dirt road that ended to the east at the 25th US Division compound, and continued to the west into Hau Nia Province. My counterpart was a Major Nguyen-Nguoc, of Catholic faith, proven by the fact that he and his wife had twelve children. After a couple of months in Cu Chi, our battalion was moved to an old Ranger camp on the road going to the 25th ARVN Division at Duc Hoa, in Hau Nia Province. Major Nguoc was a serious, but somewhat laid-back officer who did a stupid thing one day. It was SOP that when one of our vehicles turned off Highway 1 onto the dusty road towards our Ranger camp compound, the pedal would go to the metal. Major Nguoc, with his wife in the front seat, and his S-3 and S-2 in the back, drove rather slowly that Sunday afternoon, and VC from a nearby village were watching. When Nguoc got within range, the VC fired a command-detonated mine and blew the jeep off the road. In the process, Nguoc's wife was killed and he and the other two officers were wounded. What followed for the village that Major Nguoc had been so generous and helpful to is not fit for printing.

While at the Ranger camp compound, Captain Jerry Laird, 101st Airborne, visited my team and me in Hau Nia Province, III Corps.

(Jerry Laird, by then a major, was killed in action in Vietnam on a subsequent tour on January 22, 1969.)

I was wounded on June 22, 1966. What Colonel Beyer and Colonel Rienzi couldn't do, bullets and shrapnel finally did. In September 1966, I applied for a branch transfer to the Signal Corps and received a letter of welcome from Brigadier General Rienzi. After my six months in the field, I was called up to the 25th ARVN Division HQ and assigned as the Assistant G-3, Air Operations Officer as a Signal Corps branch officer. During this time in my capacity as Air Ops, I talked with Dan Telfair, former OCS classmate and then gunship pilot, at a briefing for one of our Fire-Fly missions.

All things eventually come to an end, and so in March 1967, I received PCS orders to Signal Officer Advanced Course, Fort Monmouth, NJ. I arrived back in the 'States at Travis AFB, to the chanting of "baby-killer" and "war-monger" plus other disgusting sayings by Americans against Americans (not to mention the bombardment of rocks, feces, Coke bottles and other hurtful objects), and caught another civilian aircraft to Georgia only to be divorced by my wife. Then I drove to Fort Monmouth. While in the Advanced Course, because I was so disillusioned by our lack of trying to win the war in Vietnam, due mainly to persistence in using outdated conventional warfare tactics (large unit operations) against guerilla-type operations employed by our VC opponents, I applied for a commission in the New Zealand Army. I was accepted, but they would only take me in as a first lieutenant. Not wanting to give up my captain's bars, I stayed in the US Army, and endured the Advanced Course. The Commandant at the time was Brigadier General Tom Rienzi. I also endured being in Red Bank/Monmouth, NJ, and became as near a hippy as I could with short hair. I drank a lot too.

In March, just before graduation, the Signal Corps Branch guys from the Pentagon visited with us and let us review our 201 files, and I was given a choice of an airborne assignment or Electronic Data Processing. To me, at the time, there was no choice. Following graduation in May 1968, I drove to Fort Bragg, NC to my new assignment in the XVIII Airborne Corps.

My new assignment was as Contingency Plans Officer, Corps Signal Plans Office. My job consisted of visiting telephone companies up and down the eastern seaboard to coordinate hard bunker communications in the event of civil disturbances. Other than the coordination, developing contingency plans was boring. That was exacerbated by a midget major who had a loud mouth and wouldn't tolerate the sleeves of my fatigue jacket rolled up for relief from the heat and humidity. It was hot and humid in the XVIII ABN Corps HQ. We had no central air conditioning back then. Fortune again looked my way, and Lieutenant Colonel Herb Vogel, Commander of the 50th Signal Battalion, asked the Corps Signal Officer to transfer me to his battalion to assume command of HQ Company, being the senior captain that I was. The transfer was granted, and away I went to a company command assignment and all the jumps I wanted. Life was good!

The good life only lasted four months. I was promoted to major in November 1968. There was no room in the inn for another major, so I had to go across the street to a leg (non-airborne) battalion, and off of jump status, but not until after I was Prop Blasted. I was initially assigned as the Executive Officer of the 427th Signal Battalion, Fort Bragg, NC (Theater Army Support), but only until the real XO arrived. He was a West Pointer finishing his schooling somewhere other than Bragg. It seemed like I had heard that tune before! Anyway, the ring-knocker arrived and I was relegated to being the Battalion S-3. This particular battalion had more than 1600 soldiers in its seven numbered companies. At least I was honored to be the Commander of Troops for the change of command between the retiring battalion commander and his replacement. It was probably, or should have been, one of the last large-scale battalion parades at Bragg, if not in the Army. It took a long time to troop the line! Sometime during 1968, I managed to attend and graduate from the Special Forces Operations Course, before Signal Branch caught me and told me to stay on the "conventional" side of the Army.

In December 1968, I married Gail, my (now) wife of nearly 44 years. Unfortunately, she stayed in New Jersey to complete her nursing training and graduated in August 1969, just in time to hear of my orders to return to Vietnam. I inquired of Signal Branch as to why I had to go back when so many of my Signal Corps Advanced Class mates hadn't been to Vietnam for their first tours. Signal Branch said it was my first tour. Even though I had a Combat Infantryman's Badge (CIB) and the medals to prove I had been there and done that, Signal Branch told me that this was my first deployment to Vietnam as a Signal Corps officer.

Since my wife and I had not spent any time living together after our marriage due to the distance between NC and NJ, I tried to delay my second tour. The best I could do was a one-month delay. In November 1969, I was given a delay en route to attend the Military Officer Assistance Program, at Smoke Bomb Hill, Fort Bragg, NC.

Christmas of 1969 came too quickly and passed even faster. In 1970 I went PCS to the 23rd Infantry Division (AMERICAL) in Vietnam. I ran into OCS classmate Jim Humphries, who had a patch over one eye, I assumed from a combat wound. For the first six months I served as the Communications-Electronics Officer, 23rd Division Artillery. During my last six months I served as the S-3, 523rd Signal Battalion. The only notable things I care to recall from my second tour in Vietnam are chopper rides to and from Fire Base Siberia, drinking and playing darts with a Major (later Four Star General) Colin Powell, and escaping hooch "fraggings" in the 523rd Signal Battalion area. Good bye, Vietnam!

January 1971 saw my PCS to the 31st Air Defense Artillery (ADA) Brigade, Fort Bliss TX. Being assigned to "Fort Comfort" was great, even on duty with the Air Defense Artillery. Actually, the 31st ADA was located in two different parts of the US. The field training element, commanded by an ADA Colonel James Leister, was located in the West Texas desert of Fort Bliss, and the "locked in concrete" actual missile battalions were located in Florida with the Brigade HQ, commanded by Brigadier General David Sudderth. They were located at Homestead Air Force Base just south of Miami. While in the desert, I was assigned as the Brigade Communications-Electronics Officer, and because I was the only officer wearing a CIB, I was assigned additional duty as the "Aggressor Force Commander." When the units from Florida came to Texas to undergo their field training exercises and accompanying field evaluations, I would rain on their parades by infiltrating their lines, ambushing their convoys, disrupting their communications, and other assorted aggressor actions, and I loved it. All this aggressor activity was performed exclusively by Signalers, and even resulted in at least two battery commanders being relieved because they were unable to cope with our actions.

My wife and I enjoyed many, many trips into Mexico, evenings in Juarez and other border towns, and I even learned to play golf, before learning to hate it, and ultimately gave it up. We sponsored a German sergeant, his wife and two children while the sergeant was attending the "Racketen Schule" at Fort Bliss, and we made a foray deep into Mexico. The best thing about being Sergeant Philer's sponsor though was the fact that he was able to have cases of real German beer flown in weekly on the "commissary plane" that flew from Germany to the US. The only downside of life at 5110 Snow Drive, Fort Bliss, TX was the fact that the war was winding down, followed by a reduction in force (RIF). I gave it no thought, but the next thing I knew I received a telephonic notification that I would be receiving my RIF notice. After ninety days passed, in which time we sold our horses and land in anticipation of having to go to California where I would clerk in my cousin's law office while I attended law school, my RIF letter didn't arrive. Colonel Leister, Commander of the Texas Brigade element, called Signal Branch demanding to know what was going on. He was told that it had all been a mistake and that the phone call was actually meant for another officer with only one 's' in his last name. I escaped the RIF, but all good things had to come to an end.

In June 1972, our idyllic life at Fort Comfort ended. My wife Gail and I began our PCS to the 31st ADA Brigade HQ, at Homestead AFB, FL. Gail was pregnant with our first child (who later became a HALO Ranger), and so she and I, with our two Siamese cats, drove our Mercedes Benz from El Paso along the Gulf Coast down the Florida peninsula to Homestead AFB (HAFB). I kept my assignment as the Brigade Communications-Electronics Officer, but dropped the Aggressor Commander role. Vietnam had really ended, President Nixon flew into HAFB on his way to Key Biscayne, and I collected his autograph.

I didn't have a college degree and I knew from my earlier mistaken RIF notification experience in Texas that, without a degree, I was a prime target for the RIF Board. This was complicated in September 1972 by the addition of our first born. So I applied at Florida State and one other nearby institution of higher learning, but the fall classes were full. Fortunately, Florida International University (FIU) was being built on the old Tamiami Airport and I was readily accepted. With 252 college credits on my transcripts, I only needed one year at FIU for a degree in History or two years for a degree in Business Administration. I took the shortest path to a degree, and in August 1973 I graduated in the second graduating class of FIU with a BA in History and a minor in Business Administration. One of the highlights of my graduation party in our quarters at HAFB was when those few of us who were airborne qualified officers decided that we would jump everyone off my red Coleman cooler until we had a grand total of 1000 jumps. My dad (WWII vet, 83rd Infantry Division) was doing the jumpmaster checks and when he got to the general's wife and said "equipment check!" she replied, "Only the general checks my equipment!" We fell all over each other laughing. Strangely though, the next morning we found the General's aide in a broom closet at the Officers' Club two blocks away from my quarters!

The winter of 1973 in Florida was unusually cold, which was good training because we had received orders for Germany in the fall of 1973. In January 1974 our family of three, plus our two Siamese cats, PCS'd to the 1st Infantry Division (Forward), located at Cooke Barracks, in Goeppingen, Germany. Germany was my dream assignment. I reported to Brigadier General Robert Haldane, who told me I was not just going to be assigned as the Division (Forward) Signal Officer, but also as the Battalion Commander of the 1st Support Battalion (Provisional). The change of command took place between a Quartermaster lieutenant colonel and a Signal Corps major, and I became the second commander in the battalion's history. General Haldane also gave me another assignment, which began my thirty plus years as an adult leader in Scouting. He told me that because I was an Eagle Scout, I was to be the Unit Commissioner for the Cub Scout, Boy Scout and Explorer units located in Cooke Barracks. Besides making Radio-Wire Integration work for the first time (and thereafter) to enable General Haldane to talk from his jeep in the field to his staff in buildings while we were at Hohenfels and Grafenwoehr, I tried using a point paper to re-designate the Signal Detachment in my battalion to a Signal Company. That didn't happen though until I PCS'd back to the 'States. Since I was senior in date of rank to the G-3, my rater became (then) Lieutenant Colonel Gordon Sullivan.

Our second son was born in December 1974 at Bad Cannstadt Hospital near Stuttgart, with my parents back in quarters at Goeppingen babysitting our first son. During our life in Germany, we visited distant relatives in Vienna, Austria, and hosted the German family we had sponsored in Texas. He had subsequently been promoted to the highest sergeant grade in the German Air Force. We also sponsored a German family living in Goeppingen while we were stationed at Cooke Barracks. My RIF scare back in Texas also got me to enroll in correspondence courses such as C&GSC and Industrial College of the Armed Forces. I was nearing completion of C&GSC in 1976 when I was sent a notice that I had to take the remainder of the college at Fort Leavenworth within a specific period of time, a time limit that was within my assignment dates in Germany. I broke the news to Lieutenant Colonel Sullivan, who wasn't happy to hear of this unplanned expense, but off I went TDY to Kansas. On June 25, 1976, I graduated from Army Command & General Staff College, Fort Leavenworth, KS, and then traveled back for the remainder of my tour in Germany. Next, I enrolled in the National Security Management Course. While in Germany I traveled all over Europe with my wife, plus Volksmarching and Scouting, which occupied weekends not spent in the field. However, after three REFORGERS and nearly three years and three months of battalion command time, I received PCS orders back to the 'States.

In May 1977 we PCS'd to Forces Command at Fort McPherson, GA. There I was assigned as a Force Development Officer in the Reserve Components Division, FORSCOM, again working for Major General Robert Haldane. (I think I saw OCS classmate Leighton Haselgrove visiting FORSCOM or somewhere in Atlanta.) While at FORSCOM, I completed the National Security Management Course, National Defense University in Washington, DC. In August 1979, I earned my MA in Business Management from Central Michigan University. Over the two-year period of 1977-1978, I implemented the Battalion Training Management System throughout CONUSRC, and over the three-year period of 1977-1979, I served as an evaluator of the 240th Signal Battalion, at the California Reserve Component Summer Camp.

On October 31, 1979 I was retired from the Army of the United States.

Upon retirement, I used forty-five days of accrued leave to begin my career as a "head hunter." During the period of 1979 to 1980, I worked for Del Waugh & Associates, Human Resources (Recruiting) Company in Indianapolis, IN. Del had been an Army captain and a Huey pilot during Vietnam, but a victim of the RIF in 1974. He and I were good friends while in the 31st ADA in Texas. Although I made a good compensation recruiting, it was not what I wanted to spend the rest of my working life doing, so I began looking for other opportunities. I quickly obtained an interview with the recruiter for "management trainees" for General Telephone & Electronics (GTE) of the Southwest.

On October 22, 1980, two days after interviewing, I accepted a very generous offer to work for GTE Southwest, headquartered in San Angelo, Texas. I began my twenty-three-year career with GTE working in Baytown, Texas, initially as a foreman, then as a first-line supervisor for cable installation and repair, followed by assignment as a test and dispatch supervisor in the main office in Baytown, TX. After two years, I was promoted to Local Manager of Highlands, TX where I became a member of the Rotary Club, rising to First Vice President of the club, and a member of the Highlands Chamber of Commerce where I served as Treasurer.

After four-and-one-half years in the Baytown-Highlands area, I was promoted and moved to the Southwest Region HQ in San Angelo, TX where I was assigned as one of six management consultants training and coaching managers in the field. After one-and-a-half years in the management consulting job, I was again promoted and assumed responsibilities as the Manager for Staffing and College Relations. I staffed management through lower executive positions as well as recruited on college campuses at selected locations throughout the US.

However, the good ol' boy system impeded upward mobility and working inside (versus being outside some of the time) soon became boring. In 1989 I sought and accepted a staff position in telephone operations. My first assignment was on staff in network provisioning support, and after GTE bought and merged CONTEL into GTE, I became the lead Implementation Administrator and ultimately lead

Project Manager for remote operations support in the Southwest Region.

In my personal non-work pursuits, I had nearly twenty-five years in Scouting as an adult leader in various positions from Scout troop to Council training, but Scouting didn't give me the satisfaction it had before. I looked for something more challenging, and found Civil Air Patrol (CAP). I joined CAP in August 1992, mainly just to wear a military-style uniform, but I soon found many more rewarding and fulfilling experiences in the search-and-rescue and flying aspects of CAP. In December 1992, I was appointed Commander of the San Angelo Composite Squadron and served in that capacity for four years.

In 1996 I did a civilian version of TDY to Las Colinas and Garland, TX where I was the Section Manager in the Garland Care Center managing a work force of up to 500 employees through five first-line supervisors. Upon returning to San Angelo in November of 1996, and mainly because of the twisted politics in big business (AKA GTE), I became the Staff Administrator & Acting Director in Remote Operations Support (ROS), San Angelo, TX.

However, it was to be short-lived. I had been noticed by the ROS director in Durham, NC, and in July 1998, he requested that I come to Durham (TDY) for four weeks to trouble-shoot the operations. The TDY turned into five weeks, and then I returned to Texas. In December 1999, I was offered a position and full relocation from San Angelo, TX to Durham, NC as the highest level manager in the ROS. Since our oldest son and his wife were expecting my wife's first grandchild, I had no alternative but to accept the move.

In January 1999, I moved into temporary quarters in the Durham area and began my new responsibilities, while my wife would fly from Texas to North Carolina to visit me and to hunt for a house every other weekend. In May 1999, we closed on our two-story log home in the rolling hills and horse country of Rougemont, NC. (Rougemont is French for Red Mountain, due to the red clay soil.) In June 1999, I marked my 60th birthday by showing the young-uns how to climb a pole at the GTE Education and Training Center in Durham. In 2001, GTE merged with Bell Atlantic and became Verizon. My career continued, and I became a member of the special staff and served as the Customer

Zone Project Manager in the Southeast Region-Remote Operations Support for Domestic Telephone Operations in Durham, NC.

In May through July 2003, as management and craft (union) fought bitterly while a strike loomed on the horizon, I taught management employees how to climb poles, how to use ladders to reach ready-access terminals on poles and located in the mid-span of cables, and how to do basic repair and installation. This was to provide continuity of services in the event that the strike became a reality and management had to do the craft jobs. I was assigned to New York City, NY, where managers had been shot during the last strike by Bell Atlantic! In early August 2003, the strike was averted, and I took a hard look at retirement and came to the conclusion that I would make even more money if I retired. In late August 2003, I retired, took my lump sum, and have never, ever looked back on that very sound fiscal decision. Besides, retirement gave me more time for Civil Air Patrol, my all-consuming passion.

Senior Years

Currently I am serving as the CAP Middle East Region Chief of Staff after a successful wing command tour. In December 2008, I was selected to serve as the Wing Commander of the North Carolina Wing, headquartered in Burlington, NC and I assumed command on January 1, 2009. As Wing Commander, I was a member of the CAP National Board (a corporate officer), and I dedicated most of my waking (and some not so awake) hours leading the more than 1550 volunteer members, and a fleet of ten aircraft, in North Carolina. CAP has three congressionally chartered missions: Aerospace Education, Cadet Programs, and Emergency Services. I served only three and one-half years because I was asked to accept my current duty position of Region Chief of Staff. The region has seven wings in it.

I have to brag about what I did the summer of 2012. In July 2012, I went to Kempton, PA where I served on the staff of the CAP Hawk Mountain Ranger School. In addition to teaching cutting tools, using direction finders to track and find emergency locator transmitters, and map and compass, I also dangled off the rappelling tower doing such maneuvers on the rope as tie-off, self-rescue from an obstacle in the rope, and pick-off rescue of another climber. The tower work combined with many more "ranger-type" requirements and physical requirements (push-ups, pull ups and running, to name a few) earned this 73-year-old the emergency services proficiency award of "Advanced Ranger." Hoo-ah!

In addition to CAP, I serve as a member of the Board of Directors for the Institute for Advanced Career Development, a non-profit organization located in Hillsborough, NC. I am also involved with Scouting again, and I am currently serving on the District Camping Committee, after serving over two years as the District Program Chairman.

Official Portrait, Colonel Roy Douglass, Middle East Region Chief of Staff, Civil Air Patrol.

What Has it All Meant?

My Army career made me very proud to have served my country, and especially as an officer. OCS taught me to persevere, and enabled me to be more successful in my civilian career as well as in my volunteer activities, including Civil Air Patrol. To some extent, even as a Boy Scout leader, I have used the leadership skills learned in OCS. Above all the other schools I attended in the Army, Officer Candidate School, a school where all four years of West Point were jammed into six months, was the most meaningful experience in my Army career. My major regret is that I missed our 50-year reunion.

Major (later Lieutenant Colonel) Chuck Foster, Executive Officer, 2nd Battalion, 9th Infantry, Korea, 1970.

The Early Days

My parents' sudden divorce in 1954 disrupted a very normal and stable teen development period. It resulted in a search for how I might become self-sufficient, and that meant getting a job. I worked initially as a bag boy for Kroger's grocery chain, and later in the circulation department of the LaGrange, GA *Daily News*, my hometown newspaper. While a junior at LaGrange High School I joined the news staff, pulling national wire service teletype tapes and writing sports stories. I continued working for the *News* upon graduation in 1956 and while attending LaGrange College.

My military career began rather inconspicuously. On my sixteenth birthday, I joined A Company (Recon) of the 48th Armored Division of the Georgia National Guard in LaGrange, GA. Prior to joining, I would watch them on drill nights as the Scout Jeeps and M-41 light tanks scurried over the hillside near the Armory. They seemed to be having so much fun! I served in that unit for three years, and was promoted to Specialist E-4 and squad leader in the Mortar Platoon.

When I elected to transfer in September 1959 from LaGrange College to Mercer University in Macon, GA, I was transferred to the Army Reserve. I served in that unit as Training NCO while attending college and maintaining full-time employment as a staff writer for the *Macon Telegraph* newspaper. I completed over five years of Active Reserve duty. Receipt of my first draft notice emphatically interrupted my military reserve duties only nine days after graduating from Mercer with a Bachelor of Arts degree in religion and a minor in journalism.

In early January 1961 I received instructions to report to the Armed Forces Examining and Entrance Station at Fort McPherson, GA for what I believed was my pre-induction physical. At the time, I was a full-time employee of the *Macon Telegraph* and was living in an apartment like someone who had a future. Being a college graduate, I was placed over a group of inductees for processing. A short time later I found myself on the way to Fort Benning, begging the Greyhound bus driver to stop in Molena, GA, and allow me to call my boss at the *Telegraph*. He let me make the call. I told my managing editor Jim Chapman that I could not report for work later the next day because I was in the Army and on my way to basic training!

I was incredulous at the rapidity of my induction. The explanation was that I had gone to Europe immediately following graduation to visit a former German exchange student who had been at Mercer, and to climb the Matterhorn in the Swiss Alps. I had failed to notify the local draft board that I was out of the country and therefore could not respond to any of their three requests for interview between June and September 1960. I was rewarded for this piece of ignorance with immediate induction. I later called my father and told him to clean out my apartment, pay my bills, make all necessary disengagement arrangements, and sell my car. I had no use for any of it at the moment.

On to OCS

My decision to apply for OCS was prompted by a new policy that would allow OCS graduates who had more than six months remaining on their current enlistment at the time of graduation to accept a reserve commission, and enter the Active Reserves at the end of their active duty obligation. For me it meant that I would have completed my lawful requirement for armed service, and I would be free to pursue my journalistic career without interruption short of a general call-up in time of war. Furthermore, I would be earning additional pay as a reserve officer, doing something that I truly enjoyed and at which I had demonstrated competence. It was win-win for me. All I had to do was to graduate.

In some ways, that proved a substantial challenge. I lacked the motivation common to many of my classmates of having to face their former comrades-in-arms if they failed to complete the course. I understood that the mental pressures were not directed to me in a personal way, challenging my worth. They sharpened mental skills, which are a needed and valued attribute of a leader. Prior to OCS, I never considered myself a leader. Until that time, I had only been a first-line worker bee. The hard part for me was being shaped into a leader, and accepting the notion that I wanted to be one.

A secondary challenge was the sleep deprivation and physical demands for all the candidates. These were not as challenging to me because I had experienced a lifetime of them prior to going to OCS. As the firstborn in our family, I had duties before and after school (e.g., washing dishes and clothes, ironing, some cooking, and heating the home before others got up). Additionally, I had to chop wood, collect eggs, check rabbit boxes, and work in the family subsistence garden.

Nonetheless, the mental and physical pressures were real and motivated me to perform at a higher level. The device I employed to relieve some of these pressures was to engage in verbal interplay with Candidate Fish, using language and intonations from the *Amos and Andy* TV Show (e.g., "Holy Mackerel, Andy"); hence, my OCS nickname of "Kingfish." The final hurdle was the 20th week board. Apparently my record was deemed sufficient to merit award of a reserve commission on 30 March, 1962.

Prior to graduation, we were made aware of the need for Airborne and/or Ranger-trained officers. A new Army policy was to have Airborne and/or Ranger-qualified officers in all combat units down to platoon level. These skills were then to be taught to soldiers at all levels. Volunteering for both seemed like a good way to ensure that I would remain at Fort Benning for the remainder of my obligated active duty. I applied for and was accepted for Airborne (five weeks) and Ranger (twelve weeks) training immediately following graduation.

After Graduation

I successfully completed both, but not before a disruption of my Ranger training in Florida. While serving as point guard on a patrol in the mountain phase at Dahlonega, I stepped off a cliff, mistaking the top of a sixty-foot pine for a bush. Upon arriving at that point and using my night vision to incorrectly identify the "bush," I stepped forward and bounced through the pine until landing on the ground sixty feet below. The fall resulted in a puncture of my back at the base of my spine. I did not report it and continued with the training. The hole became infected in the swamps surrounding the Yellow River at Eglin Air Force Base, FL. When a Ranger instructor observed blood and puss oozing from my back in my eleventh week of training, I was medically evacuated to Martin Army Hospital at Fort Benning for repairs. After treatment, I was re-cycled into the Florida phase of the following Ranger class.

Career Assignments

A major redirection of my life course occurred between Airborne and Ranger schools. I married my high school sweetheart Grace Brand from LaGrange, GA. Upon her graduation from Bessie Tift College in Forsyth, GA, we rented a "doll house" in the rear of a home on Cherokee Avenue in Columbus, GA. We bought a Philco black-and-white TV with stand. The refrigerator, stove, bed and bathroom came with the doll house. Shortly thereafter, I left for Ranger training.

Fort McClellan

Much to my surprise, I received orders in September 1962 to report to Fort McClellan, AL as the Post Information Officer. (NOTE: My journalism experience and history accompanied me throughout my career. DA just wouldn't forget it!) The crusty and very senior Post Commander (0-6 Armor Officer) told me when I reported in that he would never allow an Infantry Airborne Ranger officer to be his Information Officer. He ordered my reassignment as Officer-In-Charge of the Demonstration Company, the only Infantry slot allocated to the US Army Chemical Corps and Military Police Schools at Fort McClellan. At the time, that slot was occupied by a Chemical Corps Captain who was then reassigned to another position in the school. The missions of the Company were: (1) To conduct live-fire demonstrations of chemical weapons, munitions and capabilities to visiting dignitaries and (2) to administer combat arms training to Chemical Corps officers attending their Basic Officer Course (BOC). Those white-faced, scared-straight, laboratory nerds were terrified at the map-reading, obstacle course, and escape and evasion training they experienced as part of OBC. It was great fun directing their training.

Finally the day came when I had to inform the Post AG that I would be returning to my civilian career as a journalist. A very strange sequence of events resulted in my choice to change my status to Voluntary Indefinite. The AG called me in the morning and told me that I should come that afternoon to begin my out-processing or to apply for Voluntary Indefinite status. Later that morning, I noticed in the post newspaper that Third Army area funds were scarce and only mission-essential change-of-station moves would be approved.

I went to our Wherry Housing duplex apartment for lunch, and told Grace that I would begin out-processing that afternoon. She informed me that she was pregnant with our first child. This news jolted and simultaneously energized my brain cells. It occurred to me that, since there was no danger of change-of-station orders, I could change my status to Voluntary Indefinite and we could have the baby free, courtesy of the Fort McClellan Hospital. Additionally, we were saving money and we had very nice quarters. After a year in the new status, I could apply to return to Army Reserves with a family and with money in my pocket. All I needed to do was to ensure that I could return to the *Macon Telegraph* after my minimum Voluntary Indefinite commitment. A simple phone call could resolve that question.

I called my former managing editor, informed him of the situation, and asked if I could return to full employment with the *Telegraph* a year later. He told me he had been talking with Tom Johnson, a soon-to-graduate student at the University of Georgia School of Journalism whom I had mentored during his internship at the *Telegraph* a couple of years earlier. He said that Tom desired to join the staff at the Telegraph, and that I could execute my plan to stay for another year and rejoin the Telegraph upon release from the Army. What good fortune! I gleefully initiated a change of status to Voluntary Indefinite. (NOTE: Tom Johnson is the current President of CNN, former Managing Editor of the *Los Angeles Times*, and author of former President Lyndon Johnson's memoirs.)

Fort Bragg

Our first child Jeffrey was born at Fort McClellan in January 1963. The following July I was surprised upon receipt of orders to attend the Special Warfare Officers Course at Fort Bragg, NC, with subsequent assignment to 10th SF Group, Bad Tolz, Germany. I was not the only one upset with this turn of events. BG Joseph Stillwell, ("Cider Joe Stillwell", son of General "Vinegar Joe Stillwell" of WWII Burma fame), then Commandant of the Special Warfare Center, greeted me when I reported for duty with: "What in hell are you doing here?" When I told him I was responding to orders, he replied, "I'll fix that. We don't have second lieutenants in Special Forces." He instructed me to wait in my BOQ until I received additional instructions.

Those instructions came a few days later. BG Stillwell told me he had talked with Department of the Army. He informed me that I would be allowed to attend the Special Warfare Officers Course, but would not be assigned to 10th SF Group. He explained that he already had one oddball in this class, and I would be the second. He was referring to Robin Moore, for whom the Department of Military History had granted a request that he attend the course in order to collect material for his forthcoming book, *The Green Berets*.

It was a challenging period for our young family. We had expected to be planning our life as civilians. Grace was pregnant with our second child, our daughter Leigh. Our request for government housing upon my reassignment to Europe was denied. Government housing was not available in Germany and I would have to initially move unaccompanied by my family.

The military transport USS Buckner was plying the waters of the Atlantic Ocean en route to Europe when somber news arrived during the dinner meal. President John F. Kennedy had been assassinated in Texas. My orders to 10th SF Group, Bad Tolz, Germany were changed to the 3rd Armored Division. Speculation was rampant that a Russian invasion to remedy its isolation in Berlin was imminent. I was subsequently assigned to the 2nd Battalion, 2nd Armored Brigade, 48th Infantry, in Gelnhausen, Germany, and given the Armored Cavalry Platoon.

A not-so-amusing situation developed during one of my platoon tests at Grafenwoehr. My unit was conducting a screening mission for the battalion during movement to a new attack position. I received a call on my radio that the Assistant Division Commander (ADC) was on the way by helicopter to observe the training. I was controlling the unit from the cupola of my tank when I got the call, and spotted a potential position for the tank from which I would have visual contact with my scouts as well as the battalion. When I instructed my driver to move the tank into the position he said, "That's not a good idea, sir." I told him to put it there, and just as the ADC was landing, both tank treads popped off their rollers. I reported to the ADC and he asked me to tell him what I was doing then and over the next several hours. I told him my intentions, to which he replied, "Lieutenant, you're not going to be doing anything over the next several hours except figuring out how you're going to get those treads back on their rollers so you can join and direct your unit." Learning point: know how to recognize good advice when you receive it.

Major General Walter Kerwin arrived shortly thereafter as the new Division Commander. He announced dissatisfaction with the Division battle plans. My platoon was selected to go on extended assignment to identify potential battalion assembly areas, unit movement routes, and combat and combat support assembly areas, and to classify bridges in the Division area of operations. We were based for nine months at Wildflecken, a division training area sitting astride the traditional invasion route from the East (Fulda Gap).

Upon completion of that mission, I was given command of Company C and held that assignment for twenty-two months until my rotation from Germany. I recall a signature learning moment that occurred while leading my unit in off-post winter field training. I was standing in snow up to my thighs when the First Sergeant arrived in a jeep and trailer with hot coffee. He put jet black coffee in my canteen. When I asked for cream and sugar, he said, "Make a decision, sir. Drink it or pour it out." Upon reflection, I understood he was helping me learn how to lead. Those days in Germany were my formative ones. It was wonderful. I was promoted to captain during my company command stint and I received my Regular Army commission there. I was trained by the best. I loved troops and was able to communicate with them, spending fourteen of my twenty commissioned years with units no larger than battalion. Just before we returned from Germany in April 1966, our third and final child (a daughter, Tracy) was born in Frankfurt.

I didn't have much time at home while in Germany. Grace did a marvelous job explaining to our kids where I was and what I was doing, and telling them that it was important. I learned to maximize the moments we did have by letting them know I loved them and that it was fun to be with them. The unit "family" was also important to me. I enjoyed the command social hours at the end of the week, and the dining-ins where the junior lieutenant reviewed the unit history and campaigns. I was invigorated by new assignments, new locations, new challenges and new relationships throughout my career.

Vietnam

After Germany, I received orders for training at the Civil Affairs School at Fort Gordon, GA en route to assignment to 5th Special Forces Group, Vietnam. I arrived in Vietnam in August 1966 and served in a B Team. The team was located at the old, but still operational, French sugar mill in Duc Hue Province, on the Vo Cam Dong River south of Bien Hoa, in III Corps. I was the Military and Civil Affairs Advisor to the District Chief, a South Vietnamese Army captain. I spent a lot of time with him on his visits throughout his district and in coordinating civil affairs projects. Combat functions included bomb damage assessment, interdiction of Viet Cong units and supplies between War Zones C and D, searches for reported POW transport and detention sites, trail watch, combat patrols with indigenous and Regional Force/Provincial Force

(RF/PF) units, and joint operations with the 25th Infantry Division out of Cu Chi.

My experience in Vietnam was much different from that for which I had been trained up to that time. It definitely was war. We engaged Viet Cong forces and successfully repulsed one major assault by a force later believed to contain elements of two North Vietnamese Army (NVA) regiments. The District Chief's compound suffered major damage with high casualties. Our compound, bordered by the river and the District Compound, was not penetrated. My assigned .50 caliber machinegun had been sabotaged, and blew up when I first attempted to fire it. Other engagements were from extended distances and short-lived. Our casualties were light with limited loss of life.

The most striking thing to me was the persona of too many Special Forces officers and enlisted men I encountered in Vietnam. Too many dressed and acted like mercenaries, certainly far from the highly disciplined men with extraordinarily high competencies that I had encountered at Fort Bragg only four years earlier. Their employment in Vietnam bore no resemblance to the low profile, strike-and-move tactics taught and practiced in Special Warfare operations up to that time.

I did not then, and still do not now, question the necessity for the cause of freedom for which I was sent there, nor that my service there was anything but honorable. I have no apologies to make for the vigor and quality with which I prosecuted my duties. One error in judgment may have occurred when I declined the offer of command of the regional Delta Force. I thought at the time that I could make a more significant contribution in my advisory role than with the Delta Force. A good decision that I made in Vietnam was to join Grace in Hawaii for a long-delayed honeymoon while on R&R. We had a great time touring the entire island and being together for a short time without kids, though we both commented several times how much we missed them.

Back to Fort Benning

After Vietnam, the next stop was the Infantry Officer Advanced Course at the Fort Benning Infantry School. Everybody there knew that, upon graduation, we would return to Vietnam.

That was not to be the case for me. I came out on the major's promotion list near the end of the course, and received orders to be the Executive Officer of 3rd Battalion, 5th Infantry at Fort Kobbe, Panama Canal Zone. The battalion was unique in that it contained A Company, 508th Infantry (Airborne). I made my first and only over-water parachute jump while serving there. The Southern Command, housed at Fort Amador, had all four armed services represented. A major annual event was the Iguana Bowl. This was a large parade followed by the championship game between the two service teams with the best records in the seven-man touch football team league. It was played the same weekend as the Army-Navy game in the 'States, and resulted in award of the Commander's Trophy to the winning team. I was drafted and played on the Army team which won the trophy twice during my sixteen-month tour.

Certainly more significant was the overthrow of the Panamanian President (Arias) by a young Guardia Nacional Major named Torrijos. Once again, we had been denied accompanied travel, and I had rented a private home in the Embassy District of Panama City to house my family. We were quarantined in our home the night of the coup, but were later evacuated to temporary on-post quarters. The second day there, I was with A Company at the Miraflores Locks on the canal when a young Guardia Nacional Lieutenant arrived with about 20 troops and offered to relieve us of responsibility for the security of the Canal. He and the troops departed in about two hours after I emphatically informed him he was trespassing on sovereign US soil and that he and his troops must leave. The US retained control until a few years later when the Canal and all US properties were turned over to a sovereign Panama. The decision was made to come out of Vietnam before I left Panama, and I was on my way to Korea in 1969.

The 2nd Battalion, 9th Infantry was the ready reserve for the 2nd and 7th Infantry Divisions. It had the mission of manning the guard posts in the DMZ and providing security for Freedom Bridge across the Imjim River. As Executive Officer, I spent most of my time helping keep the vehicles running and visiting troop positions on the South Tape of the DMZ at night. For recreation, I tried to hit golf balls outside the compound across the Imjim, but never accomplished that feat. It was most interesting to hear the staccato sounds of .50 caliber heavy machine guns being fired by the ROK Marines located on the 2nd Division's left flank when North Korea patrols probed the South Tape. Frightened mule deer running into the fence kept our troops on high alert on most evenings.

The New Army

Coming out of Korea, I received orders for assignment as the Operations Officer of the Old Guard, but these were changed when General Kerwin, the current DCSPER, was alerted that I was en route to Washington, D.C. He called me in and told me that I was being transferred to the Recruiting Command in Newport News, VA as a plans officer with the specific task of reorganizing the Command in order to maintain an All-Volunteer Force. I told him I didn't believe in the concept, to which he replied, "I didn't ask for an opinion. Come back here in 25 days for a decision briefing on your plan." I completed it and was rewarded with attachment to a task force with responsibility for writing a plan to reorganize the Army into Forces and Training Commands. My final assignment there was to relocate the Recruiting Command to Fort Sheridan in Chicago. Upon closing the doors in Newport News, I attended the Armed Forces Staff College in Norfolk, VA. Then I was given six months to complete my master's degree in psychology from the College of William and Mary in Williamsburg, VA. I received the Masters of Education degree in August 1974, and left for an ROTC assignment at the University of Alabama.

ROTC

Toomey Hall housed the Army ROTC Detachment at the University. It was partially burned by student Vietnam war protestors. That resulted in placement of the program on probation. The new University President (David Mathews) appealed to DA to retain the program. He was allowed approval authority of officers pending assignment to the University, and he awarded them the rank of Assistant Professor upon their assignment. The program grew over the next three years until it was second only to Texas A&M in ROTC enrollment. I was given responsibility to teach juniors in the program and prepare them for Summer Camp. One of my students who received a fellowship for study in Europe told me upon graduation that he had learned more about management from our program than from the School of Business. Another student who retired as a full colonel said to me on a remote lake in Canada more than 40 years later, "I always hoped I would see you again so I could say 'thank you' for what you taught me at Alabama."

Back to Korea

The next stop was Korea again, this time as Chief Maintenance Inspector for the 8th Army Inspector General. My signature achievements on this assignment were getting a hole-in-one at the Seoul Golf Club, with a plaque there marking that achievement, and climbing the five highest peaks in South Korea.

And Back to Fort Benning

I arrived at Fort Benning in August 1978 with the assigned task of supervising the writing of the first 11B Soldiers' Manual. This was completed in approximately eleven months. When the 197th Infantry Brigade (SEP) was made a Ready Reaction Force, I left the Infantry School for assignment as its S-3. When it was decided that the 197th was "too heavy" for a reaction force, I returned to the Infantry School as Chief of Testing and Evaluation Branch, Directorate of Combat Development. In early 1981, my DA Assignments Officer informed me that I would receive PCS orders to Leavenworth Barracks, KS. I told him that my son had been accepted at Georgia Tech and my daughter had expressed a desire to go to the University of Georgia upon graduation in June 1982. I requested that I be allowed to stay at Fort Benning an additional year to satisfy those goals. I told him that I did not mind moving between Tracy's sophomore and junior year in high school.

My appeal continued until I received a telephone call from a Lieutenant General who told me that I had been assigned to him to write a plan for a project there that could not wait, and that I had no choice but to accept the assignment. I told him that for 19 years I had said, "Yes sir, three bags full," and had never requested a favor of the Army. I respectfully told him I did have a choice, and left directly for the AG Office to initiate my request for retirement. A few weeks later I received TDY orders to Ottobrunn, Germany to be part of a joint German-US task force to rewrite the NATO Defense Plan. I retired as a lieutenant colonel out of that assignment on June 30, 1982.

Retirement

On July 1, I accepted a part-time position as Public Affairs Officer for the Continuing Education Division of Columbus College, Columbus, GA. Six months later, I began a serious second career as a Licensed Professional Counselor with the Georgia Department of Corrections. In early 1983, as Senior Counselor, I initiated the first therapy program in the department for convicted sex offenders. I continued administering that program until November 1993. At that time, I was given a leave of absence without pay for up to twelve months to care for my mother who was stricken with cancer. Because she was still living at the end of that period, I had to return to work or retire. I chose the latter and cared for her until her death. I then resumed my program in private practice until I retired completely in June 2000.

I've lived a wonder-filled life, full of exciting challenges and experiences over most of this planet. The character of my life has been service, through which I've been richly blessed. I've participated in and led mission trips to the Dominican Republic, Guyana, Honduras, Paraguay, Eastern Kentucky (Appalachia), Oregon, and to Mississippi following Hurricane Katrina. I am an ordained Deacon; I have facilitated Bible studies in military chapels and local churches; sung in men's ensembles and church choirs continuously; made thousands of hospital visits; and completed twenty-five years as an active member of Gideons International. I am a member of Pi Tau Chi (National Honor Society for Religion) and Sigma Nu (National Social Fraternity). Grace and I recently celebrated our 50th wedding anniversary, surrounded for a week by our three children and five grandchildren. My current favorite recreational activities are fishing, golf and softball.

Lieutenant Colonel (Retired) Chuck Foster with bull redfish caught on Gulf of Mexico flats near Port Saint Joe, FL in September 2010.

Our children are service-oriented as well. My son is a Hydro Technician with US Geological Survey and monitors water flow rates and quality in Western Colorado. My older daughter is a Professor with the State University of New York at Oswego and teaches/conducts research in the field of Family Development. Our younger daughter is a physical trainer for median age adult women, and formerly assisted in the organization and participation of teams in charitable marathons nationwide, supporting the Children's Tumor Foundation.

As I look back over the past 50 years, I'm fascinated and dismayed by the enormous changes that have occurred in the social, moral and economic systems through which I've traveled and survived. I've had many opportunities to influence outcomes. Wherever I've been, the situation either got better or got worse. It never remained the same. I'm right proud to be able to say that. The lessons learned at Fort Benning and beyond have been integral and vital to my journey from a disheartened survivor of my parents' divorce to a proud soldier, father and leader.

*Major (later Lieutenant Colonel) Dave Harrington
near Da Nang, Vietnam, 1971.*

I was the second son born to my parents who ultimately had three more sons. My father was a minister and a strong leader in our home. My mother was a wonderful homemaker, and a remarkable asset to my father's ministry. I grew up on a typical Arkansas farm where we grew everything we needed for our family to have healthy meals. We ate lots of vegetables, plus fruit from a few trees. Season after season, Mom cooked fresh vegetables, canned or froze all kinds of vegetables and fruit, and shared them with family and friends. Her special recipes were acknowledged for their beauty as well as their taste. Because of her notable green thumb, she also maintained amazing flower gardens, which highlighted decorations she created for various special occasions in our community, and especially graced the worship services and activities in the churches they led.

Aside from the food harvested for our own family's nourishment, we also raised commercial crops, such as field peas, cucumbers, watermelons, peanuts, corn for animal feed, and the staple crop of the South, cotton. In the fall, before school resumed from the summer break, my dad would take my older brother and me into Missouri to hire out to pick cotton for about three or four weeks each year. The worst problem with cotton was keeping grass from growing up in it during the springtime.

During World War II, my dad was away for a time while serving in the Army, overseas. After the war, he returned home to our family and to resume his ministry. He attended a Bible college and also conducted Bible studies on a local radio station. He is an inspiration as he continues to be a talented and skilled musician, playing and recording his music on his harmonicas. He also plays the violin. Four generations of Harringtons gathered with him, to celebrate his 100th birthday in August 2012.

After my dad began pastoring churches fulltime, we did not have as many chores, giving us more time for school sports, etc. During that era, "preachers' kids" were expected to live up to the image as good kids, to be "above the fray," and not be trouble makers. I certainly was not perfect, but I managed to avoid many problems growing up, even though I was a very spirited, active kid who loved adventures. I am thankful I grew up in a secure home. Our school was small, but the teachers were well-prepared and committed to the students, encouraging us to study and get a good education. I was president of my senior class and an officer on the Student Council. Also, we had excellent team sports in basketball and baseball, and I lettered in both. We were proud, after competing with much larger schools, when our team made it to the Arkansas State basketball tournament.

I had made up my mind that after graduation, I would go to California with a friend and his family to work on a ranch or construction projects for the summer; to make, and save some money, and return in the fall to enter the University of Arkansas, in Fayetteville, AR. My major was pre-law studies, but my main hope was to play baseball for the Arkansas Razorbacks. I practiced with the team, but freshmen did not get playing time.

For my next job during summer break, I went to New York to work on the St. Lawrence Seaway project. Then I transferred to Ouachita Baptist University in Arkadelphia, AR to resume my studies and I was happy to get a place on the baseball team. However, no scholarships were available. It was there that I found my lovely wife, Tina, and we soon learned of an unusual bond, that we were "twins" having been born on the same day, August 6, 1938.

This was before the days of student loans, and neither of us had financial resources to complete our college education. We considered dropping out to work fulltime, before continuing college. Still, being young and very much in love, we made two important decisions regarding our course in life for the end of the spring semester; one, that I should join the Army, and two, that we get married! The only educational governmental assistance program at the time was the GI bill. My older brother's experience reminded me of this, for, after he had fulfilled military service, he had used the GI bill to go to college to study to be an architect.

We took a detour from our education to get married, and I enlisted in the Army. Tina worked as a secretary for a church in Little Rock, AR, and I went to basic training at Fort Chaffee, in Fort Smith, AR. After completing basic, my first assignment was to Fort Benjamin Harrison, in Indianapolis, IN for stenographer school. I thought at the time that might be helpful later, according to my plan to attend law school after obtaining my undergraduate degree.

During that course, we learned we were going to be parents, with the baby due around the conclusion of the stenographer course. While we were excited about the upcoming birth of our first baby, we weren't exactly happy campers when orders came for Germany. I was on leave, close to my departure date, when our baby came, and my wife, a new mom and our new son were discharged from the hospital one day before I left for what we expected would be a two or three-year separation.

I was assigned to the 7th Army Headquarters, Stuttgart, Germany, where I had the opportunity to take transcription from those involved in the planning and installation of the nuclear missile systems in Europe. I was required to have special security clearances and there were some restrictions on where I could travel. In my job, I became acquainted with the Division Commanders. One, Major General Edwin A. Walker, traded for me, because he needed a stenographer on his staff for his

Command of the 24th Infantry Division in Augsburg. (I have forgotten what he traded for me; probably not much!) That seems funny now, but it worked out well for me, and I hope for the staff of the 24th Infantry Division as well. With my transfer, I was promoted to Specialist 5, which allowed me the privileges of an "accompanied tour."

My wife and son (who was then nine months old) joined me around Thanksgiving, 1959, and on a cold New Year's Day, 1960, we were glad to move from our small apartment on the German economy near Stuttgart, to much more comfortable military quarters in Augsburg. I had a good assignment and we really enjoyed our tour there. God blessed our family with a second son in 1961, while we were in Augsburg. Amazingly, we had two other couples from the same college we had attended in Arkansas who were serving in different military units in the same town. We felt greatly blessed, joining our three families together in an "Arkansas family," which really helped us during special holidays.

In addition to a fairly heavy combat training program General Walker had set up for the division, he also was very active in promoting a "Citizenship in Service" program. The purpose of that program was to encourage all of us to be proud Americans as we served in another country; to honor our host citizens and to treat them with respect. I remember his great interest in the military being good ambassadors; to be the best example as we represented our country abroad. One of the programs General Walker began involved selecting soldiers from the various units, and preparing them for the opportunity to enroll in Officers' Candidate School (OCS). Our OCS Cadet Corps studied and traveled to a number of sites in order to enhance our experience toward becoming officers. At its onset, this Cadet Corps consisted of a number of soldiers, and from that group, as I recall, twelve of us were selected.

We left Germany and were sent to Fort Benning, GA for a six-month-period of extensive and arduous training. The challenge, if achieved by satisfactory completion, moved candidates to graduation and commission, with the potential to launch very effective careers in the United States Army. As well-trained and fully-motivated new officers, we were committed to serving our country, fulfilling whatever tasks our subsequent assignments required.

We were pleased when our primary requests for military orders were granted. My initial assignment was to the 82nd Airborne Division, Fort

Bragg, NC. Prior to departing for Fort Bragg, I continued training at Fort Benning, in Jump School and Ranger School. Completing both these schools provided tremendous satisfaction for me, acknowledging that I had accomplished my objectives. I had met goals I had set for myself. Additionally, we learned we were going to have a third child, who, being another son, we would later refer to as our little Paratrooper-Ranger.

Now this new second lieutenant was finally headed to the 82nd Airborne Division, confident he was ready to tackle any task (note: I was willing, but I soon learned I was not fully ready.) Military quarters were not available on our arrival, so we moved into a nice rental home near the post. My family spent a lot of time going and coming to see me at the airfield, as we were on alert much of the time for whatever mission our country would call on us to perform. These included flying to the University of Mississippi, setting up a tent city to provide protection for prospective students, and dealing with any type of civil unrest. We spent many hours preparing, equipping ourselves, and boarding planes to head out to hotspots around the world. Drawing worldwide attention was the historic nuclear missile crisis in Cuba, which required all military personnel to live on post. We moved just prior to the birth of our son, to a small, two-bedroom duplex. Among other crises, a particular dangerous situation erupted in Africa. In most cases, these crises were settled and the planes returned to Fort Bragg without major problems. In that era, well prepared military and civilian representatives negotiated to settle issues before they became major hostilities.

At Fort Bragg, I served in various capacities. Some jobs I really enjoyed; some I did not necessarily like, but did them anyway, to the best of my ability. As a matter of fact, those particular experiences were the ones that taught me the most. We were thankful when a four-bedroom unit opened up for our growing family. Soon after being promoted to first lieutenant, I was given command of C Company, 1/508th Battalion, 187th Battle Group. After that command position, I received orders to the 5th Special Forces in Panama, with two preparatory schools. The first did not require a transfer, since the Special Forces Course was located at Fort Bragg. Then in the spring of 1965, with my wife and three young sons, a cross country trip was on schedule, practically ocean to ocean, as I was to attend the Defense Language School at the Presidio in Monterey, CA for six months to study Spanish. We had a pleasant community life with other military friends and families, near the northern Pacific Ocean coastline. I was very proud to have learned the language and completed the course just before Thanksgiving, 1965.

I moved my family to be near relatives in Arkansas and was happy to be able to celebrate the Christmas holidays before I flew to the Panama Canal Zone the beginning of January 1966. Our two school-age sons entered a new school at mid-semester. Since military housing was not yet available for families, my first six months were spent, along with a dozen or so other officers who were also waiting for their families, living in the BOQ. I taught students in the Jungle Warfare School at Fort Gulick. In June 1966, we were overjoyed when my family was able to join me. In that same timeframe, I was selected to serve as a representative for South American senior officers during their training in Panama. Stationed at Fort Amador, I traveled throughout Central and South America. Through my work, I became acquainted with officers who later were key presidential staff, advisors, and department heads. That was such a pleasant assignment; we lived in beautiful tropical on-post housing, just across the golf course from Command Headquarters. Our sons and other children could hear and see the evening retreat ceremony and would scramble from their swings or slide to stand and proudly salute our flag.

Although my assignment was to be a three-year tour, with the buildup of the war in Vietnam, two months after my family's arrival, in August of 1966, I received orders for Vietnam, and was scheduled to leave Panama in November. Having begun the school year in Panama, our kindergartener and second grader would transfer to North Carolina for two months, then complete the school year in Arkansas. Priority being "the needs of the service" did not set well with my wife at the time. In preparing for my initial Panama assignment, my family had endured two cross country moves, half a year's separation, and finally getting together in Panama for just a few months, so another move was not on our charts. A major plus to offset disappointment at our tour being cut so short, our family enjoyed a wonderful Thanksgiving trip aboard a Grace Lines ship, an educational tour from the Pacific to Atlantic through the locks of the canal, and then a cruise back to the 'States.

Arriving on the east coast, with our sons and boxer puppy in tow, as soon as our luggage and car were off the ship, we immediately drove to the nearest mall to buy coats for our sons, since all our winter clothes had been stored before we left the 'States. We drove down to Fort Bragg for the short advisory school, where our only recourse was to live in a nice but small mobile home, to grab a bit more family time before heading back to Arkansas and the beginning of another separation.

At home in Arkansas, we reclaimed our household goods, and settled again before I left for Vietnamese study at the Defense Language School at Fort Bliss, TX. Afterward, I was blessed to have a month's family leave before the year-long separation. By then, our sons were four, six and eight years of age; our second grader had attended six schools and our six year old had three kindergartens. I missed, by mere days, his "complete with white cap and gown" graduation. My departure was May 18, 1967.

I was introduced to the sudden reality of Vietnam a few days after my arrival in country. I was traveling on a Chinook, with approximately forty soldiers aboard, when about halfway to our destination, running north along the coastline, it seemed the pilot was losing control of the helicopter. I was in the rear of the copter and looked up to see nothing but a big sheet of red hydraulic oil spewing down like a curtain! The pilot tried to get the copter under control and everyone was scrambling to prepare for what we thought was a certain crash. The copter hit the ground quite hard, but all of us complimented the pilot for his superior control in the crash landing (I didn't know helicopters could bounce that high!) Everyone was able to get out of the copter without serious injuries. However, it had taken a pretty good beating. What was really surprising to me was how fast backup helicopters, including gunships, came to provide security. Within a couple of hours we were again on our way to Pleiku. From there, the next day, I was flown into Ban Me Thuot. After a couple weeks of briefings, I was flown to our camp near the Cambodian border.

My initial assignment was to be advisor to the only Vietnamese Airborne Battalion in the country. Unfortunately, when I arrived, that had been changed. Now, I was to head up a team on the Cambodian border, training and operating with Montagnards in that area. The Montagnards (Minong) were a family-oriented, peaceable tribe, who only wanted to be left alone. They were a good, honest people, liked Americans, but did not like the Vietnamese. They became our friends, learned to trust us, and did what we asked of them, but they were not good fighters. After I wrote my sons of the plight of these poor people, they sent packages for me to give to the children. As much as I anticipated going home, when my tour ended, I hated to leave them there in that mess. There was no replacement and most of our team were rotated or, being wounded, were sent to hospitals in Germany.

I came back to the 'States exactly one year to the date I left; and was promoted to major. We moved to Fort Polk, LA where I spent the next year training troops who were scheduled to go to Vietnam. That was hard, as I knew this short course was not nearly enough to prepare these young men for what they were going to experience.

After that year, I was scheduled for the 1969-70 Infantry Officers Advanced Course at Fort Benning, GA. My family and I were traveling from Louisiana to Georgia on the day our astronauts were preparing to land on the moon. As soon as possible, we hurried to check into a motel, so that we could watch this historic and exciting event on the television. When we checked in on-post the following morning, we learned our assigned quarters were being freshly painted, and we could not move in for a week. No problem; we just took off for a vacation in Destin, FL! We enjoyed living in the old but spacious Austin Loop, just across from the Generals' quarters. The interaction and activities of the class, especially the Headquarters, was invigorating to me after my Vietnam tour and then training soldiers before they left for the war. After the completion of IOAC in 1970, I returned to Ouachita Baptist University, to complete my degree in Business Administration in 1971, having laid aside my former plan to study law.

During my second tour to Vietnam, I was operations officer of 3rd Battalion, 196th Brigade, 23rd Infantry Division. It was a good brigade and the battalions were well trained, accomplishing every mission we were assigned. Most of our contact with the enemy took place in very mountainous terrain. Had we not been provided with dogs that were also well-trained, and in most cases found booby traps before we walked into one or more of them, we would have suffered more casualties. Occasionally, we would lose a dog, especially when they had to jump across something or down to get to the next level, because the traps were placed in such a way that the dogs could not detect them until they were in the air. These dogs were really a blessing from God. In the last few months of the tour, we provided security for different noncombat units as they were leaving Vietnam. Our date to return to the 'States was changed several times. I think we were the last combat battalion out, in June 1972.

As I departed from Vietnam and started really thinking about getting back and seeing my wife and sons again, it really hit home, just how difficult these war separations had been for the families. As soldiers on a mission, we were preoccupied with our tasks, which really took our full focus, and we just had to trust that our families were doing alright. It took strong and courageous women to weather those years, in light of the many "you are there" newscasts and the loud waves of protests about this war. In my case, during my first tour, my wife was one of only two military wives in the town where she lived, whose husbands were in Vietnam. Prior to my leaving for the second tour, and being in a different location, she helped establish a military wives organization, made up of the "waiting (war) wives" as well as wives of retired military personnel and the wives of ROTC faculty at the two universities in that town. Looking back, I don't think the military did a very good job in supporting families left here in the 'States while we were deployed. Thankfully, with the continued military action requiring so many repeated tours back and forth from Iraq and Afghanistan, current sponsors and their families have had much more public recognition, national appreciation for their service and much-needed support.

A real change of venue came when I returned with orders that I did not welcome at the time; an ROTC assignment. However, after all the transfers, moving, and family separations, being in one place for three years was good timing for our family. Our sons had a stable school situation at a crucial time in their youth. Located near a beautiful lake, we purchased a big boat which provided lots of recreation and relaxation as all of us loved to water ski. At the time we had no idea how many miles we would put on that craft! Also, for me, I was surprised how teaching university students at a pivotal time in their education brought so much satisfaction. Additionally, the opportunity to counsel young men and women in leadership and service expanded and enhanced my previous experience. It has been a pleasure to continue to run into some of those former students and to know that they have done well, some of whom stayed in the military; and others, who, after serving their ROTC obligations, settled into their chosen fields.

In 1975, I received orders for Command and General Staff College in Fort Leavenworth, KS. I was pleased to have time and opportunity to also work on my master's degree in Human Resource Development along with the C&GSC studies. Our sons had good experiences; all played school sports and we had to juggle schedules to make it to all their games. Many of their classmates were there for only one year, as their dads were also C&GSC students. Through our church, the youth department developed a good musical drama which they presented in different locations.

From there I was assigned to the Navy in San Diego, CA with the Amphibious Group, Eastern Pacific. Although the assignment was rather unexpected, our family anticipated that this area would be great. With our accommodation reservations at the Navy Lodge on North Island, we immediately became very excited as we crossed the majestic bridgework separating the big city of San Diego from the quaint little town of Coronado, between San Diego Bay and the Pacific Ocean. After driving cross country, five people and a dog in two cars, one pulling a boat, and coming from the extreme heat of the desert in summer, and the humidity of the South, we welcomed the contrast of a mild temperature of seventy-three degrees! Of all the places we had been, this was definitely the most beautiful location we had ever lived! With bustling San Diego just minutes across the bay, there were many interesting things to see and do. We arrived a few days before Independence Day, just in time for a big celebration. Our family was in our boat alongside many others in the bay and ocean, being nationally televised, celebrating our nation's 1976 Bicentennial.

A rare blessing; we found a large two-story home to rent, built in 1914 by an old sea captain, right on the bay, with huge naval ships docked across from us. Coronado School, all grades through high school, was contained in one big campus complex, and located near our home. We enjoyed knowing and interacting with many Navy families. Our boat was in the water often, for regular excursions, not only for our family, but also serving as an attraction for our sons' friends. The appeal of southern California was demonstrated as we welcomed family and friends from several areas who vacationed to come to visit us while we were there. One Christmas we took our sons water skiing in wet suits to a lake, and the following week they were snow skiing with our church youth group farther north. In 1977 our oldest son graduated from Coronado High. We all still fondly recall our very fulfilling time in that beautiful area.

That assignment proved to me that an infantry ground pounder can learn new things as well as teach the Navy a little, too! An interesting aspect was that I also learned a new military language. Furthermore, I enjoyed a lot of time on ships as Plans Officer for an Amphibious Group and Liaison Officer for special warfare units. I had the special opportunity of many hours at sea with the USS Tarawa (the first helicopter carrier built). It was certainly a new experience for an Army officer to participate in the shakedown of a brand new carrier (first of its kind; and only one Army officer assigned duties on board). It was a highlight of my military experience! I was promoted to lieutenant colonel during this assignment, and also completed requirements for my master's degree. After only two years, it was hard to leave the beautiful west coast, but duty called.

We crossed the desert again, five people in three cars, still pulling our boat, but absent our beloved, but aging boxer, Duchess, who had traveled with us from her birthplace in Panama through many moves, but who was no longer able to make another cross country trip. It was "back to the South" for Executive Officer assignment with Headquarters of the 2nd Brigade, 5th Division, Fort Polk, LA, in 1978. For the first time, we built a new home off post and stayed very involved with the activities of the Brigade. In 1979, our second son graduated from Leesville High School and I was selected by Department of the Army for battalion command; a good thing, but that came with a problem; I had to go to Europe for a three-year tour. There was no negotiation; the Army would not give in to let me stay in the 'States.

Through twenty-two years of military service, I had moved my family so often; we had lived in a number of states and two other countries. Now, with two sons in college and our youngest, now a junior, soon to be making that step too, I felt it was important to all of us for me to be stateside, and Germany was too high a price to pay to be so far away from them during their college years. I was forty-two years old and sensed this was a good time to make a change. After much prayer, I chose to resign from active duty.

A good climax before my transition to civilian life was the joy of planning and participating in Steel Scorpion, the first live fire desert warfare exercise at Fort Irwin, CA, the beginning of 1980. Soon after my return from Fort Irwin, I resigned, effective June 30, 1980.

Even though I did not look back, it was hard to leave the military because of the great people with whom I had been privileged to work over the years. But I had peace in my decision, for me, my own future and my family's. After the news got around that I had resigned from my military service, I faced concern and various reactions from peers, fellow officers and colleagues at my duty station. Sincere as they were, they expressed their opinions that I was "making a big mistake in leaving the service at this particular time in my life, when my future seemed bright." I faced questions such as, "What are you going to do?" My response was consistent as I explained that I had reached this decision as I had in all major decisions of my adult life, as a result of much prayer, seeking guidance from God. I trusted God to reveal the next chapter of our life, knowing God is always faithful. Notwithstanding, I had very little time for golf and racquetball in the interim, and did not have to wait long before God revealed His plan, although it was somewhat different than we had expected.

All along our mobile lifestyle, we had assumed that after retirement, we would naturally return to Arkansas, our home state. However, within one month after my retirement ceremony, I was offered an exceptional opportunity in the private sector which would mean we would remain in Louisiana, moving to the state capitol, Baton Rouge. I became Vice President of Louisiana Association of Business and Industry, which was a combination of the State Chamber of Commerce and the Louisiana Manufacturing Association. I sensed it would be an interesting job and was thankful for the opportunity. I had no idea that I was launching my second career. We sold the home we had built, and bought another in Baton Rouge, in an area where a good school was located, as our youngest son was to begin his senior year, following the pattern of his two older brothers, who had each transferred to a new school for their senior year! By then, our second son was a premed student and playing football at Ouachita, where my life and Tina's merged all those years ago, and where I had completed my degree. Our older son transferred from University of Arkansas, Little Rock, to Louisiana State University in Baton Rouge.

I have a neat and fond memory of my former commander and his wife, coming to see us a mere three weeks after we had moved from our last military assignment and into a new home in Baton Rouge. We knew that was out of their way, for they were transferring to his new assignment at the Pentagon. From the time they entered our home, it was apparent that they were intently observing our situation, with everything unpacked and in place, from the draperies to pictures on the walls; they could readily see we were completely settled. They were sweet Christian friends, who genuinely cared for our family, and yet, had been among those who were concerned and had advised me to reconsider my decision to leave the military at that time. After a pleasant lunch, as they prepared to leave, with sly smiles, they admitted that they had wanted to come down "just to make sure we were all right" in our unlikely big change. My "boss" spoke kindly and strongly, "How good it is to see Dave dressed in a business suit, and to see your beautiful home in such order that it looks like you have been here a long time." They, too, were facing transition, and our experience seemed to encourage them.

We had a good life in Baton Rouge; our youngest son graduated from high school in 1981 and joined his oldest brother there at Louisiana State University. I thoroughly enjoyed working at LABI, my first civilian job, and learned a lot about governmental relations in a private sector environment. I did not realize I was in transition, being prepared for another profession. After about a year and a half in this position, when offered an opportunity similar to LABI, but in the public sector in our home state, that was a "no brainer" decision! Again, we put our home on the market and moved to Little Rock, Arkansas' state capitol. Our oldest son, who had begun his career in Little Rock, then continued it in Baton Rouge while a student at LSU, ultimately resumed it in Little Rock. Our youngest son joined his older brother at Ouachita. We seemed to have completed the circle begun so many years ago and praised our Heavenly Father for His loving and protective, caring hand on our family, through all the years of moving.

My new position was an appointment by the Republican Governor to be Deputy Director of the Arkansas Industrial Development

Commission, AIDC (now Arkansas Economic Development Commission). I began my job in the spring of 1982 and found it to be personally fulfilling, working toward a better economic future of our home state. In the November elections, former Governor Bill Clinton, a Democrat, was re-elected Governor, and historically, a new governor meant changes in appointments, members of the Governor's Senior Cabinet, as well as all state agency heads. However, Arkansas' political arena had recently changed, overcoming former policies, and I was appointed Director, where I remained through Governor Clinton's two successive terms.

When Bill Clinton was elected President, I chose to stay in Arkansas, as I was re-appointed by the Democratic Governor who had moved up from Lieutenant Governor. Previous AIDC directors had been in that position for only short periods, but in my tenure, I had served three governors, and had seen the economic picture of Arkansas changed dramatically. Additionally, during the administrations of Presidents Ronald Reagan, George H.W. Bush and Bill Clinton, I received Presidential appointments to work with the United States Trade Representative, serving on the Intergovernmental Policy Advisory Committee as well as advisor to the US Secretary of Commerce. I was elected Chairman of the Board of Directors for two terms on the National Association of State Agencies and successfully established and staffed three international trade offices. More importantly, I had seen goals reached that I had set when I began this job.

I had always hoped to end my working career in private business. After so many moves, we had lived in the same home in Little Rock far longer than anyplace in our marriage, and at the time we returned to Arkansas, we had sensed that this was to be our "swan song!" Each of our sons had completed their education and was married, and we had become grandparents. As the old saying goes, "the more things change, the more they stay the same!" So when my wife and I turned fifty-five years of age (on the same day!), after prayerfully considering a new opportunity to enter a private business, we accepted the challenge. I submitted my resignation as Director of AIDC to the Governor, and we were honored with a grand farewell reception at the Old State House, where Bill Clinton had first announced his entering the presidential race. We loved our home state and its people, grateful for the wonderful opportunity to serve Arkansas' economic interest.

This decision involved another move, this time to Ohio, in the middle of their coldest winter! After a few months enjoying a winter wonderland, having our sons' families visit for trips to breathtaking Niagara Falls in winter, we had had our fill of snow, so I moved the company headquarters a little closer south, both for air flight convenience, and to be nearer our aging parents and our sons' families. We bought a home on a ridge across the Ohio River from Louisville, KY. Since business travel was demanding, I bought a plane, so that I could not only expedite business trips, but also to fly us down to see our grandchildren!

After a few years, and seeing our business thriving, we found ourselves "back at home" to settle down, older, and some wiser. Our sons and "daughters in love," with our ten grandchildren, hosted a grand combined celebration for our 70th birthday and our Golden Wedding Anniversary in 2008. I am glad they all live within an hour of us.

My three careers were each completely different, requiring me to develop various strengths to adjust in every change. And I am thankful our family relationships remained united and strong during all the years. I am grateful for my wife, and cannot adequately express the benefit Tina has been in each of my careers. After working with and leading many groups of military wives, she realized the challenges they all face. So, because of her natural compassion for new wives, knowing the adjustments they would experience, she wrote a book of helpful guidance for cadet wives during my ROTC assignment, *You're In the Army Now!* Also, she was honored as "Military Wife of the Year," for the US Army Third ROTC Region. Beginning with a trip back to Europe several years ago, we continued a "pilgrimage," primarily to revisit each of our three sons' birthplaces, plus going back to several posts where we had lived. In each instance, we were glad to see those places, recalling our lives at the time we lived there. Those trips were blessed with memories.

Through this project, *The Boys of Benning*, I have reflected on the progressive path that military life opened for us. How, when we were young, simultaneously beginning both our married and military ventures, with our entire future before us, we had no idea that "God had planted us for a purpose in this vocation." Through the flexible, mobile lifestyle, God taught us so many lessons of life, seeing the "world unfold as our home," allowing each of our family to adjust, grow and mature in a myriad of adventures. God led and brought across our path a multitude of delightful relationships and friends, that we treasure and enjoy even now, albeit, many from a distance. And, as military kids, our sons learned early the benefits of being open to new, broader opportunities.

Lieutenant Colonel (Retired) Dave Harrington and wife Tina, Little Rock, AR, 1992.

Through our diversified experiences, with no promise of making a home in one place and staying there; or always seeing and knowing the same friends; or studying in the same schools; or never being touched by military family separation or a distant war impacting their young lives, our sons learned, experientially, about real, solid security. It is not to be found in a place or a position. Our foundation is a relationship with our Creator, our Lord and Savior, Jesus Christ. By necessity, through unexpected transfers, detours, and times of uncertainty during our journey, God taught us that He would not only lead us, but sustain us. Through every change, His Word is true, that He changes not. It has been a wild, and at times, a too-fast ride, but we are grateful for God's immeasurable blessings. Now that our sons are husbands and fathers, leading their own families, we are humbled, and yet smile, as we observe their steady guidance of our grandchildren from the base they built for themselves through their own passages of life, maintaining a close bond with one's family, and our daily walk of faith in God.

Lieutenant (later Colonel) Tony Newton (left foreground) reviewing the honor guard with Emperor Haile Selassie, Asmara, Ethiopia, 1963.

Prelude

I can't remember spending a day wondering what the future might hold for me or what life's responsibilities might be prior to that "shock and awe" day in October 1961. I was a kid on a treadmill; one day at a time, come as it may, with no plan and frankly few cares. Although I was a high school graduate and had "participated" in college for two years (more about that later), I was less prepared for the life that was to follow than my grandkids are today.

Like everything else I had done in life up to that point, I "tripped" into OCS almost by accident. Yes, I did submit an application, but it languished in personnel channels for months with no action. I had given up until a colonel I was working for asked personnel for a status report, and all of a sudden I was before a board and on the way to Fort Benning all within a few days. My life changed overnight.

Twenty-six weeks of Officer Candidate School provided me with a set of skills, both mental and physical, I never dreamed possible.

It took a few years for me to fully comprehend what happened over that six-month period. Without question I matured, significantly increased my self-awareness and became more confident of my abilities. Unfortunately, I did not learn humility. That came later at the hands of seasoned veterans, both officers and NCOs.

The Early Days

We lived in Bellmore, New York, a small town on Long Island's Nassau County, about an hour east of New York City. My mom, dad, brother and I lived in what I remember to be a very large house in a quiet neighborhood. (The house turned out to be pretty small when I visited it forty years later.) We stayed there long enough for me to attend the first grade in 1946. Then Mom and Dad had a difference of opinion, and Mom, my brother Walter and I headed off to Florida. Dad stayed behind. I never did fully understand what the split was all about, but as the years progressed my father was very much part of our lives and provided for all of us. Dad made a pretty good living as the sales manager of a lithography company in New York City. I remember him telling me that in the '50s he made $30,000 a year. Looking back at it, I guess that was a good salary.

Our new home was in Bradenton Beach, Florida on Anna Maria Island, located an hour or so south of Tampa on the Gulf Coast. It was a beachfront house built on stilts. I would go to sleep to the sounds of the rolling waves beneath the house. It was idyllic. I went to school in a two-room school house (second and third grades in one room and fourth and fifth grades in the other). We moved each year for the next two or three years, first to Holmes Beach and then to Anna Maria, the most northern city of the island. Our new home there was two blocks from the Gulf of Mexico. The road it was built on was and is named Newton Lane, after my family. When they built a new school I left the two-room school behind. I loved Anna Maria Island. It was comfortable and safe. At nine and ten years old, I would hitchhike up and down the island without fear.

At some point in late 1949 or early 1950, I asked my mother to send me to military school at the Florida Military Academy (FMA). I had met a former schoolmate who was going there and he made it sound so exciting that I wanted to be part of it. My mother, who cherished her privacy and freedom, got my dad to agree. In 1950 at age eleven, I was off to boarding school. My brother Walter, nine years my senior, enlisted in the Air Force in 1950, thus freeing mom from child-rearing responsibilities. The two years I spent at FMA in St. Petersburg, Florida are mostly a blur. I enjoyed regimentation and the fact that my time was planned. Not much time was left open for a youngster to sit around. Although only an hour or so from my home in Anna Maria, I only returned there for holidays and summer vacation.

As a rule, Mom and I would travel from Florida to Pine Neck (Sag Harbor), Long Island each summer to our summer home. I have fond memories of my summers there. The weather was always better than Florida in the summer. We made this trip for twelve or thirteen years.

FMA closed after the 1951-52 school year. In the fall of 1952, at age thirteen, I went to Bolles School in Jacksonville, Florida to begin the seventh grade. Bolles was a significant step up from FMA, but it was again an all-boys military school environment. Facilities, number of students, academic rigors, and the fact that boarding students came from around the world, all set Bolles apart from FMA.

I enjoyed the military environment at Bolles. I played some football and baseball and ran track. I was not particularly good at any of the sports. Bolles prided itself on being a college-prep institution, but as is the case with every academic "bell curve" environment, there had to be someone to anchor the low side of the curve. I think that's why they kept me around. When you are in a school for six years, especially as a boarder, the faculty gets to know you. I spent my share of time in trouble. There was never anything earth-shattering, but in their eyes I needed to be brought into line. The most significant incident resulted in my being reduced from second lieutenant platoon leader to private my senior year. I was most embarrassed for my dad, who was footing the bill. When I told him though, I don't believe he thought it was anything to worry about. He apparently just thought it was "boys being boys."

One shortcoming of spending eight years in an all-boys boarding school environment was the lack of interface with young ladies. From age eleven to seventeen, I never shared a classroom with a girl. It's like you don't know what you're missing until you get it back. That happened in short order with major consequences.

In the '50s, Florida law stated that any graduate from a Florida high school had the right to enter a Florida public college. In the spring of 1957, I was asked which college I wanted to attend. I knew I could not academically qualify for a college (I graduated high school by the skin on my teeth), but the law said it didn't matter. So, it was either the University of Florida (UF) at Gainesville or Florida State University (FSU) in Tallahassee. UF was the better university in every aspect. However, until 1950 or so, FSU was a teachers college. By 1957, there were still six females for every male at FSU. So, off to FSU I went.

I arrived at FSU in the fall of '57, eighteen years old and very unaware of the world around me. There were insufficient dorms for incoming freshmen, so I was sent to the Pi Kappa Alpha fraternity to live. While I didn't know it, the beginning of my college downfall was in place. I went through all of the required freshman activities including class registration. Girls were everywhere. The university required every freshman to take a three credit hour class in Speech. It was Speech 101 and that was my first college class.

That fateful Monday morning, as I took my seat in the front row, I was as excited as I could be. The instructor had us participate in an icebreaker; stand before the class and introduce the person to the left and right. I stood, and for the first time in eight years, I saw a class full of lovely ladies. It was overwhelming and the seminal event of my downfall. It took two and a half years to play itself out, but in August of 1959 the Dean of Men called me and asked if my father hadn't spent enough money on my "social experiment."

FSU was just that for me. It was making up for eight years of missed experiences. It was non-mandatory study halls (if you don't have to go, why go?). It was the social whirlwind that I had never experienced. I was part of ROTC and enjoyed that, but mostly it was just partying. While I never made my grades, I was the perennial pledge for the fraternity. The refrigerator in my room was always full of beer and booze purchased from a liquor store in a wet county 150 miles away, and sold out of my fraternity room window. Tallahassee and most of the panhandle were dry. Those were fun days. I have no idea why I was never caught. I'll skip the panty raid episode and breaking and entering the girls' dorm. It was all so silly, but I did get to know the Dean of Men rather well.

After the end of my time at FSU, I stayed in Tallahassee and worked as a salesman in a camera store for the five months until the Christmas holidays in 1959. I went home and told my family I was going to enlist in the Army. They knew it before I did.

The Decision to Apply for OCS

My nine weeks of basic training was conducted at Fort Jackson, SC. It proved to be the wakeup call I had anticipated, but all-in-all, not too bad. We were too busy to get in trouble. Time went fast and soon I had orders to Fort Devens, MA, the training school for the Army Security Agency (ASA). I had enlisted for ASA without any knowledge of what that meant. It was the old enlistment ploy of "make it sound so secretive they'll want to have it." It worked. I scored well on my entrance tests and obviously met their threshold.

My dad was living in New York City, so I spent a week with him after basic training and he drove me to Fort Devens. Upon checking in, I was put in a processing company along with all soldiers that were incoming, those outgoing and all those who had failed their advanced individual training (AIT). Fort Devens was the training ground for all enlisted ASA MOS's. I realized a couple of things right off. First, everybody in the processing company pulled KP every other day and post details on the odd days, and second, a very large percentage of the soldiers stuttered. As it turned out, most of those soldiers were dropouts from the manual Morse intercept operators training course (MOS 058). I guessed all those dits and dahs did something to your head and I wanted nothing to do with that. As it turned out, you had to run pretty fast to get away from that training, but as you may remember, I ran track in high school.

A couple of weeks later I joined a bunch of AIT newcomers in the personnel office to be in-processed to ASA and to be assigned an MOS in which to be trained. At the head of the line there were three rooms, each with a series of numbers over them. The room on the left had 058 over the door, the room in the middle also had 058 over the door, and the remaining room had a whole bunch of very different numbers, none of which I recognized, except 058 was not one of them. That's where I wanted to go. The personnel warrant officer was walking the line, and from time to time, he would take the personnel file of one of the soldiers, briefly look at it and give it back. He did that to me just as I was getting to the head of the line. He pulled me out after realizing I had studied radio and TV in college, and asked if I wanted to work in a TV station. It wasn't 058, so I was for it. I was sent back to the processing company, including KP and post details, until I heard from him. About three or four weeks later I was sure he had forgotten. I found my way back to the personnel office, and sure enough, he had. He asked me if I could type and I lied, assuring him that I could. The next morning I was off to Fort Gordon, Georgia to be a clerk typist in the ASA Liaison Office. That didn't last more than two or three months. The liaison officer had a friend at ASA Headquarters who needed a clerk for the summer. I was on the road again, this time to Headquarters, USASA, Arlington Hall Station, Virginia.

In-processing at Arlington Hall was different from in-processing at other posts because the post was secure. You needed a badge to get through the gate. Everybody there held a top secret special intelligence (TSSI) security clearance and everybody had a badge hanging from their neck to prove it. I found out that was what I enlisted for and what the recruiters wouldn't tell me about. It turned out I was to be temporarily assigned to the ASA Chief of Staff's office for the summer.

As the summer wore on, my idea of what a soldier was supposed to be became contorted. I was only a private or maybe a PFC at the time, but there appeared to be few rules. I walked the halls of the headquarters with men and women of all ranks. All was well except I had no formal Army training, had no "real" MOS, or at least not one that could get me promoted. Also, the high regard the headquarters folks had for me did not carry over to my barracks life. In fact, my platoon leader nicknamed me "gig-a-day Newton." It was clear that I did not have balance in both sides of my Army life. Rules were to be skirted and often ignored, or so I thought. Thanksgiving day 1960, I had KP and worked in the tray room. A basic rule was that smoking was forbidden in the tray room. So, when Mess Sergeant Larry Mulligan found me with a cigarette in the tray room, I paid the penalty. He gave me a soup spoon and a dessert dish, and not so gently lowered me into the grease pit with instructions to bail it out. I guessed that no-smoking rule was to be obeyed.

With little to do in the evenings, I took a job as a bartender at the NCO Club. I mixed well with the NCOs on the other side of the bar and that contributed further to my balance problem. I couldn't get into the NCO Club when I wasn't working as I was only a PFC. However, the WACs of any grade could. Talk about a double standard! I was thrown out of the club numerous times but still maintained my employment. This club was the only entertainment on the post, and a PFC made $50 or $60 a month, so Arlington and DC were out of the question.

The one upside of the NCO Club episodes was that I met a WAC, my future wife Joy, at the club. We have had numerous laughs over our fifty years together when asked how we met. I would say that I picked her up in a bar, and watch the reaction. The question of why I applied for OCS remains. There were several reasons: (1) I couldn't get promoted, (2) They wouldn't let me in the NCO Club, (3) I didn't have any money, and (4) I wanted to marry Joy. For the life of me, I couldn't figure how that was going to happen in my situation.

I filled out an OCS application and attached supporting letters from a colonel and two or three other officers I worked for in the headquarters. Months passed with no obvious result. One weekday afternoon in (I believe) September 1961, the colonel that gave me the supporting letter asked me about the application. When I told him I had heard nothing, he turned and assured me I would. That Friday afternoon I appeared before an OCS Board at Fort Myer, and on the following Sunday I was on my way to Fort Benning. The one piece of advice I was given by my platoon leader, who couldn't believe I would make it through the course, was not to report in to the OCS Company until after 5PM. Those OCS candidates reading this chapter that did report in before 5PM remember well the Tac Officer reception I missed.

Time at OCS

To me, OCS was an adventure of trying to stay under the radar one day at a time. I fully enjoyed the training, but worried that my lack of Infantry background was going to catch me short. That turned out not to be the case, but the thought was always with me.

The lessons taught outside the classroom and training areas were more important to me than those taught in more formal training. They also stood by me for an entire career. Setting and maintaining standards, attention to detail, abiding by the rules, developing a vision and establishing a set of objectives to achieve it, were but a few of many lessons I learned. One story brought them all together.

My mother had two sons in the military: my brother, an Air Force fighter jock, and me. She was convinced the services had no idea how to feed her boys, so she sent care packages. There was an OCS rule regarding food in the barracks. It had to be out by Monday morning. I forgot that rule at the wrong time. That fateful Monday morning formation, we were sent back to the barracks to unlock our footlockers for inspection. Mine was full of cans of fruit, ham, and assorted other goodies. I panicked. Not having any time, I put the cans in my field jacket and went back to formation. I thought I would dispose of them at the first break. That was a great thought, but Lieutenant Finlayson found them first. I thought my OCS days were over. Lieutenant Finlayson's response, however, was to have me carry the cans on my person from that day to graduation day. At least I knew there was a chance there was to be a graduation day for me.

Shortly after "can" day, my fiancée Joy called to say she was being transferred to Japan. We had planned to marry after OCS and she would leave the Army, but Japan would keep that from happening. I asked Lieutenant Finlayson and Captain Hadly for permission to marry as a candidate. They agreed, and on February 24, 1962, we were married at the Student Brigade Chapel. Jim Nicholas was my best man, and candidates from the Fourth Platoon were part of the ceremony. It was a great event for us.

The "can" story continues. Lieutenant and Mrs. Finlayson attended the wedding. Mrs. Finlayson took me aside, said she had a wedding present for me, and asked me to give her the cans. As happy as I was to oblige, I felt troubled. Nonetheless, she got the cans, and Joy and I were off to our one night honeymoon at a motel in Columbus. Sunday night, I arrived back in the barracks to find the cans on my pillow. I later found out that Lieutenant Finlayson was furious with his wife for getting involved in his business.

Assignments Immediately After Commissioning

My first assignment was to USASA Field Station, Asmara, Ethiopia, a place that I had neither heard of nor could find on a map. Fellow candidate Wayne Stone had been assigned there and assured me it would be a great assignment. He was right. At 9,000 ft. altitude on Eritrea's east coast, the weather was perfect and the living was good. A full time maid for $16 a month, and a half time yard boy for $8 a month were just two of the benefits.

I was initially assigned as the OIC, APO 843 (postal officer) as well as the dependent schools supply officer. Additional duties included special courts trial (later defense) counsel and honor guard commander. The latter job brings a story to mind.

His Imperial Majesty Haile Selassie visited us twice a year to get his teeth cleaned and to wipe out the commissary and PX. He was met by the honor guard on each visit. By this time in my tour I had been reassigned as Headquarters Company Executive Officer, and Mess and Supply Officer. The Post Commander told me to include a walk-through of our mess facility to show the Emperor our new Jenn Aire stoves and coolers. In Army greens and bloused boots, I started my walk-through pigeon-talking to this African leader until he put me in my place in perfect English. We then went into the kitchen and I stepped in some spilled potato water. My feet went out from under me and I slid all the way on my ass to the coolers where my feet came to rest on the doors. Before I knew it I had the Colonel pulling up on one arm and the Emperor pulling up on the other. There was no place for me to hide.

Thanksgiving day 1963 was a bad time for a lot of folks. As usual, we had Thanksgiving dinner in the mess hall for the troops and families alike. That night our hospital was full. Soldiers and dependents lined the hallways as beds were full, and all were getting IVs. They all had food poisoning, and they all had eaten in my mess hall. That was the first time I ever saw troops rally around someone to save his career.

Headquarters Company First Sergeant Larry Mulligan was the same guy that, as the Mess Sergeant at Arlington Hall Station, dropped me in that grease pit with spoon and dish for smoking in the tray room. Many of the cooks in Asmara were also part of the Arlington Hall command. They all believed that there had to be a scapegoat for the food poisoning, and I was going to be it.

We developed a plan that included emptying the mess hall totally, cleaning, painting, scraping and anything else that we could do to show that it wouldn't happen again. We set up a field mess to feed the troops. We had gone to extreme lengths, and all appeared to be forgiven. The bottom line to this story is that on that same Thanksgiving day, the Army mess in Okinawa had an outbreak of food poisoning, and the turkeys came from the same batch. The problem wasn't our cleanliness. It was the turkeys.

One Sunday morning during this period, Joy and I were having breakfast in the Officers Club when, to my surprise, Lieutenant Finlayson walked in. He and an NCO were on an advisory mission with the Ethiopian Army in their war with the Somalis. They joined us for a nice breakfast, and not a word was said about the cans.

After a year or so in Headquarters Company, I was assigned to Operations Company as a platoon leader/watch officer. My introduction to ASA/NSA operations was to begin.

In January 1965, Joy, 2 babies and I got orders for the USASA Advanced Course at Fort Devens, MA.

Subsequent Assignments

Fort Bragg

I completed the Advanced Course and got orders to the 313th ASA Battalion at Fort Bragg, NC. I was assigned as the Battalion S-1. It was the summer of 1965, and the build-up of Vietnam was beginning. My job was to fill our subordinate companies and get them ready to deploy. We knew the battalion headquarters would deploy in March 1966, but the companies came first. Those of you who have been to Fort Bragg know that it is no place for a "leg." In order to survive, I headed off to jump school at Fort Benning. I moved Joy and our kids to Dover, Delaware to be near my brother and his family while I was gone. This worked out well for all.

Vietnam

In March 1966, we loaded 28 officers and men aboard a C-130 and island-hopped from Pope AFB to Nha Trang, RVN, making stops at Hawaii, Wake and Okinawa, where we embarrassed ourselves doing PLFs off some well-meaning colonel's furniture. As we approached

Nha Trang, the Commander directed us to open the basic load of ammunition we were carrying and be prepared to defend ourselves when the aircraft landed. When the rear door dropped, we were met by two officers, both in shorts and one in shower clogs and tee shirt. We had found the enemy and it was us.

The first month was the normal havoc. No one knew what to expect, and we were all trying to act normal while a bit scared of the unknown. I was involved in normal S-1 duties for the first few weeks until I received orders to command the ASA detachment with the 1/101st Airborne, a separate brigade at Phan Thiet. My specific instructions were to travel to the base camp, find the Detachment Commander, replace him and tell him to report to ASA Brigade Headquarters in Saigon. It seemed he hadn't been answering their messages for some time. Accomplishing my instructions was easier said than done. I finally found the base camp and the detachment, but there was no commander in sight nor had he been seen for almost a week. As we were preparing for departure for Tuy Hoa, the former Commander finally showed up. I gave him the message and he left for parts unknown.

The units of the 1st Brigade of the 101st were nomads. In seven months we went from base camp to base camp using C-123s as transport. It was minimal living. My voice teams were deployed with the battalions (1/501, 2/502, 1/327), while we ran a helicopter direction finding operation and an intercept facility out of tents at the base camp. There were less than fifty of us, and everybody was busy and important to the mission.

The Army had this terrible policy of six months command, and then move on. It played hell with the continuity of command, but it was what it was. I headed back to the 313th ASA Battalion as the S-3 for my remaining time on tour. In March 1967, it was time to go home.

Bootstrap

En route to my next assignment, DA granted me the six months needed to complete my bachelor's degree from the University of Omaha. Including this as part of this chapter is important only to allow me to say that I have never met people so trusting, so welcoming and so pleasant as those I met in Omaha. They'd give you the shirts off their backs. One gave my family and me (with a big dog) his home for a week, and he had never met me. Unbelievable! (As a disclaimer, this is being written by a guy who was born, and for a while lived, in New York.) In December 1967, I graduated.

Vint Hill Farms Station, Warrenton, VA

Once again, I landed an S-1/Adjutant job. I had just been promoted to major and I thought one more of these out-of-branch assignments and I'd have to branch transfer to the Adjutant General Corps (AG). Vint Hill was a small out-of-the-way place about fifty miles due west of DC. It was close enough to able to visit our headquarters in Arlington, and far enough away to be in the country. Not much out of the ordinary happened there unless you consider the retiring Post Commander leaving his wife and child behind as he drove off post to begin his retirement. It took his wife four or five hours to figure out he was long gone and she was on her own.

Germany

The Army was kind enough to assign me to the 507th ASA Group in the Bavarian town of Augsburg. Not only did I get a great assignment, but they let my wife, two kids and me travel onboard the USS United States to Le Havre, France with car on board. After a rocky five days at sea (north Atlantic in the spring) we drove across France and arrived in Augsburg. The housing was great and the assignment was fun. Traveling through Germany, Italy, Austria and France made the assignment our best yet.

I was assigned to the S-3 as the Group Signal Officer. It was still not a Military Intelligence (MI) job, but at least not an AG position. I kept this job for a short time until I took over from the recently relieved commander of the USASA Security Company, the theatre signal security unit. It seemed he couldn't pass the command maintenance inspections.

This unit had 13 detachments spread throughout Germany and Italy with the headquarters in Augsburg. Because of the widespread detachments, I spent a lot of time on the road visiting all the supported divisions, corps, Theatre Army Support Command (TASCOM), HQ US Army Europe (USAREUR) and HQ Southern European Task Force (SETAF). The downside of having your troops and their equipment spread all over the place was the obvious training and equipment support challenges. Command and control of the troops were my daily tasks. They were compounded by the fact that each detachment was led by a second lieutenant just out of branch basic course. All of them were very recent college graduates and most still had their heads in the 1960s campus environment. It was a full-time challenge for me and my deputy, Dave Tucker. We were in Augsburg a full three years and enjoyed all of it. In the summer of 1971 it became my turn for another short tour. Joy and our three children left for a rental home in St. Petersburg, Florida while I went to Turkey.

Turkey

Sinop, Turkey is a small town located on the Black Sea and was home to Diogenes Station, or USASA Detachment 4. On a hill overlooking the town there was an intelligence collection facility manned by members of Army, Navy, Air Force and civilian agencies. It was a year-long assignment, very isolated, very cold in the winter, and a long, long twelve-month tour. Sinop, as the story goes, was kept in the dark ages because they refused to allow Ataturk to land and begin his battle to take control of Turkey. He moved down the coast, landed, began his campaign and became the father of modern Turkey. He repaid Sinop by totally ignoring them. They had almost no services. Water and electricity were spotty, roads were dirt or cut logs, and everything appeared to be 100 or so years behind Istanbul or Ankara.

I had undergone five weeks of training at National Security Agency (NSA) to be the Operations Officer of Hippodrome, a space collection facility on the hill. However, upon arrival, I was told I was needed as the S-2, and Hippodrome would wait. That was 1971 and the Army wasn't a great place to be. Racial relations were at their lowest; drug use was everywhere; few troops had much respect for their leaders; and discipline was terrible. When all of that comes together on a small hill with no place to go, trouble is a constant companion.

My turn at Hippodrome came about six months into the tour. I was able to wrap myself up in the operations and thoroughly enjoyed the mission. However, when my twelve months were up, I was ready to move on, especially after being told I was going to Command and General Staff College (C&GSC).

Leavenworth, KS

C&GSC was a great time to meet old friends again, find new friends and learn about a part of the Army with which I was not familiar. It was not academically challenging unless I wanted it to be, and I didn't. I did elect to enroll in the University of Kansas (UK) graduate program. We took UK classes after our C&GSC classes were over for the day and spent six months in Lawrence after graduation. We moved to Lawrence and rented a condo for the semester. After that, we moved back to Leavenworth where I taught electronic warfare operations in the Department of Command. That lasted less than year.

This timeframe in the USA Training and Doctrine Command (TRADOC) world was known as DuPuy time, named after General DuPuy, TRADOC CG. He was revolutionizing the Army, and we were to be part of it. A new organization was formed under LTG Thurman and MG Menetrey to write the new Army field manuals. Central to that mission was the partnership between Air Force Tactical Air Command and Army TRADOC, and in particular, the Army-Air Force battlefield intelligence and electronic warfare doctrine. I was a part of all that. It was an exciting time to sit with Intelligence and Electronic Warfare professionals from both services and write the new doctrine.

Fort Meade, MD

In the fall of 1977, I got a call from an old warrant officer friend of mine at USA Intelligence and Security Command (INSCOM) Headquarters telling me I had been selected to be an NSA Fellow. He asked if I was interested. The Director of NSA, at that time was Vice Admiral Bobby R. Inman. There were four fellows, one from each service, and one civilian, all of whom would serve in his office for a year. It was a year to learn all you could about the national intelligence system. It sounded very exciting, and I couldn't wait. They wanted me at NSA right after

Christmas to attend some preliminary classes and begin my fellowship, which meant Joy and the kids stayed in our home in Leavenworth while I "batched" it at Fort Meade. The family moved to our new home in Arnold, MD when school was over for the kids in June.

My trip from Leavenworth to Fort Meade is worth remembering, as it falls in the category of one of the stupidest things I have ever done. We had a 1971 Volvo sedan that I brought back from Europe, and a twenty-seven foot pontoon boat. In the dead of winter I hooked these two together and headed alone to Maryland via the interstate northern route. It was a particularly cold, snowy winter and the interstate, while open, was unpleasant. I had a CB radio and listened to the truckers making fun of my boat driving the car. It was a treacherous trip for me, but there was no turning back. I arrived on the Baltimore/DC I-95 stretch on Friday at 6PM with no lights on the boat trailer, slippery roads, lots of traffic and feeling very vulnerable. I was a happy camper to pull into the Fort Meade guest house that evening.

The NSA fellowship gave me an opportunity to delve into the structure of national intelligence as well as the fierce politics. We were welcome at all the usual intelligence agencies, and some not so usual, to see the how, what and why of their work. It was an eye-opening year.

At the end of the year, each fellow was allowed to find his own job in NSA. We were sought after by the civilian office heads. They all wanted to have a former fellow. I went to the NSA research and development element and worked Army ground support R&D.

The next surprise was to be offered battalion command. As a recently promoted lieutenant colonel, I was happy to be able to get command and not have to PCS. We had bought a home in Arnold, MD just off the bay, and we were not eager to leave. Part of the battalion command was also to serve as the OIC of a tactical electronic warfare training element inside NSA. Our mission was to provide the tactical EW units assigned to the Army divisions with training materials to keep them current with their wartime missions. It required lots of travel, worldwide, but it was a great assignment.

Pentagon

In 1980 I was offered a job in the military intelligence requirements branch of DA DCSOPS with then Colonel (later Lt. General) Charlie Eichelberger. He needed someone to man the tactical MI desk. The Army was combining the MI and ASA units into Combat Electronic Warfare & Military intelligence (CEWI) units in Army divisions. The major issue was force structure. All the restructuring had to be done within current manning, and it was a challenging time with manning and fiscal resources being under constant duress from both other Army priorities and Congress. This job lasted only a year, as I came out on the list for senior service college.

Fort McNair, DC

Vice Chief of Staff General Max Thurman directed that selectees to the senior service college list who were assigned in the DC area would go to Fort McNair, thus saving on PCS costs, so I was off to the Industrial College of the Armed Forces (ICAF). It turned out to be a great opportunity. Studying all aspects of mobilization, both from a historical perspective and the challenges to do it again, was fascinating. A second study track was the electronics industry, which took us to Silicon Valley and Japan to look at emerging technologies.

Fort Devens, MA

At the very end of ICAF, in the summer of 1983, I came out on the 06 list and was ordered to the Army Intelligence School at Fort Devens. We rented our Fairfax house to a Marine lieutenant colonel, packed up the family and headed off to Ayer, MA. I was assigned as Director of the Electronic Warfare Department and spent a year building a tactical training center to add some reality for the students who were headed to the tactical Army. After a year I was promoted to 06 and reassigned as Director of Training and Doctrine, replacing Colonel Frank Toomey. I was able to work with some great folks: Dr. Jack Legere, Bunny Foley, Colonel John Bennis, and a large group of long-term civilian technicians who were the underpinning of the school. The sad side of this story was the decision to close the school at Fort Devens, and send it to Fort Huachuca, AZ.

Our three years at Fort Devens were, up to that point, the most fun we had as a family in our career. Living on post, we were close-knit, our kids enjoyed themselves, and the wives had a ball. When the 06 command list came out, and Joy and I were going to Berlin, we really had mixed feelings.

Berlin, FRG

I had visited INSCOM Field Station, Berlin in the spring of 1986 and was hosted by Colonel and Mrs. Ken Roney. During the visit I met a number of the officers, visited Teufelsberg, the operational facility, and met some of the leadership of the Berlin Command. The command structure, the mission, the troops, etc., all were fairly normal, but that was where normality ended.

The Field Station Commander's home was a fifteen-room, 7,000 square foot, nicely-furnished home, complete with part time maid, the only swimming pool the US command has in Berlin, car, driver, gardener, and a lot more. All of this was paid for with Deutschmarks. Berlin was, at that time, a city occupied by the four powers, and as a result, was the scene of one social event after another, all celebrating some national event from one of the four countries. At the end of the two years, my liver was crying uncle.

My secondary mission as the Commander was to host just about anybody that was anybody, and that almost always included trips to East Berlin. I had a three-person office that did nothing other than plan for, meet, greet, escort and care for visitors.

The mission was the most exciting signals intelligence (SIGINT) mission in the world. That kept a stream of senior NSA, DoD and CIA folks headed in our direction. It was also the magnet that had INSCOM's finest technicians wanting to work there, so our talent was top of the line. The two-year command tour ended in August 1988, and Joy and I headed back to Washington.

Pentagon (again)

We moved back into the Kings Park West home we had bought in 1981 when we moved from Fort Meade to the first Pentagon assignment. The development was off Braddock Road just before the road ended.

By 1988 the whole landscape had changed. I couldn't find the house without much hunting. In the intervening years, we had rented to a succession of senior service college officers, and as a result returned to a home that was in better shape than we had left it.

My assignment was twofold: Director of the Army Intelligence Master Plan, replacing BG Paul Menhour, with offices in the Skyline building; and Director of a division within Deputy Chief of Staff, Intelligence (DCSINT) in the Pentagon. Each day I would drive to Skyline before daylight, get my gym time in and work until noon. Then the rest of the day would be in the Pentagon with my other duties. I'd get home around 7PM or so each evening. That got old fast. The Army has its way of letting you know when you have reached the top rung of your ladder, and with twenty-eight years of commissioned time plus two-and-a-half years of enlisted service, I knew I was there.

Sometimes unexpected things happen. One evening in early 1989, a lady knocked on our door and said she represented a couple who wanted to buy a home, the same model as ours, in Kings Park West. The prices of KPW homes were no secret. Each month we got a newsletter that showed all home listings and sales with prices to include time on market. She offered the top price, and without any hesitation, we took it. That is what you call committed.

We decided to make a clean break of it and turned down offers with local contractors. I saw what some of my friends had gone through, opening doors, selling their friendships, and generally being used because of their contacts, and I wanted no part of that.

In April, Joy and I took a road trip to find our retirement location. After very little research (before computers), we selected Sarasota, Florida. In July 1989, we packed up and headed south.

Post-Military Civilian Life

I chose to take my leave as opposed to selling it, so my actual retirement date was October. We rented a waterfront home on Longboat Key while searching for a more permanent home. Our first purchase was a twenty-four foot Sea Ray, and the Gulf of Mexico became our playground. It didn't take long for us to realize that retirement was expensive and I needed to find work. I dabbled in a couple of ventures which didn't suit me, but I kept looking. One day I ran into a guy at the golf course who decided he was going to be my solution.

Don Duncan was a crusty old Korean War Navy guy with an artificial leg. He was the county Veterans' Employment Manager and he felt I was just the guy to help him put Vietnam veterans to work. For the next three years that's just what I did. I got to know Sarasota County's employers, politicians and all-around important people. It was both successful and fun. Working with Vietnam vets was challenging, but at their core they were all the same. They had all served, doing different things, but they possessed the same sense of right and wrong. They knew just how little they could BS one of their own, and I could talk to them in a way no one else could. The economy was pretty bad. Unemployment was high and we were at war again (Desert Storm). The employers were open to giving a vet a chance if the vet was willing. That went down well.

In 1993 I was offered a job with the bi-county Workforce Development Board doing essentially the same thing, but for a larger population. That time I was challenged to put welfare folks to work. You have to be a special person to commiserate with a welfare mom who doesn't want to work, won't get out of bed in the morning, and yells at you when she doesn't get what she wants. I'm not that person, and fortunately the director recognized it. I went back into my comfort zone of working with the employers, now in two counties, to develop job training opportunities.

For the next three years I continued working for the same folks, but the jobs changed. I ended up the Director of a youth program with the mission of preparing high and middle school students for the world of work. We worked with all area middle and high schools with emphasis on those with the highest dropout rates. We worked with teachers and administrators to find ways to keep kids in school while at the same time giving them workplace experience and training.

One day a lady came by my office and offered to donate a fully operating Ben and Jerry's ice cream store. She thought it would be a great training ground for high school kids. Absolutely everybody I talked with told me not to take it. It was an operating failure, bad location and losing money daily. My board of directors insisted I take it. We operated it for 14 months before we needed a grant to close it. What a mess!

In 1997, the federal law changed and required all the workforce development boards country-wide to contract with private industry to provide their services. Lockheed Martin, the builders of everything military, decided to get into this business. They bid on our area, won and hired me to run it. I now had two bosses: my employer, Lockheed Martin, and our customer, the Suncoast Workforce Board. The years I spent with the board put me in a special place. I was a trusted friend. That relationship stood me in great stead through good times and not so good times. I had 150 or so people, five facilities and $5 million a year. Over nine years we had a lot of success, but the law governing this program was going to be changed again, and it was my time to retire.

In late 2005, Joy and I were in our "think tank" (other folks call it a pool) and we were talking about really retiring. She said that she had gone wherever the Army sent us for thirty years, and retired to Florida where I wanted to go. Now, maybe it was her turn to pick where we retire. You can't fault that logic. Her ideal place would have to have four seasons and some land. With a terrific housing market in Florida, much research and six visits, it was east Tennessee.

In July 2006 we sold our Florida home for an obscene amount and moved into our retirement home in Lenoir City, TN. The 3,600 square foot house on two (+) acres gives us plenty of space to live and enough land for a vegetable garden and places to plant shrubs, flowers and trees. We went through the University of Tennessee Master Gardeners program to get an idea on how to manage Tennessee's clay soil.

*Colonel (Retired) Tony Newton and Joy, his wife
of 50 years, Lenoir City, TN, 2012.*

Joy got her four seasons and we got our retirement home. The story is not over yet. We continue to travel, cruise, and see our kids and grandkids in Baltimore, Clarksville, TN, Medina, NY and Knoxville. Also I shouldn't forget the fishing in Alaska, and the hunting in Maine, North Carolina, Utah and Colorado.

Lieutenant (later Captain) James K. Nicholas Jr.,
Jump School, Fort Benning, GA 1962

Prelude: Duty, Honor, Country

Those words had not yet been immortalized when 119 brand new second lieutenants graduated from Infantry OCS in March 1962, but we were all taught and knew them in various forms and contexts. Those words were first publicly spoken by General Douglas MacArthur on May 12, 1962, to the cadets at West Point when he accepted the Sylvanus Thayer Award. They reverently dictate what we ought to be, what we could be, and what we would be. They were our rallying points to build courage when courage seemed to fail, to regain faith when there seemed to be little cause for faith, and to create hope when hope seemed forlorn.

I will always believe my classmates, my heroes, all 118 of them, lived those famous words and used them, knowingly or not, as their personal codes of conduct. Their applicability to both military and civilian life is profound. I have used them as a guiding beacon all my adult life.

Duty, Honor, Country.

The Early Days

Life began for me in the little sleepy, southern border town of Brownsville, Texas, on February 5, 1940. I have often joked that had I been born a mile further south, I would have been a Mexican. My parents' heritages were significantly different. My mother, a native Texan of modest means, was born into a family of strong women of pioneer stock primarily of English extraction. My dad was a geographical Greek orphan who spent his early life in a Catholic Orphanage in Philadelphia. He and his father came to America from Greece when my dad was five. The plan was to temporarily put my dad in an orphanage while his father went back to Greece to get the rest of the family. His father went back to Greece, but neither he nor any family members ever made it back to America. After completing the seventh grade, my father left the orphanage and went to work at a confectionary store in the subway in Philadelphia. With no peer or parental guidance, he made his way from Philadelphia to Brownsville, via Memphis and Galveston, primarily working in or owning restaurants. He owned one in Brownsville when he met and married my mother.

World War II was the catalyst for a family move from Brownsville to Ballinger in 1942. My mother's aunt owned property in Ballinger, where a new training field was constructed to train military pilots for the war. She convinced my parents to open a new ten-cent hamburger joint in the little dusty central West Texas town. The Broadway Cafe grew from seating four to eighty by the time I was five, when I became the cashier for several hours most days. As the years passed I swept floors, washed dishes, cooked and waited tables. Like many kids working in a family business, I wanted to do something else, something new and exciting.

Ballinger seemed to be the Mayberry of the 1950s. In a town of

4000 population, everyone knew almost everything about everyone. There was not a great disparity of wealth, so most were modest class equals. Kids could go where they wanted with no fear or limitations other than parental constraints. When boys were not working on the farm or at their family business, they abandoned play only to go home to eat and sleep. No activities outside of school were organized, so inventiveness and imagination borne of boredom dominated activities. Should a youngster do something wrong, the news usually preceded him home. Old traditions prevailed so children were taught to respect property and adults. Adults were addressed as "Mr." or "Mrs." and replied to as "ma'am" or "sir". Teachers, policemen, and adults were usually right, and common sense prevailed. Most parents had weapons and taught their children of both sexes how to safely use them. Life through a child's eyes was idyllic.

Boys and guns of all kinds were always prevalent and age dependent. We started with cap guns while playing cowboys and Indians followed by rubber band guns. Rubber band guns using bands cut from old inner tubes as ammunition were great when playing war. When hit from close range, tears and welts most often followed, putting the battle on hold for a few minutes. New adventures followed with BB guns for shooting birds, snakes, frogs and turtles on the creek, or anything that moved, including each other. When we finally got shotguns or .22 caliber rifles or larger, we wisely quit shooting at each other. We used 22's exclusively for hunting, because we could afford low cost ammunition. Rabbits, doves, turkeys, ducks, deer and vermin of all kinds were prey to our 22's. One only shot deer in the head, particularly at night. Poachers had to be quiet and 22's were quiet. As hunters we neither bought a license, nor paid attention to hunting seasons. Most of us were excellent marksmen.

My life changed dramatically at age eleven, when my parents divorced. My mother remarried and moved forty miles away to another town. My older sister and I moved with her. I stayed for a year. My dad was alone, so I decided to move in with him. We initially lived in a rented three-room and bath, an uninsulated garage, which had been poorly converted to an apartment. It was frigid in the winter and blazing hot in the summer. From that time on, I was almost completely on my own. My dad expected me to work at the café, but gave little or no guidance on how to grow up and be a man. He loved me, but he had neither the tools nor experience to guide a boy to manhood. He just asked that I work at the café and make good grades. I did both. From the seventh grade forward, I made all decisions for myself without consulting anyone. Some fathers involved in Boy Scouts encouraged me and others to work and complete the requirements for advancement in scouting. At age fourteen, nine of us became Eagle Scouts.

School was too easy and often boring. Even though our school system had outstanding teachers, most never really challenged me. Reading was always a delightful escape from a small town. I voraciously read every book in our library in grammar school and a large number in our high school. After reading textbooks in a matter of days, I just listened in class and made A's. I was the junior high school salutatorian, missing by 0.01 point being valedictorian. In high school, I became embarrassed by the ease of academics and began to hide it. Most often I would intentionally answer a few exam questions incorrectly to put me back in the pack. Once, I wanted to be exempt from taking a final exam in a course, but my average of 94.7 was below the 95 required for exemption. Since the teacher would not round up the grade for final exam exemption, I took the exam. I think I needed a 15 to pass the course, so I answered enough questions to get the required grade. I then answered the rest of the fill in the blank questions with one word per blank, "I—only—need—to—make—a—15—to—pass—this—course". My teacher arranged for me to meet with my high school principal, Mr. Joe Forester, possibly the wisest man I have ever known. He counseled me about retaking the test and making a score of at least 95 or I would take the course again the following year. I passed. He also counseled me several other times involving situations both in school and those which had nothing to do with school. One stroke of his seldom used paddle would bring tears to the toughest teen, but honesty was the only policy with him. The other outstanding teacher in my life was Miss Marryatt Smith, a single lady who dedicated her life to teaching and inspiring students. She was our town's Miss Dove after the primary character in the book titled, *Good Morning, Miss Dove*. While still teaching in her seventies, she suffered a heart attack. After two or three weeks for recovery but still too weak to return to school, she resumed math and Latin classes in her living room across the street from the school. Later, strong boys, we all were then, were assigned to literally carry her in a chair to and from home each day to her second-floor classroom.

In Texas, the only sport was football. Basketball and track only kept one in shape to play football. I started playing football in the seventh grade and continued until graduation. My classmates picked me to be a co-captain my senior year prior to being selected to the all-district first team and all-area second team. I was a ferocious 150-pound lineman who was lucky enough to make more tackles than anyone else on the team and to have the most rushing yardage over my guard position on offense. The band members chose me to be captain of the band as well.

Staying in shape meant hard work each summer. Strenuous jobs without governmental restrictions to age, working conditions or danger were sought. My jobs included farm tractor driver, National Guard summer camp, truck driver, concrete mixer operator, bricklayers' helper, construction laborer, and combine driver. At age sixteen, the hardest and most dangerous of all was roughneck on an oil drilling rig. Pay in the oil patch was always the highest as were the number of employees with missing digits. Getting to those jobs was easy with a driver's license obtained at fourteen, even though I had been driving for the prior two years. I was even allowed to drive to Georgia by myself at fifteen to bring my sister back to Texas when her husband went overseas.

In the Army

College was a question of where, not if, so I chose North Texas State College. The first year was an easy rehash of high school–little study for A's or B's. More time was spent playing poker than studying. My sophomore year focus was income from poker with diminishing attention to academics, so I decided to begin my military obligation. Basic training began at Fort Leonard Wood followed by Army Security Agency training at Fort Devens, where my adult life really began.

Another soldier and I were aimlessly driving one weekend when we stopped at Weirs Beach, New Hampshire. He met a lovely girl who introduced me to her friend, Dolores Tata. She was not my first girlfriend, but she became my last, for it was love at first sight. She was the complete package: striking black hair, beauty, figure and personality. I was dumbstruck almost fifty-two years ago, and I still am today. It took her a bit longer, but the love bug bit her a short time later. We decided to marry a couple of months after we first met, but not as quickly as we anticipated. Uncle Sam was indecisive concerning where I should go next. I had orders to Eritrea, Japan and finally Korea. There is nothing like having one's orders changed almost weekly and never getting to leave. Doe and I were married almost four months after we first met and two weeks before I went to Korea in December 1960. Thank goodness she had a great family to support her in my absence.

Going to Korea on a troop transport was unique. I had never seen anything much larger than a rowboat, much less a ship. The five-high bunks were assigned by rank, lowest rank lowest bunk. I was lucky that no one above me got seasick. I quickly adapted to the ship's routine and my job working in the cold cuts butcher shop. After a couple of unpalatable meals in the enlisted mess, with vomiting seasick soldiers nearby, I discovered that a few cold cuts could be swapped for almost anything—laundered fatigues, meals in the officers mess kitchen, fresh fruit or no other details. However, they could not get me off the ship when we spent one night in Pearl Harbor. I actually enjoyed most of my cruise. Christmas in the middle of the Pacific was unusual, as was ringing in the New Year at Inchon. The 177th ASA Company at Pyeongtaek was my home for eight months before returning to Texas for funeral services for my dad. After completing my dad's affairs, Doe and I drove to Boston.

On to OCS

Doe worked as a laboratory technician at Boston City Hospital. She had a friend and coworker there whose father was an influential congressman. The friend told her dad about my anticipated return to Korea, and shortly thereafter, I received unrequested orders for an immediate transfer from Korea to the Boston Army Base. I had applied for OCS while in Korea and was notified of my acceptance almost simultaneously with the Boston orders, so "Hello, Fort Benning." The military had been an easy adventure; be invisible, do the work and be positive; until September, 1961. Little did I realize that same approach, when coupled with tenacity and time management, would help get me through OCS. Insufficient sleep was more bothersome than the physical demands. I kept quiet and watched and listened to others in class who were more mature and militarily experienced. Tony Newton was a leader for me. I was honored to be his best man when he wed during OCS.

Breaking starch, immaculate appearance, spit shined boots, spit shined floors, not enough time, teamwork, dusty trucks, running everywhere, cockroach races, latrine cleaning, Kotex pads under the footlocker, walking on as few room tiles as possible, no boots in the barracks, square meals, washouts on KP before shipping out, "Blues" harassing, turning Blue, ribald jokes starting each class, escape and evasion, tanks, artillery and rifle ranges fill my memories. "Old" captains who would never be promoted were running rifle ranges—the Army took care of its Medal of Honor soldiers. We were all growing and becoming well-educated leaders, although many of us did not realize it. And then it was over. We, all 119 newly-minted second lieutenants wearing brightly shining brown bars, who had shared six intense months together, were scattered to the winds to seldom, if ever, see each other again.

Commissioned Active Duty

Most of us went directly to jump school, which was a vacation after OCS, but that did not diminish my pride in wearing jump wings. Doe joined me for the month of jump school. We lived in a small apartment just outside the main gate with Ben and Carol Genise as neighbors. Young wives usually cannot cook well and both proved it for a short while.

The next assignment was with Co B, 313th ASA Bn, at Fort Bragg for four months. A large number of reservists were completing their one year Berlin Crisis activation at Fort Bragg, so quarters were difficult to find. We found a dumpy apartment with no air conditioner next door to one of the reservists. Both husband and wife were millionaires from Brooklyn. What a contrast we made. They were wealthy and we were poor. I was by the book and he could not find the book. It took me a month to understand their rapid, accented speech, but Doe had no problem. We became good friends with them and several others in the New York contingent. Most were somewhat older civilian professionals including Broadway writers or directors, CPAs, architects, and business owners. Fort Bragg was quite an education for me. Jumping with the 82nd Airborne on huge drop zones was a treat. Watching General House arrive for lunch at the Officers Club with his armada of helicopters was quite a sight. Little did I realize what workhorses helicopters would become in Vietnam.

In August 1962, Co B moved from Fort Bragg to Fort Campbell in support of the 101st Division. Quarters were available on post, but empty for us with no furniture. The waiting list for furniture was somewhat lengthy. Military wives get things done, as Doe found out at a wives meeting. Some colonel's wife at the meeting was appalled that our borrowed furnishings consisted of a card table and two folding chairs. Enough military household furniture was delivered the next day to completely furnish our place. In early September, a small group of us went to Fort Knox as part of a demonstration team, where I meet a former acquaintance who had just returned from MacDill Air Force Base. He told me to get ready to go to Cuba.

When we returned to Fort Campbell, my unit was on alert. As the alerts escalated, reaching DEFCON 3 by October 22, preparations for a Cuban invasion became intensive. Everyone needed a map, and gas stations supplied them in those times, so most gas stations within fifty miles of post supplied us with maps of Cuba. Surely it was not too difficult for the civilian population to figure out we were not planning a division vacation trip. My CO lived across from the rail yard. His wife, the unofficial head of intelligence and primary communicator, kept all the wives informed about the amazing amount of equipment and material arriving daily. Every woman on post had to know we were going to Cuba, but few discussed it. Our units received all TOE equipment and personnel to include linguists from the National Security Agency (NSA) in preparation to invade Cuba. The riggers were super-busy getting the division ready for a drop into Havana. Aircraft were waiting on the runway. President Kennedy spoke on television about Russian nuclear missiles en route to Cuba and forced Khrushchev to back down. That was as close to combat as I ever wanted to be, but I did want to make one combat jump.

Army life became routine after the Cuban Crisis. I went to Ranger School in February 1963, where I learned as much about my capabilities under adverse conditions as I did from the school curriculum. A trip followed in July to Grassy Key, where our battalion had electronic intercept sites in the Florida Keys. Doe and I got to spend three months living in a fisherman's motel, where I only occasionally wore fatigues, supervising two of those sites. Fishing was great. After returning to Fort Campbell, we were the first occupants of new housing, three bedrooms for just Doe and me. Jumpmaster school, a couple of major maneuvers, and a month of TDY at Fort Monmouth filled the months before I became a civilian on August 29, 1964, on my way back to college in Texas.

Civilian Career

Doe gave birth to our daughter, Maria, in October. Then we were three. Seventeen-hour class loads with labs were a different challenge for a pre-med major. During my senior year, I decided that I did not want to go to medical school, so I became a business major. Finally, in 1967, I finished my BBA and began to work on my MBA. Speculation of activation of my Special Forces Reserve Unit was rampant. I thought I should be better trained, so I completed Special Forces school at Fort Bragg during the summer. The MBA still needed completion, so we returned to college. My typical day was up at 4:00AM to run a newspaper delivery route, go to class, do research for a professor and work as a welder for four hours each evening. Study was stuck in the middle of that somewhere. We were probably the poorest couple to ever consider adoption, but we adopted Claudine in 1968.

General Electric in Lynn, Massachusetts, was my first civilian employer, where I was a financial management trainee in the aircraft engine group. Doe was delighted to once again be home with her family. I was still searching for the perfect job, so I left GE to become Controller of a small venture firm, Machine Control Company. The company was one of the first to match machine tools with computers, but alas, it failed. Modicon, a company which successfully designed and built a small, slow and simple computer, followed Machine Control. Life was great. A friend and professor in Texas had become involved with a young life insurance holding company that needed a treasurer. The decision was difficult. The responsibilities, challenges and pay were greater, and once again a new adventure began for us in Denton, Texas.

My new employer, LSL, managed an initial public offering a few months after my arrival, so it was flush with cash and profitable, as were its two life insurance subsidiaries. My professor friend left the company shortly after the public offering. Things were going well until I began to have a problem with stock certificate reconciliation. Imagine my surprise to discover that the charismatic president possibly had more shares pledged as collateral on loans than he officially owned. His nephew would print as many stock certificates as his uncle needed. Everyone in power chose to believe the president, and I got fired for the first time in my life. What a bummer for my ego! I had a difficult decision to make. Was I going to remain a number cruncher, controller/treasurer or was I going to use my finance and investments education? Merrill Lynch hired me in May 1972, to be a stockbroker trainee. About a year later the life insurance company began to implode with the arrest, conviction and imprisonment of several employees including the president. LSL was gone in two years, and remains a great memory for me.

After six months of training at Merrill, three in New York and three in Dallas, a fresh faced, newly licensed broker was unleashed on the public. The Dow Jones Industrial Average had the audacity to decline almost 50% in my first two years in business, and it took ten years to recover that loss. Compounding the decline in the Dow was the rise in interest rates to 18% in 1980. No one is ever completely prepared for the terrible markets in both stocks and bonds, but I was educationally prepared and believed in sound investment fundamentals. At last, I was a single entrepreneur working under a corporate umbrella. I was doing what I really wanted to do. Sixty and seventy-hour work weeks were the norm to make my business prosper which left insufficient time to continue in the reserves. Captain Nicholas no longer existed. I was also an adjunct instructor at the University of North Texas for over a decade. Thank God that Doe was there to run our home and support me during those long work hours. As I matured in the securities industry, my work week declined to approximately fifty hours.

Helping people reach their investment goals began to show results. Always putting their investment interests first helped me build a successful business. The lessons learned from OCS, time management, understanding the mission, setting goals, tenacity and plain hard work were all applied at Merrill Lynch. The market, my investors, Merrill and I all prospered. Bond buyers, usually more conservative than stock buyers, dominated my business in the eighties. Thirty year US Treasury bonds maximum yields were 14% while long term tax free bonds yielded 12%. Repetitively doing the right thing over and over grew my business.

One of my career highlights was being the originator of the forty-two million dollars initial public offering of Computer Language Research, one of the better offerings of 1983. I am proud to say that I have worked with three generations of some families. I have overseen my oldest, age 93, customer's investments for 40 years. Many customers were like family members and we have grown old together. Rejoicing with their good times and despairing with their sad times and going to their funerals were my business life. Their stories about growing up in Europe have helped me walk in their footsteps in London, Vienna, Paris and Budapest. Management beckoned in the 1980s, but I said "No", for I was doing exactly what I wanted to do.

Most of us like rewards and recognition. Trips to some great cities and fine resorts were a common reward for a job well done during the decades of the eighties and nineties in the industry. We went to three different countries and several states, most of them multiple times. As my business prospered, the trips became more frequent. Doe and I would usually take an extra few days when the official part of the trip was over, for sightseeing on our own. We quit counting reward trips at one hundred. Our first and most impressionable trip was to Maui. A Holiday Inn impressed then. I had been to Hawaii twice before, the airport and Pearl Harbor, but had never seen any of it. We had never stayed in a luxury hotel with unlimited food, drink, golf and tours. We hicks just could not believe our good fortune. Go home, work hard, and earn another trip.

Our daughters turned out to be as different as night and day. Our younger daughter Claudine, the artist, went to Texas A&M, while Maria, the academic, went to the University of Texas. UT and A&M are bitter rivals and the two kibitz today about their college rivalry. After Maria completed her MBA at UT, she decided to work at Merrill. She, too, grew her business by putting her customers' interest first. Claudine also worked at Merrill for a few years in an administrative position. Maria became my junior partner after a few years. The somewhat rigid corporate culture at Merrill was easy for me, but always chafed Maria. Both of us have the same incorrigibly independent personality. She left Merrill in 1999 for Morgan Stanley.

A Failed Retirement

The completion of our new home in 1999 and Maria's departure were the catalysts for my retirement after 28 years at age 59. Customers' assets under my supervision had grown to one hundred and fifty million at my retirement. I had never developed any hobbies, but I had played a little golf, so that was my temporary retirement pursuit. Family and work were my life. Retirement was not ready for me. I was bored, so Maria hired me to be her junior partner the next year. I started having fun again helping Maria to oversee almost two hundred million in investments for customers around the world.

Life has not been perfect, but it has been great. I have truly been blest to have accomplished most of my lifetime goals, in spite of a plethora of bad decisions and mistakes. Analyze, regroup and start again. I have worked for 67 years and I am uncertain when I will retire. I have been in class as a student or teacher for 64 years and still think education is the key to the future. Helping others has rewarded me more than the help I have given them. I often think of sayings of the late Satchel Paige, one of the Negro Baseball League's greatest players. My favorite is, "Never look back. Something may be gaining on you."

Duty, Honor, Country.

Jim Nicholas "Retirement Years", Dallas, TX, 2013

Captain (later Lieutenant Colonel) Dan Telfair with his first helicopter in Vietnam, the PHOENIX, Duc Hoa, Vietnam, 1966.

Prelude

Officer Candidate School was a part of a singular change of direction in my life that began a short time before. It was a major milestone in a process that involved putting away childish things to become a man, and a very important step in becoming who I am today.

The Early Days

I was born at the end of the Great Depression, a timing that colored my early years. My paternal grandfather had been a successful businessman in Greenwood, a Mississippi Delta town that was relatively affluent and where "Cotton was King." The money that came into town from the surrounding cotton plantations fueled a healthy economy where retail establishments flourished. He owned what I have been told was the town's largest department store, and had an antebellum house in an affluent part of town. He must have been a very good businessman.

Unfortunately, he died in the middle of the Depression, and my father, his elder son, took over the business. Dad was not the astute businessman that my grandfather was, and under his management, the store failed. In order to protect what was left of her assets, my grandmother basically cut off my father from dealing any further with family finances. Although she never again had the affluence she had when my grandfather was alive, she did manage to hold on to the family home and live a modest lifestyle. When she died in 1974, my share of the remaining estate was around $500.

My father, having lost the family business, took work where he could find it. He drove a Coca Cola distribution truck, managed a small farm, and worked as a handyman and electrician to support my mother, my older brother, and me. In 1943, despite being ineligible for the draft because of wife and children, he enlisted in the Army. He served as a stateside Military Policeman, without ever having an overseas assignment. While he was in the Army, my mother divorced him and ran off with another man, taking my brother and me with her.

Although my father eventually became somewhat successful, I don't believe he ever fully recovered from being born relatively well off, and going downhill from there, rather than rising above his beginnings. He was an alcoholic when he died in his early sixties. My mother was also an alcoholic, but started earlier and lasted longer. I never held much affection for either. When they died, my only feeling was regret that neither ever had a better or happier life. The one relative I loved and respected was my stepmother, a WWII WAC who had served over two years in combat zones in Africa and Europe. She was quite a lady, and served as a role model for me.

I did learn two lessons from my father, though. The first was that I did not deserve anything I did not earn for myself. That lesson has stood me in good stead. The second was that I should grow up to be like John Wayne: talk low and slow, don't talk too much, treat ladies with respect, never start a fight, and never run from one. I tried to follow those rules, but about the only one I didn't break at one point or another was that I never ran from a fight, although I lost several.

The other person who influenced my early life was my brother, Charlie (RIP). His tombstone reads simply, "Charles Ward Telfair, Sergeant Major, Special Forces."

He was my senior by two years. Neither of us was much of a scholar, nor did we get along very well with our contemporaries or our teachers. When Charlie was seventeen, he quit school and joined the Army, volunteering for Airborne with assignment to the 82nd Airborne

Division. I don't know what made him do either. In any case, once he had taken that course of action, my immediate future was determined. A year after he enlisted, I lied about my age and entered active duty at sixteen, volunteered for Airborne and was assigned to the 82nd. That was in 1954. I turned seventeen just before jump week of Airborne training.

I spent four years in the 82nd and 11th Airborne Divisions, of which nearly three years were in Germany. In 1955, ten years after the war, Germany was a great place for a seventeen-year-old boy/man to grow up. In 1958, when the 11th Airborne Division was deactivated, and I was taken off jump status, I allowed my enlistment to expire, and returned to the 'States. In my first four years in the Army, I achieved the exalted rank of Specialist E-4, and barely managed to hold on to that. I was not a particularly good soldier.

After returning to Mississippi, and at my stepmother's urging, I entered Mississippi Southern College as a freshman. At that time, a veteran could take entry exams and begin college without a high school degree or equivalency. I never did obtain my high school diploma or even a GED equivalent. I had the Korean era GI bill ($110 per month), and that went a long way toward supporting me in college. Unfortunately, the lack of work ethic that typified my first four years in the Army continued in college. I spent fifteen months there and earned about nine months of credit, with a C average. Those were the days of Jack Kerouac and the Beat Generation. Being a bum was an acceptable self-image.

Toward the end of my first college experience, my girlfriend learned that she was pregnant. We never considered anything but marriage. That was the turning point in my life and the beginning of reasonable respectability. While it was completely acceptable for a single man to be a bum, it wasn't acceptable for a husband facing fatherhood.

Lacking any other form of livelihood, I re-enlisted in the Army, retaining my rank of E-4 by virtue of staying in the Mississippi National Guard during my brief college career. My family responsibilities worked a considerable change in me. Almost overnight, I went from bum to semi-respectability.

I was assigned again to the 82nd Airborne Division, and within a few months, was promoted to Sergeant E-5. My first daughter was born in the Womack Army Hospital at Fort Bragg. I attended three enlisted schools at Fort Bragg, and made Honor Graduate in two of them, including the XVIII Airborne Corps NCO Academy. In short order, I racked up an impressive number of letters of commendation and other attaboys. With those in hand, I applied for OCS. While I had made sergeant shortly after re-entering the service, I knew that further promotions would be a long time in coming. Also, I believed that being an officer and gentleman would be more in keeping with being a husband and father.

When I appeared before the OCS selection board, my biggest problem was my short and less-than-stellar college record. Against that, I had my Honor Graduate accomplishments and an impressive array of letters of commendation. When asked about my poor college performance, the only excuse I could give was "youthful stupidity." It must have been sufficient. In short order, about eighteen months after re-entering the Army, I was on my way to Officer Candidate School at Fort Benning.

My Time at OCS

I arrived at Infantry OCS as a fairly impressive prospect. I was a sergeant with almost six years of active duty in two Airborne Divisions, Senior Parachute Wings, and a few "been there" medals. I was "lean and mean," and ready to give it my all. I believe I had a number of advantages over many of the younger and less-experienced candidates, and even detected some gleam of hope for me in the Tac Officers' eyes. Things went downhill from there.

I mentioned previously that neither my brother nor I got along very well with our contemporaries. That character flaw followed me into OCS, and stays with me today. I believe it was during 22nd week counseling that my Tac Officer called me in and showed me three stacks of paper. The first was the thickest, the second less so, and the third being only a few sheets. These were my "buddy reports."

At that time, all candidates rated the other members of their platoons three times. I don't remember the exact points in the program, but it was something like the 11th, 18th, and 22nd week of training. The candidate doing the rating had to provide a written evaluation for those of his platoon mates that he placed in the top five and the bottom five of the rated group.

My first stack of buddy reports represented most of my platoon placing me in the top five during the initial rating period. The second stack represented about half that number placing me in the top five during the second rating period. The third stack consisted of two reports placing me in the top five and one report placing me in the bottom five! My Tac Officer, who had previously had great hopes for me, asked me if I could explain. I replied that one of the reports placing me in the top five was probably from my good friend and OCS roommate, Monte Tate (RIP). I could not think of who might have written the other top-five report.

I don't recount this as a criticism of my classmates. The fault was mine. Even my Tac Officer evaluations declined as the training progressed. While I generally get along with people in other than a work environment, and people who work for me, I have never gotten along very well with many of my fellow workers and superiors. I didn't then, and I don't now. Although this character flaw has caused problems throughout my working life, it did have an enormous benefit on one occasion. (More on that in the post-military portion of this chapter.) In any event, my problems were not sufficiently severe to prevent my graduation and commissioning, although it may have been a close thing.

In my defense: My problem is mainly one of intolerance. If I like and respect someone, equal, superior or subordinate, my feelings show through, and are appreciated. If something causes me to dislike or lose respect for someone, equal, superior or subordinate, those feelings also show through. With subordinates, I get rid of those I don't like or respect, and those I do like and respect generally like working for me. With equals and superiors, I don't have the option of eliminating them, so a situation of mutual dislike generally ensues. That isn't an excuse. It is an explanation. I could choose to be more tolerant. I just never have.

One final comment on my days as an officer candidate: At that time, any officer who hoped for a Regular Army commission, as opposed to a Reserve commission, was expected to go to Airborne, Ranger, or Flight School. One day, our Tac Officer came through the platoon with forms to be filled out indicating which, if any, of these schools we wished to attend. I had already been to Airborne School, so it was not necessary for me to even fill out the form. However, in an attempt to impress the Tac Officer with my positive attitude, I volunteered for Ranger and Flight schools, a decision I was to regret after graduation.

At that point in time, it was very difficult to get into Ranger School, and almost impossible to get into Flight School. No worries. When I received my assignment orders for after graduation, much to my surprise, they were for Flight School, after first attending Ranger School. I was delighted at the opportunity to attend Flight School; less so at the thought of Ranger School.

A few words about goals and aspirations: Most motivational writers and speakers exhort everyone to aim high and shoot for the stars. In one of the few motivational talks I have ever given, I urged the audience to "Shoot low; they are riding Shetlands." This phrase has always meant something special to me; that you should set reasonably attainable goals. If you aim too high, you are likely to fail, if nothing else, because you can never convince yourself that success is possible. Given that frame of reference, success is very unlikely. On the other hand, if you aim to be something well above your present station in life; not too high but for a major improvement, you are much more likely to succeed.

As an example, I began long-distance running late in life, and ran my first full marathon when I was forty years old. I did not run the race to win. I ran it to complete the course in less than four hours; approximately a nine-minute-per-mile pace for 26.2 miles. That was a difficult, but achievable goal. To win the marathon, I would have had to maintain an under five-minute-per-mile pace; impossible for a man my age, weight, and lack of athletic history. Had I set out to win the marathon, I would have likely given up the attempt after a few months of training. By setting a realistic goal, I completed twenty-four full marathons before I was forced to give up long-distance running twenty-five years later.

When I received my commission, the general practice was that if you had held a previous enlisted rank, and could hold onto your commission for ten years before losing it to a reduction in force (RIF), you were secure. Even if you lost your commission after ten years, you could revert back to your enlisted rank, and stay in the Army until you reached twenty years for retirement. Then, you could retire at the highest rank you had held. In other words, if I could make captain, and keep my commission for a minimum of ten years before losing it, I could retire at half-pay for a captain. For someone who started as a poorly-educated private soldier, that seemed like a significant but reasonable goal.

Several of my OCS classmates made full colonel. One was even promoted to brigadier general. None of them would have made it had they espoused my personal philosophy or had my particular character flaws. On the other hand, retiring as I did as a lieutenant colonel so far exceeded my initial goals that I was reasonably satisfied.

Ranger School

After a short leave, I returned to Fort Benning and reported for duty as a student at Ranger School. Several of my OCS classmates joined me, but I can't remember who, other than my good friend, newly commissioned Lieutenant Robert Brooks. I nearly failed out of Ranger School in the first few days.

While at OCS, I had scored in the top five of my class on the physical fitness test, and was even granted special privileges for that reason. As previously mentioned, I was "lean and mean." When it came time to take the initial physical fitness test at Ranger School, I was not worried, and skated through it without much effort. As a result, I failed the timed "low crawl" portion of the test by a half-second. That was sufficient to be eliminated from the program. Those of us who failed the test, but were not ready to give up, were allowed to retake the entire test, not just the portion we failed, the following day. That was after a full day's activities, including water survival training and a twelve-mile speed march. I managed to pass everything the second time around, and was allowed to stay in Ranger School. Lucky me!

I spent the next nine weeks in the woods at Fort Benning, the mountains at Dahlonega, and the swamps at Eglin, regretting both volunteering for Ranger School and passing the physical fitness test the second time around. However, I am proud of one accomplishment while in Ranger School. I was the squad leader of a twelve-man squad, including a thirty-five-year-old Iranian captain, and a forty-three-year-old National Guard major/used car salesman; neither a prime candidate for Ranger School. In an institution where attrition is generally maintained at 50%, all twelve men in my squad graduated and earned their Ranger Tabs. We were known as the "minimum squad," never doing more than necessary to pass any given event. We didn't excel at anything other than survival, teamwork and mutual support, but we all graduated.

On to Flight School

After Ranger School, and a short period with my buddy Brooks as a temporary Tac Officer back at Officer Candidate School, I proceeded with wife and daughter to Camp Wolters, Texas and began Rotary Wing (helicopter) Flight School. There, we took basic flight instruction on the H-23D Hiller Helicopter. The first thing I learned was that there are those who are natural pilots and those who are not natural pilots. I, unfortunately, was and am in the latter category. With enough practice, almost anyone can learn to fly, and fly very well. It just took me more practice than most. I got through primary flight school by the skin of my teeth, excelling at academics and being near the bottom of my class insofar as flight evaluations were concerned.

Satisfactory flights during training resulted in white evaluation slips from our instructors. Unsatisfactory flights resulted in pink slips. Outstanding flights resulted in blue slips. I am not aware of anyone ever receiving a blue slip during our primary training. We managed five flights a week, and each flight resulted in a white or pink slip. If a fledgling pilot received three pink slips out of five flights, he was given a check ride on his way out the door.

I think I faced almost every Friday flight with two pink slips out of four, dreading, but somehow squeaking through on the final flight of the week. I did receive three pink slips one week, and had to take a check ride. Fortunately, instead of being kicked out, I was assigned to another instructor, where I continued my regular two-pink-slips-a week performance. Somehow though, I managed to pass basic flight training and proceeded to Fort Rucker, Alabama, where I began advanced training on the CH-34 Choctaw cargo helicopter.

The CH-34 Choctaw is a big, extremely ugly, Sikorski helicopter, powered by one of the last of the military aircraft radial engines. All Sikorski helicopters are ugly, but the CH-34 is uglier than most. I believe it is the origin of the classic definition of a helicopter: "A large number of rapidly rotating parts, flying in close formation, surrounding an oil leak."

Problems that began at Camp Wolters followed me to Fort Rucker, where I continued my two-pink-slips-a-week performance. Finally, toward the end of training, I managed to get three pink slips in one week, and was required to take a "washing machine" check ride; the check ride that was required before formally washing out of flight school.

At that point, I was sick of the whole business. If I couldn't fly, I needed to get out of the torment, and go back to ground-pounding as God obviously intended me to do. I think I had a good bit to drink the night before my washing machine check ride, and approached it with an attitude. I can't remember much that happened during that check ride. However, I do remember one interesting part. There were "confined areas" surrounded by tall trees and other obstructions, where students were trained to get a helicopter in and out with maximum power. Students were also expected to be able to land without power, using an auto-rotation, and landing on a road, field, or similar large, open area. When my check ride pilot cut the throttle, simulating an engine failure, I performed a successful auto-rotation into a very small confined area. He appeared shaken, but impressed. God's Truth: I was given a blue slip for an outstanding flight on what was supposed to be my washout ride. My regular instructor never forgave me.

Germany

After Flight School, wife, daughter, and I went to Germany. I joined the 2nd/4th Cavalry, as the Aero-Rifle Platoon Leader in their Air Cavalry Troop. That was the highest Infantry "command" slot I ever held. I did reasonably well there, receiving maximum efficiency reports. Of course at that time, Officer Efficiency Reports were inflated, and everyone who was not intended for end-of-career reports pretty much received the same ratings. I served there for a little over two years, being promoted to first lieutenant at the obligatory eighteen-month mark. I was happy with that, and settled in to wait another four or five years before being promoted to captain.

While in Germany, our second daughter was born. I was never a very good father. My concept was that the father provided for, and the mother raised and entertained the children. I was a responsible provider, but otherwise, a poor husband and father. Somehow, probably due to my wife's influence, our daughters grew up to be fine adults, with responsible jobs and generally more success than I ever dreamed of achieving. I am exceedingly proud of them both.

The only other accomplishments of note during my first unit tour was that I transitioned into the UH-1 "Huey" helicopter, soon to be the mainstay of Army Aviation in Vietnam, and the world's first "gunship."

Vietnam-First Tour

In 1965, President Johnson decided to "surge" the US military presence in Vietnam. It was known as the Johnson year—the same year in which *We Were Soldiers Once…and Young* was set. We were asked to consider volunteering to go to help out in Vietnam. Realizing that there was a choice between volunteering today, and being sent against my will in a few months, I opted to volunteer.

After returning to the 'States, and setting up family in Memphis, Tennessee, where my wife could continue her interrupted college education, I joined a unit at Fort Benning that was forming up for deployment to Vietnam. Because of my "extensive" experience in the UH-1 Huey helicopter (about thirty hours), I was assigned to the gun platoon as a Fire Team Leader (two or three armed helicopters), where I would be flying gunships instead of troop-carrying helicopters. I could not have been happier.

While still at Fort Benning, I was promoted to captain, two years after making first lieutenant, instead of the four or five years I expected. The early promotion was not due to anything I had accomplished. It was in keeping with the more rapid promotions everyone received during the Vietnam buildup. As the saying goes, "It is an ill wind that blows no one good."

My unit went by sea to Vietnam, where we off-loaded and set up our helicopters and operations in Vung Tau. Vung Tau is a port city and was an entry location for many of the troop and supply ships coming into Vietnam. It was also a resort area where, before and during the war, both civilian Vietnamese and US Army troops came for vacations and R&R. It was not exactly a hardship assignment.

That began a strange and cognitively dissonant existence, wherein we flew combat missions during the day; shot at people and were shot at in return; and returned to our lodging at night to air-conditioned rooms, showers, reasonably good food, drink, and (optional) female companionship. If it were not for the two-way gunfire, it would have been a great assignment. My subsequent assignments in Vietnam were not nearly as plush, but still reasonably comfortable.

This existence is not to be confused with the experience of the average grunt ground-pounder in Vietnam. In two years as a gunship pilot in Vietnam, I only spent a short period on my feet, in the swamp, at night (in this case, by myself), and other brief periods under direct and indirect enemy fire on the ground. Most of my armed conflict was from the relative comfort of a Huey gunship or Cobra. True Infantry officers and enlisted men spent a good bit of their time in Vietnam in the mud.

A person is as likely to be killed in the air as on the ground, if not more so, but it is a lot more comfortable in the air. I have never suffered from post traumatic stress disorder, possibly because of the comparative comfort in which I fought my version of the war. I suspect that most who do suffer from PTSD fought on the ground.

After a period as a Fire Team Leader with my initial unit in Vietnam, I was transferred to the 197th Armed Helicopter Company in Bien Hoa, the only all-gunship company in Vietnam. I became the platoon leader of the Dragon Platoon, the third platoon of the 197th.

Despite being the frequent target of hostile gunfire, and flying a good part of my first tour in slow, underpowered UH-1B gunships, my helicopter suffered very few hits. My perception at the time was that everyone had guns, but nobody had sights. I kept count of the number of times my helicopter was actually hit (number of occasions; not number of hits), and, if memory serves, it was only hit on 24 separate occasions in a year of flying. I attributed this to my unquestionably excellent tactics. That explanation was somewhat undermined one day when inspection following the day's missions revealed a .45 caliber slug lodged in the bottom of my rotating beacon. I can only hope that it was at least from a Thompson or "grease gun" submachine gun, and not from a 1911 Colt pistol!

I finished my first combat tour with a handful of Air Medals and a Distinguished Flying Cross, which may or may not have really been deserved. Decorations in combat depend on who is watching at the time.

After returning to the 'States, I went back to Fort Benning, where I attended Infantry Officer Career Course and Nuclear Weapons Employment Course, earning Distinguished Graduate in both. After that, I spent six months or so at Fort Benning as the Operations Officer of the Infantry School flight element. During that time, I taught aerial gunnery and ran an armed helicopter transition program for the US Navy. Also during that time, I worked on a movie with my hero, John Wayne. He was filming *The Green Berets*, with a lot of scenes shot at Fort Benning. I coordinated air support for the movie, and flew in a few of the gunship scenes. The movie is a real stinker, but I will always value the time I spent with "The Duke." He never learned to act. What you saw in the movies was the real John Wayne.

Vietnam—Second Tour

Shortly after I finished Career Course and Nuclear Weapons Employment School, the first class of the new AH1G Cobra gunship opened up. All I needed to do to get a slot in the new school, and become qualified in the world's first real attack helicopter, was volunteer to go back to Vietnam. The choice was obvious. With little regard for my family, I jumped at the opportunity.

My second tour in Vietnam began with the 1968 Tet Offensive and was mainly with another Air Cavalry unit, the 7th/1st Cavalry. I did reasonably well there, in spite of being an Infantry officer in an Armor unit. While there, I earned a Silver Star, the first to be awarded to anyone in the unit. Again, it was mainly a matter of who was watching at the time.

This was before the North Vietnamese Army began using surface-to-air missiles in the south. The most effective anti-aircraft weapon the

Viet Cong and the North Vietnamese Army had at the time was the 12.75 mm machine gun on an anti-aircraft mount. It accounted for the loss of many helicopters and even some Air Force fighter/bombers. I led my gun teammates on an attack against one in an anti-aircraft emplacement. Two things ensued. First, we knocked it out. Second, General Ware (RIP) witnessed our attack. He awarded me the Silver Star, and my teammates all received Distinguished Flying Crosses. He also presented me with the anti-aircraft gun that his troops recovered in a sweep through the area after the battle.

Like my first tour, everyone still had guns, but now it seemed someone had also provided sights. I can honestly recount that there was not a day during that tour that my helicopter was not hit at least once, even though I was then flying the faster and more maneuverable UH-1C and AH-1G Cobra gunships. Throughout that time though, I was only shot down once, and that was because of two unlucky hits in my tail rotor drive shaft that resulted in tail rotor failure. I was flying a UH-1C at the time, and managed to put it down without further damage and without injury to the five people on board; the four-man crew plus a Special Forces officer observer. I received a minor award for "gallantry" for that, the Army Commendation Medal with V device for Valor. The citation read that I had saved the lives of five people on board. It neglected to mention that one of the five was me. In that the Army doesn't issue parachutes to helicopter pilots, I really didn't have much choice of the "above and beyond the call of duty" variety.

In nearly 1,300 hours of combat assault time in helicopter gunships, not one of my crew members was ever killed or even wounded. I must have been doing something right.

The other thing of note during this period was that I was selected for a "below-the-zone" promotion to major. I still think that may have resulted from a flaw in the selection process. I was an OCS graduate of no particular distinction, a Reserve officer, and I only had about a year of college credit. As an Infantry officer, I had only served in combat as a gunship pilot. I was probably one of the least likely captains in the Army to be selected for a below-the-zone early promotion. Regardless, I left my second tour in Vietnam as a major. I had advanced from sergeant E-5 to major, O-4 in about six-and-a-half years. As an ancillary benefit of my early promotion to major, I was given a Regular Army commission without so much as asking for the privilege. The Regular Army Commission pretty much guaranteed that I could stay in for a career. So much for my ambition to make captain and hold on to my commission for ten years.

Back to School

After my second tour in Vietnam, I was allowed to attend the University of Nebraska at Omaha (UNO) military "Bootstrap" program. That was a program that provided bachelor's degrees to officers who had not yet earned that distinction. They gave management course credit for OCS and NCO Schools, Physical Education credit for Ranger and Airborne Schools, and God only knows what else. I only know that after six months of on-campus work, I was awarded a Bachelor of General Studies (BGS) degree, for whatever that is worth.

Back to Fort Bragg

After my stint at the University of Omaha, I returned to Fort Bragg, first as an aviation staff officer, and then as Commander, A Company, 82nd Aviation Battalion, a position I held for eighteen months. That was probably the most successful period of my Army experience. It seemed that neither my company nor I could do any wrong, and we did a great deal right. Following my last aviation assignment, I returned to Infantry duty as the S-3 of the 3rd Brigade, 82nd Airborne Division. Consider for a moment becoming the operations officer of an Airborne Infantry Brigade (about 4,000 troops), when my last real Infantry assignment was as a platoon leader (about 40 troops)! I did very well in the job, but it was a difficult time for me.

And Back to School

After about three years in the 82nd, I was offered the opportunity to return to the University of Nebraska at Omaha for an eighteen-month, legitimate, master's degree program. I jumped at the opportunity and said goodbye to Fort Bragg for the last time. While at UNO, I did very well, finishing my only real degree with honors.

Back to Southeast Asia

After the master's program at UNO, I attended Armed Forces Staff College, where I also finished as a Distinguished Graduate. Immediately thereafter, I volunteered for a third tour in Southeast Asia; this time stationed in Thailand and flying back and forth between there and Vietnam. I was assigned as the Assistant J-3 (Operations) for the Joint Casualty Resolution Center (JCRC). That organization was supposedly responsible for accounting for all the Missing in Action and war dead whose remains had not been recovered (BNR) from the Vietnam conflict. I won't go into detail concerning that assignment, as it stands out as the least useful endeavor in which I have ever engaged. The one bright spot in the tour was working directly under the J-3, Marine Lieutenant Colonel Charles Ward (RIP), the best, most honorable officer I encountered in twenty-four years of active duty. I left Vietnam for the last time two weeks before Saigon fell. It was not a happy time.

Back to School Yet Again

After my third Southeast Asia tour, I was assigned as the Assistant Professor of Military Science in the ROTC program at West Texas State University (WTSU). Like many post-Vietnam ROTC programs, the one at WTSU was in trouble. The Professor of Military Science (PMS) was having a very difficult time, through no fault of his own, in keeping the cadet numbers up to a point where the program was worth maintaining. The performance of the cadets at competitive summer camps was abysmal, nearly at the bottom compared to other ROTC programs in the Region. I set to work changing the performance level, but did little or nothing to solve the numbers problem. In one year, I managed to raise the standing of our cadets from close to the lowest in the Region to 21st out of 119. However, in raising the quality, I made it even harder for the PMS to keep the numbers up. He was not happy with me. (More of the not being able to get along well in a work environment.) I can't say I blame him.

While at WTSU, my generally unhappy marriage ended in divorce. I would say that the fault was 90/10 with 90% my fault and 10% my wife's fault, although she might argue with my assignment of 10% of the blame to her.

Toward the end of my ROTC tour, I was finally promoted to lieutenant colonel. I was never passed over in the primary zone. Still, it took almost nine years to be promoted from major to lieutenant colonel. I decided then and there that I would retire in exactly two years, the minimum time after promotion to be retired at the new pay grade.

Back to Fort Benning

Shortly after my promotion, I left for my final assignment; Executive Officer for the Basic Training/Advanced Infantry Training Brigade at Fort Benning. After a stint as Brigade XO, I was transferred to Infantry School Headquarters, where I led a team to revise and rewrite the Army Basic Training program. My Army career ended "not with a bang, but with a whimper." Once you have been in combat, everything else is drab. I think it was Winston Churchill who said, "Nothing is quite so exciting as having someone try unsuccessfully to shoot you." He was right.

Eighteen months after arriving at Fort Benning, I hung up my uniform for the last time on December 31, 1979. I had entered the Army as a sixteen-year-old boy with a tenth grade education from a Mississippi County Agricultural High School. I left twenty-four years later as a Regular Army lieutenant colonel, a Senior Army Aviator, Master Parachutist and Ranger, with a chest full of medals, a commercial helicopter pilot license, and a master's degree. It had been a good run.

Civilian Life

At 41 years of age, I found myself unemployed. I had purchased a modest new car shortly before retirement and the payments, around $140 per month, came out of my retirement pay. The entire remainder of my retirement pay went to my ex-wife in the form of alimony and child support. I was at zero income for the first time since entering the Army twenty-four years earlier. I calculated my net worth, including the pay for my final month of service and accrued leave time, and all my personal belongings, and it came out around $5,000; not much to show for twenty-four years.

On the other hand, all my family financial responsibilities were covered by my retired pay, and the only thing I owed was remaining car payments, which were also covered by retired pay. I was confident that I could support myself, and looked forward to my first job interview. In my naive view, the civilian world would welcome someone with my impressive military credentials with open arms. Wrong! At first, I had difficulty fitting my illustrious military career into a two-page resumé. Eight years later, the entire military career entry on my resumé was reduced to, "Served in US Army for twenty-four years, advancing from private to lieutenant colonel."

My first job was as a consultant in an 8a, minority-owned firm in Washington, DC. I lasted there less than a year. Immediately thereafter, I opened my own consulting firm, with me as president and sole employee. Over the next few years, I built the company to a staff of seven, with six consultants and one secretary/office manager. The firm was very successful, dealing mainly with contracts and subcontracts for the Defense Programs Office of the Department of Energy. We provided security evaluation of nuclear weapons facilities and other duties for the DOE/DP Office of Safeguards and Security.

Everyone in the firm, with the exception of the secretary/office manager, was ex-military, ex-FBI, or ex-state police. We were a good team. My future wife Zia came to work for me there and proved very valuable. She had recently left the Army after eight years active duty, but stayed in the National Guard and Army Reserve, where she was eventually promoted to lieutenant colonel before retiring. She was married at the time. I had a live-in girlfriend, and did not condone office romances, so it took us six years or so before we had our first date.

Over the next several years, we developed programs and practices that made the company just about indispensable to our customers. Seven years after opening the firm, we had a lucrative, multi-year contract with DOE, through Battelle Laboratory. Our company and all our employees had Q clearances. We were recognized as a leading organization in the world of nuclear weapon and nuclear materials security. And I had had enough. My inability to get along with fellow workers and superiors came back to haunt me. I was particularly unsuited for work with Civil Service workers and politicians. My opinions of these people can best be summed up by a quote from the British author and engineer, Nevil Shute Norway:

"I am very willing to recognize the good in men of these two classes, but a politician or a civil servant to me is still an arrogant fool till he is proved otherwise."

I decided to sell the company and move on. A retiring Air Force lieutenant colonel, looking for an organization to take over, made an offer for the full asking price. There are two types of entrepreneurs; those who start firms, and those who take over firms that are already established. I am of the former category; my prospective buyer was of the latter. In addition to being an established firm, having talented and Q-cleared employees and national recognition, the most valuable asset of the company was a new, multi-year contract. The problem was ensuring that the contract would be continued under a new owner. That is where my inability to get along with people finally paid off.

Neither Battelle nor our DOE masters could easily do without the services my company provided. On the other hand, they had had more than enough of me. The idea of having the personnel and assets of the company available, led by someone more reasonable, was a godsend to them. Both Battelle and DOE staffs worked night and day to make sure the company sale, including the existing contract, went through. Sometimes, being unpopular has its advantages.

Approximately seven years after starting the company, I found myself retired and unemployed again, albeit in somewhat better circumstances than when I left the Army. I used a portion of the funds I received from the sale of the company to buy back my retirement pay from my ex-wife. My younger daughter was out of college by then, and my older daughter had finished law school. Both had good jobs, and were no longer dependent on me. I also had a reasonable nest egg to carry me into my second retirement, a new car paid for, and a modest but perfectly suitable house. I was still single, and had no one to take care of but myself. I could theoretically live on my little nest egg and my retirement pay in reasonable comfort for the remainder of my years. I was 49 years old, and things were looking up.

Back to Work

I have never been very good at leisure. Shortly after selling the company, I was back at work as a consultant, helping the Sandia National

Laboratory in Livermore, California prepare for a DOE Safeguards and Security re-inspection. They had failed their last inspection and were in considerable difficulty. Partially due to my efforts, they passed the re-inspection with flying colors. I was offered and accepted a permanent position on their security staff.

Not long after going to work at the Sandia National Laboratory, I found myself in need of an assistant. Zia, who had left my original company about the time I sold it, had divorced her husband, gone to graduate school, finished her master's degree, and was looking for a job. I brought her to Livermore as a consultant, and she was hired as a regular employee shortly thereafter. Zia is a talented lady, a fact not lost on the Sandia Livermore managers. She had not worked under my supervision much over a month when they transferred her to another area of the Lab, where we were no longer in a supervisor/supervised relationship. We were married a few months later.

After I had been with the Sandia Livermore Laboratory for three years, Zia was transferred to the main Sandia Laboratory in Albuquerque, New Mexico. With the lab picking up the tab for our move, I went with her. We bought a traditional adobe home in the foothills of the Sandia Mountains, and settled down to work and live happily ever after. The living happily continued, but the work didn't. A little over a year later, we both resigned from Sandia National Laboratory, and I entered my third retirement. I was 54 years old, and determined to make it work. Zia was 41.

Retirement

This time, we made retirement work. It has been twenty years, and neither of us has any inclination to re-enter the work force. Zia has found full-time occupations as a volunteer puppy raiser for Canine Companions for Independence, an organization that provides service dogs to people with physical disabilities; teaching and taking Bikram Yoga; volunteering at the New Mexico Animal Humane Association as a dog handler and teacher, and a myriad of other activities. Due to the yoga and her generally healthy lifestyle, she has the body of an eighteen-year-old. I am blessed in more ways than one.

I have gone through a number of items on my bucket list in the years since retiring. I have run 24 full 26.2 mile marathons plus several mountain races; learned to read, write and speak passable Spanish; acquired Level I and II SCUBA certification; obtained my private airplane license and, together with Zia, bought the family plane. While I was going through learning to fly airplanes instead of helicopters, Zia also obtained her private pilot license.

We have traveled a good bit; Central and South America for Spanish practice, and Australia for general interest. Several years ago, following an international convention we sponsored in Victoria, Australia, we obtained our Australian pilot licenses, and flew 5,000 miles around the Australian Outback; the most fun flying I have ever experienced. More recently, we spent three months in a tiny town (2,500 population) in the middle of the Queensland Outback, 750 miles by recently-paved two-lane road from the coast and the nearest city. Those people know how to live.

My more-or-less full time volunteer occupation for the past six years was as the New Mexico Wing Leader of Angel Flight. In that organization, we use our private airplanes to fly unpaid charity missions, transporting needy patients between outlying areas and central medical facilities in Albuquerque. In addition to my administrative duties, I flew many of the missions. After twelve years with Angel Flight, I recently flew my 500th mission.

This past year, I was presented the Spirit of New Mexico Award for my charity work by New Mexico Governor Susana Martinez, one of the very few politicians I admire. In addition to the award, I got a hug from the Governor!

Once again though, my impatience with those above me came to bear. I was recently removed as the (volunteer) Angel Flight New Mexico Wing Leader, primarily due to disagreements with the (paid) Executive Director of our parent organization, Angel Flight South Central. I am quite happy with the change, as I have more time to fly missions, without the burden of administrative duties. It has always been the same. No matter how carefully and politely I explain to others the stupidity of their policies, they never seem to learn.

Angel Flight Pilot Dan Telfair on his 500th mission, flying a two-year old girl and her parents back to their home in Las Cruces after her treatment at an Albuquerque hospital, Albuquerque, NM, March 2012.

What has it all been about? I really don't know. I do know that my time at OCS was instrumental in everything that followed. I know that events and circumstances have led me to a place in life far better than any I ever expected.

I will soon have my seventy-fifth birthday. Although I have had to give up long-distance running, I am still in decent shape, without any of the medical conditions frequently associated with my age. I do not take any medications. I can still easily pass my flight physicals, and with several thousand hours in the family plane, I have come to be a very good pilot.

I have a wonderful wife, two successful daughters, a beautiful home in a great part of the country, a comfortable income, a fun airplane, and the health and leisure time to enjoy it all. It would be very ungrateful of me not to be happy.

Captain (Later Lieutenant Colonel) Tyrone Trbovich (Center),
Bastogne Fire Support Base, Vietnam, May 1968.

I was born on July 19, 1937 and raised in Lorain, Ohio on the shores of Lake Erie and the confluence of the Black River. Lorain is 25 miles due west of Cleveland. Fortunately for me, I was raised in a simpler time when instant gratification was not a necessity, and we all could have fun and grow up without the stress I see in some of today's lifestyles.

Lorain was an industrial town, with US Steel (the largest continuous pipe mill in the world) as the county's largest employer; Thew Shovel (manufacturer of industrial cranes); American Ship Building (a Steinbrenner company); and Fruehauf Trailer Company. Prior to my enlistment in the US Army, Ford Motor Company also came to town. I believe the city population was around 50,000 people. Sad to say, as I write this chapter of my life, the only major business left in Lorain is a portion of the US Steel Company.

At one time in my formative years, our entire family lived on the same street within a radius of four city blocks. To this day I fondly remember the summer picnics in the back yard with all the grandparents, aunts, uncles and cousins, along with my brother Ron (six years younger), playing stick ball, wiffle ball or hide and seek. We even had a large victory garden.

At one time growing up, our two-story house held my mom, dad, my brother, three renters and me. We had one full bath on the first floor and a quarter bath in the basement. Can you believe we never had any problems!?

My Grandfather Puskas owned a bar and grill, the Crystal Rock Inn near one of the main entrances to the steel mill, a short two blocks from our house. My Grandfather Trbovich worked in the steel mill along with my dad Michael, my uncles John Gimben, Pete Kuzela and Ben Polny. My uncle Nick Puskas worked at Thew Shovel. The summers just prior to and during college, I also worked in the steel mill, for the county cutting grass, and one summer at the Ford Motor plant.

My dad was a combat engineer, Uncle Nick was a B-26 gunner and Uncle Ben was an infantry soldier, all serving in WW II. I still have a memory of my father coming home for a surprise visit prior to heading overseas. They all returned home safely. I also remember when President Roosevelt died, and running home from my cousin's house to tell my mother Victoria the news.

Growing up in Lorain was a great experience and I would not trade a minute of the time spent with my family and friends. I went to Oakwood Elementary School, three blocks away. I became a great school crossing guard in the fifth and sixth grades. Also in the sixth grade I was in the band (played the clarinet), and I started playing organized football for the first time in the Catholic Youth League, playing quarterback for St. John's Church.

I attended Whittier Junior High School (grades 7-9). We either walked (approximately seven blocks) or rode our bicycles to school. At Whittier, I was in the choir, played Tom Sawyer in the school play, and played and lettered in football and basketball. I think we still hold the city record of 25 straight wins on the basketball court. We were junior high champs three years in a row.

In addition, all the neighborhood guys got together and played baseball, softball, tackle football (no pads) and basketball in Oakwood Park, or pickup games in some empty lot. We just had fun. There was a period of time when either a fire station or a local bar would sponsor a team and we would play softball in the city recreation league or basketball in the YMCA league. I still have some news clippings from those days.

When we were not playing some sport, we were either down the flats in the Black River area or exploring the French Creek area playing BB gun games and cooking potatoes we borrowed from the farmer's field. Going to the lake was special because our dad or uncle had to drive us to Lake Erie Park or Beaver Park on Lake Erie. No fears because we all learned how to swim at the YMCA.

I attended Lorain High School (school bus was the mode of transportation), made National Honor Society and lettered in basketball and football. Our first football game in my senior year, we played Bluffton Junior College and won. I also broke my left wrist late in the first half of my last game against our arch rival, Elyria High School. I can tell you it was really fun practicing basketball with a cast on my left arm. No one wanted to guard me.

I was very fortunate and received full scholarship offers from Colgate University, the University of Kansas, and the University of Wisconsin to play football. I committed to the University of Wisconsin (UW), mainly because my high school teammate Paul Gray was there in his first semester, and his brother Wells was the Captain of the 1955 UW football team. When I made my first visit to campus, it was the first time that I was out of the state of Ohio on my own. What an eye opener!

I took my first train ride and had to change trains in Chicago to get up to Madison, Wisconsin. I felt like a country bumpkin. I do not remember who met me at the train station in Madison, but it had to be Paul Gray or one of the assistant coaches. Unfortunately, after all these years, I do not remember too many things about that first visit. One thing for sure though, I found out that they served beer in the Student Union.

I started college in September 1955 and declared Mechanical Engineering as my degree discipline. The Athletic Department arranged off campus housing for me, a neat apartment very close to campus that I shared with other freshmen athletes.

College life was too much fun as it turned out. What study discipline I had disappeared, and unfortunately between 1955 and 1959, I was expelled on three separate occasions for not achieving a 2.0 grade average. On the plus side, I did make lifelong friends with some of my football teammates and fraternity brothers in Phi Gamma Delta. I left Madison in September 1959 for Lorain, and my dad helped me decide to join the US Army in October 1959.

My induction center was at Fort Knox, KY, and I spent seven days there getting orientation and GI-issued clothing. I was then assigned to "The Big Red One," the 1st Infantry Division at Fort Riley, KS, for basic training. The Army flew us to Fort Riley, so I had my first airplane ride in a commercial DC-3.

The next eight weeks of my life were interesting. We had a great platoon leader, Master Sergeant John Francis Michael McGuire. We saw him first thing in the morning and the last thing before lights out. Obviously, our Platoon Sergeant made a lasting impression on me. He was a Korean War veteran who made sure we knew what we were doing. Fort Riley was bitter cold, and many a day we all stumbled back to our barracks and just walked into a hot shower, weapon, clothes and all.

In 1960, I took my advanced training at Fort Devens, MA, where I learned Morse code intercept. From Fort Devens, I was assigned to the 177th Army Security Agency Company at K-6, in Pyeongtaek, Korea (now know as Camp Humphries). It was an amazing experience to witness the culture of South Korea so close to the end of the Korean Conflict. I did visit Seoul, the DMZ, and the Peace Village. Sports were a big pastime and we won the K-6 Post, 508th ASA Group, and 8th Army Logistics Command flag football titles.

Mid-point in my Korean tour, I decided that I wanted to become an officer, and applied for Infantry Officer Candidate School. I was accepted and was assigned to Fort Benning, GA OCS Class 2-62.

My experiences at OCS were and still are a blur, and I was happy when Blue Day arrived and when we finally graduated on March 30, 1962. My mantra through OCS was, "Don't screw up, take responsibility, and succeed." Our overall class motto was "cooperate and graduate." You helped your classmates as much as possible. We graduated on a Friday and on Monday, 21 of my classmates and I reported for Airborne Class #30, where we all received our jump wings on April 27, 1962.

My first assignment after Jump School was with Company C, 313th Army Security Agency (ASA) Battalion, XVIII Airborne Corps. (It later became Company C, 303rd ASA Battalion, III Corps.) We were the only airborne unit in support of the 4th Infantry Division at Fort

Lewis, WA. The odd thing about the assignment was that Company C was stationed at Two Rock Station, Petaluma, CA. Our company would convoy up to Fort Lewis to join the 4th Infantry Division for major exercises. Fortunately, the company moved and was permanently stationed at Fort Lewis in late 1962, while I was away undergoing Ranger training. I received my Ranger Tab on November 21, 1962 (Class 3-62), and rejoined my company back at Fort Lewis. While at Fort Lewis, I was a platoon leader and a company XO.

Our company participated in three Polar Siege exercises in Alaska (winter training) and two Desert Strike exercises in the Mojave Desert (believe it or not, summer maneuvers). I was also on TDY to Company B, 313th ASA Battalion for exercises supporting the 101st Airborne Division. I ran into OCS classmates Robert Collins at Fort Campbell, and Wayne Stone at Fort Bragg and Fort. Lewis. When Wayne and I were together at Fort Lewis, I talked the Operations Officer of a C-124 squadron at McChord AFB into letting us jump out of their planes (two jumps) over Weir Prairie (Fort Lewis) instead of dropping several 55 gallon barrels of water on their practice missions. Then we talked our way into an HH-43 helicopter jump at McChord AFB adjacent to Fort Lewis. That was before our Battalion Executive Officer found out what we were doing and told us to knock it off.

While at Fort Lewis, I saw several OCS classmates: Merritte Wilson, Bill Hunter and Robert Burke. I was in Merritte Wilson's wedding party, my first and only dress blues military wedding. Our company flag football team won the Post, Northwest Military, and the Sixth Army flag football championships.

I left Fort Lewis in late 1964 and was assigned to the 401st ASA Detachment (ABN), supporting the 8th Special Forces Group (SFG) at Fort Gulick, Panama Canal Zone. My initial job was Detachment Team Leader in support of various A Teams in the 8th Special Forces Group, and later as the 401st Detachment Commander. While there, I received my senior and then my master parachute wings. OCS classmates Mario Burdick and Alvin (Buff) Morris were also with the 8th SFG, and we had a great party celebrating our promotions to captain while we were there.

In mid-1966, I was sent to Fort Devens for captains' career course training. Michael J. Remick, another OCS classmate, was in my class.

After completion of the career course, I was assigned to Headquarters, USASA, in the Operations Division for six months (tactical contingency planning) before landing my dream assignment.

That assignment was as the Commanding Officer of the 265th Radio Research Company (ABN) in direct support of the 101st Airborne Division at Fort Campbell, KY. I had the privilege of organizing and training our company for deployment to the Republic of Vietnam (RVN). I had the added assignment of being on the Commanding General's special staff. A side note: I made my 67th and last parachute jump while at Fort Campbell.

On December 1, 1967, we deployed with the Division staff and the 2nd and 3rd Brigades of the 101st ABN Div, on the longest airlift in military history (Operation Eagle Thrust) from Fort Campbell to Ben Hoa Air Base, RVN. One of my platoons was assigned to each Brigade. Our company was recognized for exemplary duty during Tet 1968, during the Viet Cong attack on the Ben Hoa Air Base. The main attack came directly across our company front. Our troopers did a great job in slowing and confusing the VC thrust to the Air Base. We were fortunate to only have three men wounded.

In February, the Division moved to Camp Eagle, and what a lovely place that was! I was very proud of my troopers and how they completed their mission in the harshest of circumstances. The Division's 2nd Brigade Commanding Officer awarded our 2nd Platoon troopers the Combat Infantry Badge. Prior to my departure, our 1st Platoon suffered four wounded soldiers. I received my promotion to major on November 13. When I left Vietnam in mid-November 1968, I thanked God that He brought all my troopers safely home.

In 1968, I was assigned as an instructor in the Military Intelligence Career Course at Fort Holabird, MD for a short time. In late May 1969, the Army sent me back to the University of Wisconsin to complete my BS degree in Economics, which I did in January 1971.

Now a good story for me: Just prior to my graduation, I called Department of the Army Personnel and asked where my next assignment would be. After some thought, the individual with whom I was talking said they had a great job for me, in Cambodia. Yikes! I responded with words to the effect that it sounded interesting, but since I just recently returned from Vietnam, I wondered if there were any other options.

I was told that I would get a call back in a couple of weeks. When I received the call back, I was asked if I wanted to take an assignment at the Supreme Headquarters Allied Powers Europe (SHAPE). I thought long and hard on the right decision (maybe 2 seconds) and off I went to SHAPE in Mons, Belgium.

I was at SHAPE from January 1971 to January 1974. I was assigned to the Communications and Electronics Staff reporting to a British Royal Signals lieutenant colonel. My job was to write policy on Operations Security. While I was at SHAPE, I completed my master's degree in Systems Management from the University of Southern California, and the Security Management Course from the Industrial College of the Armed Forces.

From SHAPE, I went to the Armed Forces Staff College (AFSC) in Norfolk, VA. As I reviewed my records for this chapter, I discovered that Dan Telfair (OCS classmate) was in the same class, but I do not remember ever running into him.

In mid-1974, from AFSC, I went to Washington, DC, and spent my last seven years in the Pentagon. My first assignment (four years) was with the Assistant Chief of Staff for Intelligence (ACSI), and then three years with J-3, Joint Chiefs of Staff. I was promoted to Lieutenant Colonel while on the ACSI Staff. During my tour with JCS, I ran into another OCS classmate, Thomas Vaughn.

Even though our OCS Class 2-62 would be up for promotion to Colonel in the near future, I decided to retire and forgo the potential for promotion. I did not believe I would ever be promoted to Brigadier General, and I had a good job offer. I could not see spending another six years in the Army, considering salary and benefits, compared to starting my civilian career. I called DA Personnel to let them know my plans, and retired in June 1981, having completed 22 years of military service.

My entire military career focused on gathering tactical intelligence in support of Division or Special Forces missions. My staff jobs at SHAPE, DA ACSI and J-3 JCS were also related to policy and guidance for disseminating tactical intelligence. I was awarded the following decorations: Bronze Star for Meritorious Service w/OLC, Defense Meritorious Service Medal, Meritorious Service Medal, Joint Service Medal, Army Commendation Medal w/OLC, Good Conduct Medal,

National Defense Service Medal, Republic of Vietnam Service Medal, Korea Defense Service Medal and the Republic of Vietnam Campaign Medal. I also was awarded the Army Staff and Joint Chiefs of Staff Badges.

I spent the next 26 years (1981-2007) in the aerospace business: seven years with Emerson Electric Company's Electronics and Space Division in St. Louis, MO, and their Rantec Division in Calabasas, CA, and then nineteen years with Lear Astronics Corporation, that eventually became part of BAE Systems, a $22 billion corporation. I held various positions in business development my entire civilian career. I retired for good in January 2007 at the age of 69, going on 70.

I had an enjoyable and successful business career. One of the highlights was participating in a Junior Achievement program, "Project Business," while in St. Louis. Project Business was supported by private industry and taught business principles to eighth through twelfth graders. The experiences of junior and senior high teaching, and the participants' discussions and questions were a blast.

Sherrie and I have been married for 26 years and have two sons and five granddaughters. The weather in Southern California is great. We live in La Quinta, CA in the PGA WEST golf community. Now, my time is spent golfing, traveling, and spending time with our granddaughters. As a public service activity, I have organized a golf tournament, "The Feature at PGA West—A Cancer Research Charity," that my brother and I have hosted for the past four years. The proceeds go to the Carbone Cancer Center at the University of Wisconsin.

It has been a pleasure to take part in this project to produce a quasi history of the members of OCS Class 2-62. The 50th class reunion on March 30, 2012 at Fort Benning brought back a lot of memories. It was a great opportunity to reunite with classmates from my OCS platoon (the Fifth Platoon Spartans) and those with whom I had the opportunity to serve in various later assignments. It has left a memory forever etched in my mind.

Back row center: Lieutenant Colonel (Retired) Ty Trbovich with wife Sherrie. Left to right, back row ends: sons Jim Lent and Dan Lent; second row: daughter-in-law Monica Lent, granddaughters Samantha Lent, Allison Lent, and Sydney Lent and daughter-in-law Miranda Lent; front row: granddaughters Amanda and Camille Lent.

Colonel Thomas B. Vaughn, Task Force Lancer Commander,
Operation Orient Shield, Camp Fuji, Japan, 1985.

The Early Days

From a very early age, I dreamed of becoming a soldier. Those dreams were fueled by books and movies, most notably, the James Jones novel, *From Here to Eternity*, a best-selling book and Oscar-winning movie about Army life in an Infantry company at Schofield Barracks, Hawaii on the eve of Pearl Harbor. I was transported in time and place by the book, and more so by the movie. Little did I know I would someday command a battalion and later a brigade at Schofield Barracks.

Back home, I was inspired by several former real-life soldiers, including WWII veterans John Cox and Joe Nunley. They were my football coaches, teachers, mentors, and friends for life. McMinnville native Sergeant Major Charlie Hillis was another Army role model. He personified what an Airborne Infantryman should look and act like. A highly-decorated combat veteran of Korea and Vietnam, Charlie was my hero and also a lifelong friend. Other Army influences came from my National Guard mentor, J.S. Carr, Army Reserve Colonel and Korean War veteran James Dillon, and my high school principal and WWII veteran Jonah Fitch. They too, were role models and mentors.

That said, my main mentor and role model was my Mother, Gertrude Simons-Vaughn-Grissom. She worked long hours at the local hosiery mill, washed and ironed clothes, and cleaned houses for other families, just to keep our family together. Most of that time she did all that on her own, while raising my sisters Doris, Geneva and me. I never knew my father-and after the way he treated my Mother-I never really wanted to. Mother had only an 8th grade education, but she was incredibly wise and kind. She instilled in me a lifelong love of learning. I can still hear her words ringing out across the years, "Get a good education, son. No one can ever take that away from you."

Acting on my Army ambitions began modestly when, at age fifteen, I joined our local Tennessee National Guard unit. At age sixteen, I took a leap of faith and joined the Regular Army. My motivation was partly patriotic and partly wounded pride, the latter from being jilted by my girlfriend, who preferred a top trombone player to an average athlete. I "fixed" her by quitting school and signing up with Uncle Sam. The second time I lied about my age seemed to work for a while, but the Army caught up with me three months before I turned seventeen, and turned me out with a "Minority Discharge under Honorable Conditions." I guess that was their way of saying I was a patriotic liar.

I returned home to McMinnville, Tennessee in late May 1955, somewhat in limbo regarding my Army ambitions; a Regular Army veteran, still too young to rejoin the National Guard! To add insult to injury, I had to repeat my sophomore year, and sit out the fall football season. Ego firmly in check, I made many new and lifelong friends among my new classmates, including Jeff Golden and Dickie Hillis. I even worked with the football team as an equipment manager until I was reinstated as a player the following spring.

I rejoined my Tennessee National Guard unit as soon as I became eligible in August 1955, enlisted by the same J.S. Carr who had witnessed my earlier indiscretions in pursuit of my boyhood dream of living the soldier's life. If forgiveness is a virtue, and surely it is, J.S. was a saint on earth. He not only forgave me, he was a mentor when I most needed one.

Upon graduation from McMinnville City High School in 1958, I left for Fort Knox, KY with my best friend Homer Kirby, Jr. to attend the Armor Advanced NCO Course. I was its youngest member and an undistinguished graduate, attracted more to the winsome WACs across the street than to the stacks of Field and Technical Manuals lining my barracks lockers.

I began my Regular Army career in earnest in 1959 by re-enlisting for six years, thereby earning a $1,200 bonus. To me, that seemed like a fortune. I carefully counted the dozen "Ben Franklins," first with the somewhat petulant finance clerk, then for myself. Ignoring old Ben's advice about "A penny saved is a penny earned," I spent some of my many pennies on a TV set for my mother and a barbell set for myself. I spent most extravagantly on a down payment for a brand-new Chevy Impala Sports Coupe. It seemed like the thing to do at the time.

As over three years had passed since I took Basic Combat Training at Fort Knox, KY, I had to take it again, this time at Fort Jackson, South Carolina. I reminded the Personnel NCO that I had recently graduated from the Armor Advanced NCO Course. His remedy for that was to assign me to Infantry Advanced Individual Training, also held at Fort Jackson. Whether that was his idea of cross-training or a cruel joke on a young NCO, was known only to him, and he is long gone. Anyway, it was a fortuitous experience for me, preparing me well for my rising ambition to become an Infantry officer. After serving briefly at Fort Hood, Texas with the 2nd Armored Division, I was ordered to South Korea for duty in the 1st Cavalry Division. Days of processing in California and Tokyo were followed by more days of processing in Seoul before I was deemed fit for duty with a rifle company near the DMZ. I was first assigned to lead a five-man fire team. Then, upon promotion to Staff Sergeant, E-6, I was given command of a two-man squad, consisting of a Korean Augmentation to the US Army (KATUSA) soldier named Kim Sung Koon and me. Things improved markedly thereafter. I even acted as platoon sergeant and platoon leader from time to time. It was heady experience for a twenty-two-year-old NCO, and invaluable preparation for OCS.

My Time at OCS

I reported to OCS in October 1961. As I climbed the steps of the 52nd Company barracks, I saluted the Company Commander, Captain William McKell Hadly. He returned my salute, shook my hand firmly, and greeted me warmly. "Welcome to OCS, Sergeant Vaughn! Go ahead and sign in, then come back out here on the porch." My sigh of relief was premature; the worst was about to come. After signing in, I was pinned between two Tac Officers screaming at me for being "grossly out of uniform" and ripping the staff sergeant stripes off my sleeves with pleasure bordering on perversity.

That was the first of many days of challenge to come at the "Benning School for Boys." I say "challenge" because that's what OCS was essentially all about, physically, mentally, and emotionally. Numbers tell the tale. As I recall, we started with 238 candidates and we graduated 119, a 50% attrition rate. That was March 30, 1962, three years before LBJ sent the first ground combat troops to South Vietnam, so the supply of potential officers vastly exceeded the demand for them that year. Highlights in OCS for me included earning the coveted Expert Infantry Badge and being named a Distinguished Graduate of my class.

My Career as an Infantry Officer

My Officer career began auspiciously when I married my high school sweetheart, Nancy Aycock. We crammed our wedding and honeymoon into a three-day pass, packed and moved to Camp Wolters, TX for Rotary Wing (helicopter) Flight School. It turned inauspicious when I flunked out of flight school because I couldn't master the nuances of hovering a helicopter. In retrospect, that was a good thing, for the Army, and for me. I went on to serve in the 1st Infantry Division with the 1st Battle Group, 13th Infantry, later renamed the 1st Battalion, 18th Infantry. I was pleasantly surprised to see a few classmates there, notably Ed Burke and Jim Hamilton.

Ed, Jim, and I were promoted to first lieutenant in the same ceremony. Duty in the 18th involved a series of successful assignments: Rifle Platoon Leader, Weapons Platoon Leader, Rifle Company XO, Heavy Mortar/Davy Crockett Platoon Leader, and Battalion Assistant S-3 Air. Highlights included a trip to Pierre, SD to serve as one of the escort officers for President John F. Kennedy when he came to dedicate the Oahe Dam. Meeting him was a significant emotional experience. He was nattily attired, perfectly coiffed, well-tanned, and the picture of perfect health. Later, we would learn he was actually in poor health, but hid it well.

Another highlight was our deployment to Berlin, where I was attached to the Berlin Brigade, running recon patrols into East Berlin. As I recall, we made some thirty-three clandestine patrols in about three months, gathering intelligence on Soviet and East German military units, and reporting back to the Brigade S-2 on our findings. I was struck by the stark contrast between the flourishing free West Berlin and the floundering fiefdom in East Berlin. The dream of a unified Germany would take decades to realize, as would the demise of the Soviet Union. My first son, Tom Jr. was born prematurely during my deployment. Nancy endured that experience without me by her side. I still regret that very much.

I volunteered for combat duty in Vietnam in early 1964, and attended the Special Warfare School's Military Advisor's Training and Assistance (MATA) course, facetiously called "Mill Around Till Ambushed" by irreverent students, including OCS classmates "Roger the Ranger" Anderson and Dave Davis.

I left Fort Bragg, went back to McMinnville, picked up Nancy and Tom Jr., and headed west to Monterey, CA to attend the Defense Language Institute's twelve-week Vietnamese language course. It was a difficult course, but a delightful experience. Former OCS roommate Dick White dropped by to visit, bringing a six-pack of beer. OCS classmates Dave Davis and Stan Wisniewski were in the class too, and we shared some good times together. Blackjack games were a lot of fun until I won all the money one night, which went over like a pork chop in Palestine with the wives. My lame attempt to curry favor with them by paying for our Mexican dinner that night was not successful. As I recall, that was the end of our card games. In November 1964, I deployed to Vietnam, serving first with the ARVN 1st Battalion, 50th Infantry

Regiment, a Light Infantry unit of some 400 Vietnamese soldiers and four American Advisors. I worked for Captain Charlie Harrell, son of Major General Ben Harrell, who was the Commandant of the Infantry School during our OCS class, and who later retired as a four-star General. Charlie was a real character and a great guy to serve with. He had an almost demented desire to demolish things, as in "Blow them up!" The Vietnamese loved him. He was replaced by Captain Roger Horner from, as I recall, Deer Harbor, Michigan. He was a strapping, somewhat-scholarly man with a totally different personality. He was also a good man to work for and with.

Our primary Area of Operations was in the countryside around Tan An, the capital city of Long An Province. However, we also conducted extensive combat operations from bases as far away as Luong Hoa, a village some eighteen miles west of Saigon. Strategically situated on the rim of the Viet Cong-controlled Plain of Reeds, it was surrounded by four Viet Cong battalions. We had to fight our way into Luong Hoa; then aggressively defend it against repeated enemy assaults. Offensive missions in both AOs included search and clear, search and destroy, raids, and ambushes. Battalion and company-size operations were mostly "walks in the sun," with rare contact with the elusive VC. Raids and ambushes, conducted at night by squads and platoons were more successful, though often risky and violent.

After some seven months "in the bush," I was drafted by our Division Senior Advisor, Colonel Jesse Ugalde, to be one of his G-3 briefers. He was a hard man to work for, but he taught me lessons about tact and diplomacy when briefing senior officers, which I grasped intellectually, but practiced poorly, then and throughout my military career.

In November 1965, I left Vietnam en route to Airborne School at Fort Benning, GA. Airborne School was fun, despite injuring my left shoulder on my fourth jump. Luckily, due to weather delays earlier, we made our fourth and fifth jumps back-to-back. Otherwise, I probably would not have been able to make the last one, owing to severe inflammation in my shoulder.

I reported to Fort Jackson in January 1966, eager to assume command of a Basic Combat Training Company, only to find that the G-1 Officer Assignments Officer had picked me to be the commandant of the local NCO Academy. I told him I had orders from Infantry

Branch to command a BCT Company, and that's what I intended to do. After a half-hour of verbal jousting, I tactfully suggested he peruse his roster of current BCT Company Commanders, pick one with long tenure, send him to the NCO Academy, and send me to command that company. He reluctantly agreed, and I took command of Company B, 9th Battalion, 2nd Training Regiment. Captain Buck Jones and his winsome wife Jean were among the first to welcome my wife Nancy and me. They became lifelong friends.

In those days, command of a BCT Company was not exactly a "stairway to the stars" career-wise, but it was an opportunity to command and train soldiers, which was just what I wanted to do. Our trainees were a mix of Regular Army volunteers and draftees, plus National Guard and Army reservists on active duty for training under the Reserve Forces Act. Thanks to my cadre of well-trained and certified drill sergeants, Company B typically excelled in rifle marksmanship, physical fitness, drill and ceremonies, and other challenging events crammed into our eight-week training cycles.

In late 1966, Infantry Branch selected me to attend the University of Omaha for the Degree Completion Program, commonly known as "Bootstrap". I spent a year there, earning a Bachelor of General Studies Degree. Intellectually speaking, Omaha was a real eye-opening experience for me, enriched by motivational mentors, notably Dr. Winston Churchill Breckenridge Lambert. He taught me a lot about politics, and a lot more about living a meaningful life of public and private service above self. My second son, Larry, was born in February 1967, back in Tennessee. Again, Nancy went through birthing a son without me, which I also regret.

In early 1968, it was back to Fort Benning for the Infantry Officer Advanced Course, after a brief hiatus at the Infantry Agency, where LTC Mel Drisko and I co-wrote the Long Range Reconnaissance Patrol Field Manual. That was my main written contribution to the Infantry Agency annals in the few months I was there as a "Snowbird" awaiting the next IOAC class. The course was interesting and useful, but many of us viewed it mainly as a brief respite between Vietnam tours. We allocated precious time for family, friends, fun, and academics, usually in that order. The highlight for me was being promoted to Major, AUS, just six years and eight months after graduating from OCS. Little did

I know that I would remain a major for the next seven years and nine months. I finally received an "accelerated" promotion to lieutenant colonel in the Pentagon, alongside my OCS classmate and good friend Dave Davis.

In March 1969, I returned to Vietnam as a so-called "Second Tour Volunteer," fully expecting to go to one of the airborne units already there. My expectations were thwarted by "the needs of the Army," when classmate Eric Mackintosh and I were diverted to the 23rd (Americal) Infantry Division, near Chu Lai. We had to catch our own flight north to the airfield that serviced the Division. Upon arrival, there was nobody to meet us. We "rode our thumbs" to Division Headquarters, only to find they weren't expecting us that day. Adding insult to injury, the G-1 Officer Assignments Officer informed me I was being sent to the S & T Battalion, as in Supply and Transportation! With due disregard for previous lessons in tact and diplomacy, I told him I would not do it, unless ordered to by someone higher than him, such as the Division Chief of Staff. He then approached another just-arrived Infantry major, who cheerfully accepted the S&T S-3 job. Eric and I were assigned to the 11th Light Infantry Brigade and further posted to proper Infantry battalions where we belonged. By the way, we were also both wounded in action the same night.

My first assignment with the 3rd Battalion, 1st Infantry Regiment was as S-3. When the XO left, I replaced him. We had a succession of battalion commanders, including one relieved, and one killed in action. The best one was the last one, LTC George V. Ellis. He was a bold, brave leader, and a tried and true tactician. He respected his men and they respected him. He was a mentor and role model for me. I left the Battalion shortly before he did, but I never forgot him, and I never will.

I left the Battalion to be the Division Deputy G-2, working for LTC "CY" Nerone, a brilliant Infantryman, who gave me free reign to run the G-2 office, based on his broad, often visionary guidance. Meanwhile, he was "chomping at the bit" to command an Infantry battalion, which he soon did and well. During my G-2 stint, Eric and I got embroiled in the Peers Investigation into the infamous "My Lai Massacre."

In late 1969, I received a call from USARV headquarters informing me I had been selected for Leavenworth (the Command & General Staff College, not the Federal Prison). In a rare moment of modesty, I asked them to double-check my name and service number just to be sure they had the right man, because I had only recently completed the Advanced Course. They confirmed it was indeed me, so I left Vietnam in March 1970 to attend C&GSC.

Arriving at Fort Leavenworth early, I was tapped to teach our foreign students "Conversational English," and "The American Way of Life." The latter included tours to nearby attractions in Kansas City, Lawrence, and Topeka. It was a lot of fun, and a learning experience for me. I even made friends with our Iranian students. I often wonder whatever happened to them and their families. I hope it was good, but fear it was bad, given what has happened in Iran since then.

My Leavenworth experience was a happy one for my family and me, with one exception. The housing lady informed me that coming to C&GSC in my first year of eligibility entitled me to live in St. Joseph, MO, some 35 miles northeast of the college. Fortunately, my lovely and resourceful wife Nancy resolved that problem by managing a 35-unit "luxury" apartment complex in Leavenworth, complete with swimming pool. We lived there in relative comfort with a very short commute. My sole duty was to maintain the pool.

In addition to my C&GSC studies, I took graduate-level courses from Kansas University and competed for a slot in their Graduate School, which I attended in 1971-72. We moved to Lawrence in June and I graduated the following summer with an M.A. in Political Science.

To my deep disappointment, I was assigned to CONARC headquarters as a Manpower Survey Officer. However, I did manage to convince Infantry Branch to let me go to Ranger School on the way. They thought I was nuts, but my persistence paid off. Two previous attempts in the 1960s were thwarted by knee and shoulder injuries, but I finally earned my Ranger Tab on November 9, 1972, at age 34. That was and remains among my proudest achievements in the Army.

During the mountain phase of Ranger training, I received a call from the Infantry Branch Chief, Colonel (later LTG) Bob Arter. He asked me to come to Infantry Branch instead of going to CONARC. I said, "YES!" of course, even though I had already moved my family to Fort Monroe, VA. I left them there until Tommy and Larry finished school. Meanwhile, I lived in a BOQ at Fort McNair, within walking distance of the old Infantry Branch location.

Duty in Infantry Branch was challenging, rewarding and, sometimes frustrating. I worked directly for LTC (later MG) Charles Bussey. He was a brilliant officer who demanded high standards of conduct and performance from his men, and he led more by example than by exhortation. When he left for the War College, LTC (later Colonel) Dave White replaced him. Dave was more laid-back, with a wry sense of humor, but he was also a great leader and a pleasure to work for. The 1970s were trying times for the Army. We were coming out of Vietnam after a long, arduous, and unpopular war that left the nation deeply divided. It was up to our civilian and military leadership to set things right, and restore the Army to its traditional and honored role as guardian of our Nation, and defender of our Constitution. To do all this while downsizing the force, doing away with the draft, and launching the new All-Volunteer Army was a tall order indeed.

In Infantry Branch, we had our share of challenges, too. One of our most onerous and odious tasks was the infamous Reduction in Force (RIF) program. We had to cut the Infantry Officer Corps in half through a series of ever-tightening RIFs that were devastating to the officers and their families who experienced them. The RIFs also hurt the morale and esprit de corps of officers not yet involuntarily released, but fearing they could be next. I will never forget sitting across my desk from a young Airborne, Ranger, Special Forces, Combat Infantry captain, with two Vietnam tours and a chest lined with ribbons, including the Purple Heart with Oak Leaf Cluster. He had just received his RIF notice, and had driven through the night to visit Infantry Branch for help in sorting out his options. Though I never let it show, I was seething with anger and frustration over the prospect of losing such a hero and good man to the vagaries of the RIF. I tried my best to explain the inexplicable to him, but could tell he was skeptical. Who wouldn't be, after serving and sacrificing so much, then being given the boot? The only saving grace for that officer was his prior enlisted service. Since he had served six years and attained Staff Sergeant, E-6 before being commissioned, he was eligible for reduction to that rank and retention in the Army. It was a bitter pill to swallow, but better than being tossed out of the Army he and his family so loved. Thousands of other fine officers would not be so fortunate.

I left Infantry Branch to work for Hal Moore, the Commanding

General, Military Personnel Center. I juggled a variety of administrative duties, including mountains of paperwork, speechwriting, and trip coordination for him. I thoroughly enjoyed working for General Moore and learned a lot from him. When he was promoted to LTG and appointed Army DCSPER, MG (later LTG) Robert Gard replaced him as CG, MILPERCEN. Bobby Gard was a gifted intellectual, a dynamic personality, and a workaholic to boot. He was also a visionary who saw the Army as it was, and imagined what it might become, if we all worked together to make it so. He was a joy to work with, and like General Moore, a mentor to me and countless others.

I left MILPERCEN to join the Office of the Secretary of the Army as a Legislative Liaison Officer, with duties in the Pentagon, and on Capitol Hill. Succinctly stated, I was one link in the critical chain of communications and coordination between the Army and Congress. My tasks were to explain the Army to Congress, and Congress to the Army. That meant working 24/7, when necessary, writing speeches, handling hearings, coordinating congressional trips, and so on.

After paying my penance to the Pentagon and vowing never to return if I could help it, I gladly departed for Hawaii and battalion command. I was honored and humbled to lead the 1st Battalion, 19th Infantry for eighteen months. Fortunately, I inherited a good unit. With the help of rock-solid officers, notably Major (later Colonel) Gorham Black, Captain (later Colonel) Clint Williams, Captain (later Colonel) Rich Kiper, and Lieutenant (later Colonel) Mike Bingham, plus topnotch NCOs, young soldiers, and families, I believe we made the unit even better.

We were also blessed with solid leadership from our 1st Brigade Commanders, Colonel Henry Doctor, Colonel Bill Klein and Colonel Burton (Pat) Patrick. Different in personality, they all led by example, did their duty and empowered us to do ours. I will cherish those memories until the day they lay me down. By the way, all three of these dynamic leaders went on to become general officers, deservedly so.

We returned to the mainland in 1979 and settled in lovely Lexington, VA, where I served for nearly two years as Chair of the Military Science Department at Washington & Lee University (W&L), a prestigious private college with roots dating back to 1749. Upon arrival, I discovered that Rank Hath Its Privileges (RHIP) among faculty was strictly observed. The Athletic Director informed me that as a full professor, I rated a wall locker in the faculty dressing room. He handed me an "official" W&L laundry bag, told me to toss my used racquetball clothes and towel in the hamper, and they would be promptly washed and returned to my locker the same day. They always were.

The ROTC Program at W&L was struggling with recruitment and retention when I took over. Our cadets were long on quality, but short on quantity. To cope with those challenges, I chaired several brainstorming strategy sessions with my staff and key cadet leaders. Based on recommendations from the latter, we decided to train our cadet leaders to become committed recruiters and retainers for ROTC at W&L. Once trained, they exceeded our expectations by attracting and retaining both quality and quantity scholars and athletes to our program. When I found out W&L did not award athletic scholarships, I persuaded the Athletic Director and some of his coaches to help us recruit and retain ROTC cadets and athletes. Armed with a sufficient number of ROTC scholarships, and looking for the same kind of potential leaders they were, it was a win-win situation for all.

We also re-energized our Adventure Training Program, which included getting cadet slots for Airborne, Ranger, and Air Assault training. The cumulative effect of these two innovations was to vastly increase our enrollment and retention of W&L ROTC cadets. I loved Lexington and I thoroughly enjoyed my W&L ROTC stint. So did my family. I told the W&L President if I had not been selected for promotion to colonel and to attend the Army War College, I would have stayed there until they made me leave, and I meant it. For me, ROTC duty was the next best thing to command of active duty soldiers, with many of the same challenges and rewards.

War College was another great experience. I learned a lot and met many excellent fellow students, some of whom would become lifelong friends. As I recall, Leighton O. Haselgrove and I were the only two there from our OCS class.

My next assignment was Deputy Chief of Staff/Executive Officer to the CINC, US Southern Command, General Wallace Nutting. It was an interesting time to be in Panama. We were in the implementation phase of the Carter-Torrijos Treaty. As with any treaty, the devil was in the details. So we spent a lot of time with our Panamanian counterparts and the Panama Canal Commission, hammering out those details. We got more "help" than we wanted from the US Department of State. Without getting bogged down in all that here, our challenge was to see the treaty commitments were smoothly executed in an orderly way that gradually transferred the Panama Canal, the trans-isthmus railway train, and all major US military installations to the Panamanian government. That challenge was complicated by events in other Central and South American countries, especially El Salvador, Nicaragua and Peru. We had a huge area of operations and responsibility, with a relatively small force structure, consisting of all services, with their Guard and Reserve components, carrying out a variety of missions. General Nutting was a dynamic leader with high standards of conduct and performance. He was a pleasure to work for.

When General Nutting left USSOUTHCOM in 1983 to command USREDCOM, and the new CINC brought in his own Executive Officer, I was offered the J-1 job, but turned it down. I was ready to leave Panama. At first, Colonels' Division urged me to take a joint staff assignment in the Pentagon, but I turned that down too. Instead, I went to the Air University at Maxwell Air Force Base in Montgomery, Alabama. My title was Chief, US Army Advisory Group. However, a typo in my orders indicated "Chef." We all got a laugh out of that! To be honest about it, Maxwell was like an extended R&R after the fast-paced, high-pressure environment at USSOUTHCOM Headquarters.

In addition to being the top Army advisor to the President, Air University, and the Commandant, Air War College, I taught various seminars at the college. I was also responsible for all the Army students attending classes there. To my surprise, I received a Legion of Merit for my service there, and was inducted into the Infantry OCS Hall of Fame at Fort Benning, GA. Still, Maxwell duty was a far cry from what I really wanted to do, command an Infantry brigade. Thank God and the US Army leadership, I was able to do just that.

In August 1985, I assumed command of the 1st Brigade, 25th Infantry Division, Schofield Barracks, Hawaii. My old friend and colleague, then-Colonel (P), Jerry White turned over to me a very good brigade indeed, and told me to make it better. During my two-year tenure, I did my best to follow his charge. I adopted the motto, "Lancers lead the way!", borrowed from the Ranger motto. My top priorities were to improve the Brigade's combat readiness across the board, even as we made the historic transition to "Light Infantry" status and took on a new cohort battalion. To test our readiness, we conducted a number of tactical and strategic deployments, including joint and combined exercises with the Air Force, Navy, Marines, and our allies around the Pacific Theater. Back at Schofield, we placed renewed emphasis on Expert Infantry training and testing, marksmanship, physical fitness, combined arms tactics, and maintenance. One of my first initiatives was the Lancer Leader Development Program, which covered officers and NCOs, all the way down to corporal. In essence, it identified, recognized, and rewarded leadership performance and potential by moving our officers and NCOs through positions of increasing authority, responsibility, and accountability, with the goal of preparing them to "be all they could be" as servant leaders in the Army.

Thanks to outstanding battalion commanders like LTC (later MG) George Close, LTC (later MG) Jim Mitchell, and LTC (later COL) Ben Wedding, Brigade XOs like Major (later COL) John Sullivan and Major (later COL) Cole Kingseed, CSMs like "Bernie" Bernier and "Rabbit" Stanfill, plus a superb brigade staff, we really did lead the way in all matters great and small, including hosting Vice President George Bush and commanding the All-Service Honor Guard for President Ronald Reagan's stopover in Hawaii on his way to Asia. We were also fortunate to have friendly competition from the 2nd Brigade, led by Colonel Roger McElroy, and the 3rd Brigade, led by Colonel Mike Sierra. We were doubly blessed to have my esteemed OCS classmate, Colonel (later Brigadier General) Joe Jellison commanding the Division Support Command. Joe's logistical experience and expertise were buttressed by his can-do attitude toward mission accomplishment. He was especially helpful to my brigade and to me personally, during the planning, preparation, and conduct of our many off-island deployments, most notably, to Japan and Thailand. By the way, his "better half" Evelyn was a great DISCOM First Lady, both gracious and helpful to my wife, Nancy.

For the most part, the command climate at Division and higher levels in Hawaii was conducive to outstanding mission accomplishment and taking care of soldiers and their families. For example, the 25th Infantry Division Commanding General when I arrived in Hawaii was "Mickey" Kicklighter. He and his wife, Betty were an excellent command team. They met us at the airport and were a pleasure to work for and with during our service together. General Kicklighter was replaced by General Jim Crysel, a tough taskmaster, who was eager to apply his considerable 101st Airborne and Air Assault experience and expertise to the new challenges of leading a Light Infantry division. Professionally speaking, I respected him, but personally speaking, I never really got to know him. Moreover, neither Nancy nor I got to know his wife, whose name escapes me. The ADC for Maneuver was BG Chuck Armstrong, a prickly personality and a difficult man to deal with. I can't speak for the other brigade commanders, but for my part, he was often more a hindrance than a help. I'll just leave it at that.

I left Hawaii for a brief, frustrating tour at US Forces Command, where I served as Chief, War Plans Division. After brigade command, it was, to put it mildly, a letdown, so I decided to retire in June 1988. I wanted to leave the Army I loved without fanfare, but Nancy insisted on a retirement ceremony worthy of my long service. Thanks to my regimental affiliation with the 187th RCT, 101st Airborne Division, we went out in style. My old friend and Infantry Branch colleague, BG (later MG) Bob "Fox" Frix presided over the ceremony and presented me with my second Legion of Merit. Following a reception at the Officers Club, attended by many Army friends and my own family and hometown friends, it was all over. Nancy, Tommy, Larry and I enjoyed a brief respite at the Fort Campbell Barsanti House with our dear friends Homer and Sue Kirby; then returned to our newly acquired home in our hometown of McMinnville, TN.

The Retirement Years

My retirement lasted about six weeks. I read six books and mowed the lawn six times, then realized I needed some new challenges, including a job! Thanks to radio stations owner, civic leader and new friend, Thorold Ramsey, I landed a job in radio, first as a country DJ, then as a "Town Talk" co-host, with Rob Jones. I also began a long and rewarding career as an adjunct instructor at Motlow State Community College. Working with McMinnville Center Director Melody Edmonds and our Administrative Assistant Monica Burgess was a special joy. Thanks to lifelong friend and hit songwriter, Jack White, I even embarked on fulfilling my dreams of being a songwriter myself. Together, we formed and founded Bob White

Music, Inc. At first, we were "all hat and no cattle," as they say in Texas. Then came hits by Neal McCoy, Charley Pride, Steve Wariner, and others. Since then, we continue to write and publish, more for fun than profit, but still solvent after all these years. Since Jack has done the lion's share of the songwriting, and all of the hits, I thank him for carrying me as a co-writer, and indulging me as President and CEO of our company. Another labor of love for me is my weekly newspaper column, My Turn, where I get to opine on whatever interests me.

Unfortunately, we lost Nancy to cancer in December 2005. After nearly forty-four years of marriage, I held her fragile hand, as her heart of gold stopped beating. She was a much better wife than I was a husband. She loved the Army, warts and all, just as I did. We had our ups and downs, as most couples do, but made some great memories along the way. RIP, my "Green-eyed Girl."

In May 2007, I met Betty Lusk, a former high school classmate, at our 50th class reunion. After a shaky start and a "non-date" dinner the next night, we didn't see each other for several months. Gradually, though, we became closer and closer, and became husband and wife on March 12, 2011. Now, when I count my blessings, I count Betty twice. She helped me find the faith I had lost in recent years, and to embrace that faith more fervently in words and deeds. Thanks to her, I now look forward to going to New Union United Methodist Church, and even filling in occasionally for our minister, Brother Tim Lewis.

Our blended family includes my two sons, Tommy and Larry; her three daughters, Delois, Donna, and Doris; five grandchildren, Dylan, Katelyn, Jacob, Josh, and Taylor; plus two great-grandchildren, Sophi and Rawley. Along with in-laws, we draw a good crowd for dinners and holidays in Pleasant Cove, TN.

As for the obligatory "What has it all meant?", I suppose I'm still sorting it out. For starters, OCS was a defining experience for me. It was a life-changing period, with a profound promise for a larger, more purposeful life. I entered OCS as a relatively new Staff Sergeant, E-6; I graduated as a Second Lieutenant of Infantry, a lowly O-1 on the officer totem pole, but with high hopes and a more professional attitude. Being with some of my OCS "Band of Brothers" and their ladies on our 50th Year Anniversary in Columbus and Fort Benning, GA recently, I was reminded to my core of that special time and special place, when "We were soldiers once... and young..." Now the years have flown and carried our youth along. Old soldiers now, we reminisce, and carry on. From the vantage point of fifty years, OCS was the gateway to greater service and success, in the Army, and far beyond. The proof of that shines in the lives of those of us who survive, and in the memories we share of those who have gone on.

My own life beyond OCS, and even beyond my Army career, continues to be fulfilling, made richer by faith, family, friends, and community service. Betty and I live a full and active life, and that's the way we like it. I've made the transition from "Rambling Man" to "Country Squire" with relative ease, thanks to Betty. Meanwhile, she's gone from tolerating dogs to liking Big Dog and Buddy "in their place," as in "outdoors." We both love to eat out or in, and we love to travel, but home in Pleasant Cove is where our hearts are.

A Thorn among Roses—Colonel (Retired) Thomas B. Vaughn with (left to right) Daughter Donna Manus, Wife Betty and Daughters Doris Stephens and Delois Bratcher, Miramar Beach, FL, June 8, 2012.

*Graduation Day for OCS Class 2-62, March 30, 1962,
Fort Benning, GA. Second Lieutenant Terry Vestermark
with his brother Gary, USMC, doing the honors.*

Prelude

My name is H. W. Vestermark. I was born in Iowa City, Iowa at a time
when The Great Depression was leaving by the back door and World
War II was on the front steps.

Although the patriotic fervor in the decade after my birth could
hardly have reached a higher pitch, it never occurred to me that I would
be a soldier someday. There was no military tradition in my family.
The least physically able of my uncles was the only family member to
serve, drafted, in a war zone, North Africa, in the 1940s. I didn't know

what OCS was until I began to consider military alternatives after high school and then only after I had enlisted in the Army.

Youth in Iowa

My father was an attorney. His father was Danish, and his mother was German. He was the fourth of seven children. His family moved from my father's birthplace, Rock Island, Illinois, to a farm near Wilton Junction, Iowa during World War I.

My grandfather abandoned his family and went to Chicago. My grandmother moved her children to Iowa City, a university town, where she could find work cooking and cleaning. Her children were all big and energetic. Four of them had school ability. My father was my grandmother's biggest challenge. In Rock Island he had climbed a black walnut tree with his brothers. He fell and broke both arms and one leg. Surgery saved the leg, but not the arms. My father heard his father tell the surgeon, "Let him die." The arms were amputated above the elbow. He was fitted with crude prostheses, but rejected them and never tried to use them again.

I never saw my father pick up a tool, but I saw him mow the lawn cushioning the handle against his stomach, paint the trim inside and outside the house holding the paint brush in his mouth, garden with a steel claw riveted to one shoe of an old pair of wingtips, harrow the garden pulling behind him like a draft horse a three-foot long platform with dozens of spikes driven through it and expose a broken sewer line by digging a trench the length of the backyard and five feet deep at the alley end of the property using a spade with a round and padded handle. He could never hold a wrench, but he could grasp words, writing by holding a pencil in his mouth and speaking, as a lawyer must be able to do.

My mother was an elementary school teacher. She was Scotch, the third of four children of my grandfather's three wives. Her mother died before she was ten, the second of my grandfather's wives to die young, and she was raised by her father and a half-sister. My grandfather worked in a bank in Vinton, Iowa where my mother was born. On the side, he bought and sold real estate and farmed. My mother taught in Dike, Fort Dodge and Grinnell, Iowa before her marriage. She cared for my father until the end, mothered four children and worked full-time as a teacher for three years when I, the oldest, was twelve and her youngest was two. She would have worked, as the Scotch would say, "on her bloody stumps," if necessary. In every respect, she was my father's equal. Unlike my "unchurched" father, my mother was a devout and earnest Presbyterian. (In college I had to read a book titled, *On God and Political Duty*, a book I still have in my library. It is a compilation of certain writings of John Calvin from his *Institutes of the Christian Religion* and his commentaries on the biblical books of Daniel and Romans. It evoked in me a zealous and moral thrill comparable to the martial thrill of hearing a bagpipe play "the tunes of glory.")

My parents' marriage, after a time, was not very comfortable, as are many marriages I suspect, but they endured. My relationships with them were uneasy after my early teenage years. They were, without question, the most remarkable people I have ever known. They gave me what I have that I value most, and what anyone might know about me that is of any importance may be discovered from what I have said here about them. It is a truism, but I am very much the child of my parents.

Time in Iowa City in the 1940s—the Iowa decade of my early life—was of two kinds: going off to war; returning from war. In the first half of the decade, we paid tokens for rationed gas, recycled all of our tin cans and saved grease. My father's garden was then called a Victory Garden. The mood was dark. In the second half of the decade, the town exploded with the return of veterans. The oldest brother of a neighborhood friend who delivered milk to our door sweated in winter. He had been in the Philippines and had contracted malaria. Amazing, we thought, to sweat in winter. Quonset huts sprouted like mushrooms on the university campus providing cheap places to live for the many who were the first to take advantage of the GI Bill.

During these two kinds of time, I was, for the most part, able to be a kid. I played every sport available to me, but liked baseball best. I sang in a quartet. There was dancing and delivering tons of newspapers and playing in the snow until I had to shovel the now packed-down stuff. I wandered around the campus of the University of Iowa and fished in the ponds near the Quonset hut communities and rode my bike all over town and out into the country, once to West Liberty to visit the birthplace of President Herbert Hoover. Actually, I wanted to see where one of my teachers lived. My father, who had participated in track at the university and was a good swimmer (he loved athletics and even tried golfing) was frequently asked to be a lane judge at track and swim meets and often invited me to go along. We went to football, basketball and baseball games and wrestling matches, too. And my father took me on long walks across the university golf course and into the fields and woods beyond. He was a great walker.

I was an indifferent student through 8th grade. I only cared about baseball, singing and girls, in that order. However, during those school years there were two adumbrations of the future. In 4th grade, one day staying after class to read a history book, I discovered that "narrative" interested me. This was promising, I felt and quickly filed the thought. In 7th grade, we <u>had</u> to read a long story. After avoiding a decision for weeks, I finally chose from the list, *The Black Arrow*. The first hundred pages were painful, but then the narrative suddenly left the earth behind for me. Again, I set the experience aside. Too much else was going on, and I wanted to focus on geography, which was the only subject I was good at because it was the only subject I liked.

My California decade, the 1950s, began to fall into place while we were still in Iowa when it became necessary for my mother to go to work. A university town in the midwest is an attractive place for lawyers to practice. The returning veterans were now educated, hungry and ambitious. The law can be a brutally competitive profession. It was a tough time for us. There were four children to support. We all stepped up. My mother got a job teaching in a little town west of Iowa City. My mother's father and brother helped. There wasn't enough day for my parents to do everything that needed doing. She was gone all day driving a beat-up 1937 Ford Coupe over treacherous winter roads. He was gone all day without bathroom care from morning until night. We were a ragtag and bobtail bunch, trailer trash kids living in a brick house, but we had been blessed with able bodies and minds, and parents who were doing all they could.

Youth in California

In the summer of 1952, a school friend asked me to help him unload a trailer piled high with watermelons trucked up from Arkansas. His parents owned a grocery store downtown. The melons were big, slippery and heavy, and it was hot, and once in awhile we would drop one, and it would split open. So sad! Later, in August 1952, we moved my mother and my two brothers and sister into a small apartment above a dry cleaners in Cedar Rapids, Iowa where she had gotten another teaching job. My father and I caught the train in downtown Cedar Rapids, destination Long Beach, California, "The Capital of Iowa," the ticket agent told us, which made no sense to me until later when I learned many former Iowans had moved to Long Beach, in addition to two of my father's brothers, which was what had decided us on the destination. The plan was for my father to find a job lawyering in California and reunite the family in 1953.

My father and I lived in one room without sink or private bathroom, two beds, two windows, two dressers, one table and one chair on the third floor of the downtown branch of the Long Beach YMCA near a fire escape above an alley. We were there for a year. One of my uncles paid our rent: $50 a month. Breakfast was a fresh pastry from a bakery around the corner, dry cereal, some fruit and milk, which we "refrigerated" when we could on the fire escape. I got a hot lunch at school. I don't know where my father ate lunch. I didn't ask. For supper, we would go to one of a half-dozen downtown restaurants, including a cafeteria where we discovered beef could be sliced so thin it was transparent. My 9th grade teachers knew our story—found out somehow—and circled the wagons. I got a second breakfast at school. One of the other residents at the Y told us drinking warm water helped. He was right. The staff at the Y and the residents also rallied around us.

My father studied California law all day. I studied all day too, and evenings and weekends, and I became a good student. It was a discovery! No more baseball, ever. No more singing, ever. No more girls, for awhile. The baseball and the singing were losses from which I have never stopped bleeding. No one had the psychic space to even think to ask me what I missed and might need, and I could not ask for what I needed because the needs of others were so critical to the family's survival. And, after all, I was living in a mansion in downtown Long Beach, the Pacific a half-mile away, and downstairs, television, pool and ping-pong tables, a weight room, a swimming pool, a sauna, two basketball courts, handball courts and an inside track. And, instead of fields and woods, my father and I could walk along the beach from the edges of the Port of Long Beach, south through The Pike, past Rainbow Pier to Belmont Pier and beyond to the jetty bordering Seal Beach and then back home. Today, where the Y once stood at the corner of 6th and Long Beach Boulevard, there is a CVS Drugstore, and across the street on the corner at 7th, still standing, is Ward's Drugstore where a pharmacist by the name of Trotter was kind enough to give me a job stocking shelves sixty years ago.

August 1953, my two brothers, sister and mother, bag and baggage, piled off a Greyhound bus at the station four blocks from the Y. They had hitched a ride from Iowa City to Barstow, California with someone from the University of Iowa and taken the bus from there to Long Beach. We rented a house for a year less than a mile from the Y, and my father started a 20-year commute to Los Angeles where he worked as a tax attorney for the US Treasury Department. I continued to be a good student in 10th grade.

The next year my parents bought a home not far from Belmont Pier. I commuted across town to the high school I had been able to walk to the year before and became not just an indifferent student, but a poor student. Study? Been there, done that. Basketball substituted for baseball and everything else. And the girls were very attractive. I had "a good time" in 11th and 12th grade. I got thrown out of second year Spanish, I repeatedly fell asleep in chemistry and I thought I was at least as good a clown as any of Shakespeare's.

But several interesting "academic" things did happen in high school. As a junior, I had to read *My Antonia*. It was the perfect story for an émigré from the flatland to read in California. It rended me from neck to navel, and marked a significant step up from *The Black Arrow*. And, as a senior, I wrote an essay on the poem, "Old Ironsides," for my girlfriend. The teacher remarked on her essay in class. I had never done anything like that before, and I never did again, though the combination of deceit and recognition was heady stuff. These two experiences gave me a better feel for how well-written narrative might sound.

The California scene in the 50s and the Iowa scene in the 40s, on the surface, closely resembled an episode from the sitcom "Happy

Days" and a Norman Rockwell painting, respectively, but the surface was prone to rupture: the sister of my friend with whom I unloaded watermelons was brutally murdered; a high school classmate was mysteriously electrocuted while taking a bath.

Officially, I did graduate from high school, but that was not how it felt. Somehow, I had managed not to be present, and it all just came to an unceremonious end. The years between 12 and 18 had been clouded by preoccupation with survival and transition. They had been lost to me, and I was lost, and I would spend the next three years floundering, trying to understand my sense of displacement, which was far more complicated than I realized at the time. Nonetheless, I managed to persuade a college admissions officer that my less-than-mediocre secondary school performance ought to be taken seriously, and I should have a chance. I got the chance and dropped out after a month. Determined to restore some semblance of promise to my future and get a second chance, I went to work to earn tuition money, enrolled in night school and applied for admission to another college. I got a second chance. And again, I dropped out after a month. Once again, in the course of fooling myself, I fooled and hurt others. The Director of Admissions bumped into me on the sidewalk as I was leaving the college library where I had been cleared for departure, and he said to me, "Well, you were a committee case anyway." My parents were only slightly less unhappy with me. I slept in the garage for a few weeks.

Now my drift was public. During the time I had been applying myself to a second chance at college, I had read *Letters From The Underworld*. As with *My Antonia*, this book seemed to have a similar physical effect; the top of my head had gone missing. Letters has been a great comfort to me throughout my "committee case" life.

I worked, but now aimlessly. I read. I hitchhiked to the Mardi Gras and back and then up the coast of California to Oregon and home again. I was a solitary beatnik and pre-hippie without the music, the clothes and the drugs and nonsense.

Through an acquaintance from my days of dutifully attending Presbyterian services, I was introduced to a small group of conservative Christians who were committed to a consistent translation and interpretation of the testaments fundamental to this religion. My association with this group was prolonged by a young woman, which proved fortuitous. I used this opportunity to thoroughly acquaint myself with the texts that are the foundation of the religious practice of the culture in which I grew up.

The shelf-life of the relationship with the young woman was brief and marked the beginning of the end of this three-year period of trying to find what seemed missing, as well as the end of my California decade. I hitchhiked to Denver in February of 1959 to convince the young woman I could be taken seriously as a marriage partner. She was wise. She loaned me her hooded winter coat, whose sleeves were too short, and I was soon on the road again, south across the Raton Pass to Albuquerque where I slept in the cab of a truck and then on to Grants, New Mexico, when there was only what seemed like a two-lane goat path through that town and where I stood for eight hours on the side of the road waiting for a ride farther west.

During this post-high school period of drift, I had worked very briefly for a cabinet maker, a Linotyper and a banker and for longer stretches as a school camp counselor, parking garage attendant and in warehouses in Long Beach and Los Angeles. There seemed to be no way through the malaise until the relative, who had nicknamed me "Terry," suggested the military. (The nickname derives from the Milton Caniff comic strip, *Terry and the Pirates*.)

Regular Army

I enlisted in the Army early in the morning, August 24, 1959, at an induction center on Figueroa Street close to downtown Los Angeles. My intention was to survive and behave honorably. My expectations were that I would be clothed, fed, billeted, nursed if necessary and challenged. I never intended to make a career of the Army, and I had no real understanding of what OCS might mean until basic training at Fort Ord.

I was discharged on September 11, 1964, a still very young First Lieutenant, finishing up at Fort Bragg. On the back of my discharge orders were orders assigning a number of the junior officers from the 82nd Airborne, some of whom I knew, to Vietnam. I was on my way out to try going to school, again. They were going into harm's way. I still remember standing outside battalion headquarters looking at the back of my orders. I had decided long ago this was what I wanted to do—move on, go to school. My time in the Army had finally put a foundation under my house. I had chosen, was choosing and would always choose to do something difficult for me to do, even though it may not seem like that to someone looking in from the outside, and I dimly recognized the consequential fork in the road this moment represented for me and others. I was very much like the inhabitant of a town hearing heavy artillery off in the distance firing the first rounds of a long siege from which I knew I would not escape without harm, a harm cousin to that experienced by many, many others like me who lived through the Vietnam War Era, of which I now had become a military member, suffering on the civilian side of the fence. I learned later that one of those named on the back of my orders, a graduate of The Citadel, had been killed in a mess hall when a Vietnamese child lobbed a grenade through an open window. For those many of us looking through the fence, some with an intimate knowledge of what it meant to serve in the armed forces, there would be other kinds of death and wounds: "We can find no scar, But internal difference, Where the meanings, are" as expressed in the poem, "There's a certain Slant of light."

During the enlistment process in 1959 at the main post office three blocks away from the Y on Long Beach Boulevard I had been unable to pick the Military Occupational Specialty I wanted: Army Security Agency. Why should I have thought the ASA would want a dreamy kid? I became a medic and went through two sessions at Fort Sam Houston after basic training. In the spring of 1960, I was back at Fort Ord, assigned to CDEC, Combat Development and Experimentation Center and administratively attached to an artillery battery. My unit was involved in field exercises at Camp Hunter Liggett about twenty miles west of King City, California on the edge of the Los Padres National Forest. We worked with staff from the Stanford Research Institute to figure out better ways to evacuate wounded from a battlefield.

Early in 1960 I had set my sights on OCS because it would be harder than what I could envision doing for the balance of my three year enlistment. I was beginning to acquire, let's call it, an enhanced capacity for focus. (The cost of not being a focused soldier is very high.) I began the process of applying to OCS: the paperwork and the requirement to have passed a recent PT test, which I had to take more than once because of the delay in the processing of my application. This version of the Army's PT test, destructive of joints and muscles in my opinion, was soon to be replaced, but until it was, it always left me almost unable to move and nauseous the next day.

In the late spring of 1960, I got my orders, but they were not to attend the 6th Army NCO Academy. Instead, I was on my way to an artillery battalion near a rural town in Germany about halfway between Nuremberg and Stuttgart. I had it on good authority that the battery clerk had repeatedly buried my OCS application, among other things necessitating the repeated PT tests. Nothing had ever passed between us and the only reason I could ever determine for the sabotage was that since he wasn't going to OCS, and to the best of my knowledge didn't want to, I wasn't going either. I have been indebted to him ever since with no way to express my gratitude for the delay I believe him to have caused.

I hitchhiked from San Francisco to Philadelphia, in less than three days, and in August, 1960, I boarded the USNS *Maurice Rose* in New York City, the same transport ship that on August 16, 1965 would take the two Ia Drang battalions of the 7th US Cavalry from Charleston, South Carolina to Qui Nhon, South Vietnam, with one port call in Long Beach, California. I was in steerage on the *Rose*. It was a rough crossing. I spent as much time as I could on deck, regardless of the rain and cool weather, trying to avoid seasickness, which I did.

Bremerhaven and all of Germany seemed to me a beautiful place, but the kaserne in Germany was about as unhappy a spot to work as any I ever experienced. There were a few World War II vets and a lot of Korean War vets in the battalion and a lot of young, homesick kids from the USA. Drink was a problem. Racial tension was more than just palpable. It was brutally acted upon on more than one occasion. This was a unit integrated in name only. I didn't always behave well and seriously thought of behaving even worse than I did. I would never have made it out of this duty station without my black friends: Bill Jones, Willie Williams and Crawford J. Parker.

I got off post in Germany every chance I could, and there were a lot of chances. They were giving three-day passes to anyone who was chosen Colonel's Orderly from the guard mount. They got sick of seeing my face around battalion headquarters. I was gone on a three-day pass almost every time I had guard duty. It was embarrassing. And, of course, I took vacations on top of my passes: Oberammergau in October to see the 1960 passion play; two or three times to Stuttgart and Heidelberg; to Salzburg, with Willie; Geneva and about ten days in Paris, walking from one end of the city to the other before going home and to Fort Benning.

My battery commander in Germany persuaded me to change my MOS to that of a chart operator in the fire direction center of one of the gun batteries: self-propelled 105's. It didn't take much persuading. I saw Grafenwoehr up close and participated in a Winter Shield exercise. We sent a scout at night to the closest gasthaus to bring back beer during Winter Shield, but not even cherry brandy could keep you warm in the damp cold of a German winter.

I attended 7th Army NCO Academy in Bad Tolz. At the time, it had a reputation for being the best in the Army. If my experience was any indication, it was the best. The kaserne itself was an amazing space built around a quadrangle. I shared a huge room with a sergeant who finished at or very near the top of the class. I was a somewhat fogged over PFC, and I learned a lot from him. Out our window of the kaserne, I saw Special Forces troops from the Bad Tolz detachment wending their way into the Bavarian Alps. I feasted on the terrain navigation and the compass course at Bad Tolz. It was a great experience for me, and I finished well.

Back with the artillery battery, and after weeks of rehearsing for port call, which consisted of some short-timer coming into the barracks and shouting out the news which triggered a response from every short-timer who was in the barracks—the response consisting of furiously unloading everything in your foot and wall lockers and stuffing it all into your duffel bag so that on the big day you wouldn't miss the boat—the big day came for me in August 1961; my ship came in: Bremerhaven and the *Rose* again.

It was an easier crossing. I had learned some things. This trip I had food in my duffel bag so I could eat when I wanted. And, I disregarded the Army dictum, "Never volunteer for anything." On the principle that nothing could be worse than confinement in steerage, I volunteered for an upper deck work assignment. It was where all the American teachers hung out, returning from a year abroad working in schools teaching the kids of soldiers.

Stateside, the same uncle who had been in North Africa during World War II, who had helped us during the hard times of my youth and who would continue to help us even in death, took me to see one of the last professional baseball games played in the Washington, DC area until the recent return of the Nationals. This same uncle watched in shock, utter disbelief, as I packed starched fatigues for OCS. "Starched fatigues!" He wouldn't let it go. I can still hear his voice. And to make matters worse, they were <u>fitted and starched</u>, and they didn't fit anymore, and I had to rip out all the stitching and have them tailored again.

OCS and Post-OCS Training

I don't remember much about my first day at OCS, except it was sunny and very warm, and there were a bunch of cadre hanging out on the steps of the barracks, a kind of knotted gauntlet I had to get past if I was going to report for duty. I do remember I was very glad I hadn't arrived earlier in the day.

I was assigned to the 5th platoon, which was the tail end of the alphabet, and though I was recently reminded by my first OCS roommate that the first candidate Company Commander was from the 5th, someone else from the 5th is the first one I can recall. I think there is a good reason for that. I was slowly shaking off being dazed, and this platoon mate was doing a clearly superior job with the assignment. I remember standing in the ranks and thinking to myself, "This guy is really good, and there is no way I am going to come close to this performance." From this ferret-like perception, there emerged rather quickly the realization that on the performance of the unit, inspired by its leader, my own survival and success was utterly dependent. This candidate went on to become one of the three distinguished graduates from the 5th platoon.

All three distinguished graduates of the 5th platoon, like those I am sure of the other platoons' distinguished graduates, wanted the honor, worked for it and earned and deserved it, which suggests what seems to me the most important and memorable aspects of OCS. It was a meritocracy. Achievement was impossible without mentoring and without that thing commonly identified as esprit de corps. The austerity of the life was not imposed, not something sterile, something like a prison sentence, as someone looking in from the outside might imagine, but rather something organic that arose from and served merit, achievement and the camaraderie which resulted in the training company and the 5th platoon becoming more than just a confederation of capable soldiers.

Every candidate understood they were being watched and judged by everyone for what felt like 25 hours a day. All knew this evaluation was critical, not merely for them personally, but most importantly for the group, because the group would someday become the unit whose success would enable the life of the individual, the unit and the larger civilian community to be sustained. We were being graded. There would be a ranking. There had to be a ranking and the ranking would be based, insofar as humanly possible, on the basis of who could best lead a unit on a mission and succeed. At the end of the course, based on my performance in the course, I knew where I stood, and I have always felt they got it right.

I had never seen before and I have never seen since the quality of mentoring I received in OCS. I don't think that assessment is vulnerable to the criticism it was mentoring uniquely suitable to the training of highly-disciplined, genteel killers. It is hard to characterize this mentoring. While I know of one instance where it may be the case that sadistic hazing occurred, what I experienced and witnessed was a form of support that was based on affection and an understanding of the course's difficulty. That difficulty for me had a certain twist. I lacked bona fide experience as an infantry leader. I had been an Army "specialist." I was not the only one in the 5th platoon or the company disadvantaged in this way, and while no one cut us any slack because of it, we were, I believe, mentored by cadre and peers taking this missing piece into consideration. Platoon mates and platoon tactical officers took us under their wings. In the case of the 5th platoon, this matter was dramatically illustrated for me by a change in tactical officers soon after the beginning of the course. I do not know what occasioned the change and only recently have I compared notes with my first roommate and learned his experience had been similar to mine in the sense that there seemed to be a negative tone to comments and assessments of performance by the platoon's first tactical officer, which with my lack of experience took on an insidious dimension weighted toward failure. My roommate on the other hand had genuine, relevant infantry experience under his belt. He was as committed and successful an infantry soldier, both as candidate and commissioned officer, as anyone in the company, and was one of the 5th platoon's distinguished graduates. His reaction to these critiques, in so many words, was, "Yes, sir. I will take it under advisement." Thus, he was able to shrug off what I allowed to become a festering doubt—until the change in platoon leadership.

I have not polled others in the 5th platoon, but I am as certain as I can be that Powell Moore's assumption of leadership of the platoon reversed the polarity from negative to positive for most of us. The tone of things now was, "We do think you have what it takes to be an infantry officer. You wouldn't be here if we didn't think so. How about trying…?" I really question whether I would have graduated if Powell had not taken over, and I am absolutely certain that if I had been able to stumble across the finish line under the leadership of his predecessor, I would have been unable to remember my OCS experience as a highlight and proud moment in my life, to say nothing of how it would have affected my post-OCS service.

Powell was not the only tactical officer who led in a way that built one up, and he was not the only tactical officer named Moore. The 3rd platoon had their own Moore, Charles A., and while I could only observe the 3rd's Moore and other tactical officers from a distance, their leadership style seemed to be the same or very similar to Powell's. Criticism usually took the form of an exaggerated, mock-disbelief that we could possibly have shown ourselves to be so wanting. Thus, what was true and disappointing, even perhaps disgraceful, was wrapped in a brotherly affection communicating that, no matter how far you had fallen short, the bond was not broken, and wouldn't be unless you summarily broke it. And any upbraiding was, I believe in the case of both Moores, delivered in a slow drawl, the affect of which was to make it just about impossible for the candidate to keep a straight face while at the same time enabling him to take the commentary with the utmost seriousness and not forget it. There is a picture of each Moore in the OCS 2-62 Classbook which conveys, as they say, "a thousand" times better what has been expressed here by me with words. (Note their facial expression and body language.)

"Esprit de corps" is another one of those "Humpty Dumpty" expressions. It's broken. And so is "team play." Of these two cracked usages, I prefer the latter because at some point in their life most have been on a team, at least a nominal team. I was lucky enough in school to play on a team once, only once. I came to understand what that meant when I subsequently played on a nominal team, which was like Major League Baseball's annual All-Star game. (I couldn't care less about watching a collection of talented individuals.) My experience on the nominal team had been pretty much the coup de grace for me for school athletics' esprit de corps. All five of us on the nominal team were good enough to play first string. We had all the tools. We were racially diverse: a black, a Latino, an Asian and two white guys. We lived around town at different points of the compass. We only saw each other on the court. We only looked like we were playing together. I thought there were no other five players as individually talented on any team in town. Our play was pathetic. We were not a team. It was just five kids who assembled for a few minutes each day.

There is an altogether different kind of pathos that occurs when there is no team and the circumstances are a matter of life and death. While the goal of the military unit may obscure, may even be used to consciously obscure, the possible ultimate consequence of the team effort, the goal is to avoid death and keep the community, the unit and the individual alive—in that order. Only because everyone is prepared to "leave it all on the court" is success a possible outcome. The thing that most bound us together in OCS 2-62, that trumped everything, even our tactical officers, is the same thing that binds us together today and would make it possible, should we have to do it, to assemble again. It is that, in spite of all our differences and because of our various competencies and diverse experiences, we understand this larger thing—the community that must be sustained—could die, if we fail to build and behave as a team. "If you build it, they will come," from the book *Shoeless Joe* and the movie *Field of Dreams* is a variation on the same theme. The Confederacy, after all, was a Union, and with or without it, there would be a Union.

It is a commonplace that this phenomenon made Sparta formidable.

If one hasn't experienced this *e pluribus unum* phenomenon, a military unit's movement, whether marching or maneuvering, gives the appearance of a childish, silly and ghastly choreography. A.N. Whitehead was not thinking of small unit tactics when he wrote this, but it is, I believe, not inappropriate to give his comment a passing glance: "The many become one and are increased by one."

I do not exaggerate when I say that I loved my time at Fort Benning—OCS and especially jump school and Ranger training. I thought it was a beautiful place. There was nothing on post that didn't need to be there, even the museum, such as it was at the time. It was like a good story: every word mattered. It was the right kind of cloister for me at the right time. Fort Benning has been and still is one of the country's most important posts. Returning for our reunion fifty years to the day after our Gold Bar Day, I was saddened to note many buildings that seemed to want for care. Other needs, it appears, as they no doubt should, have taken priority. Still, it is too bad that a place as important as it has been, and still is could use some buffing up, which it is unlikely to get.

Until we "turned blue," and among other things no longer had to run everywhere instead of walk, I cannot remember any sensual pleasure except going to the bathroom and showering. After "Blue Day," my idea of a good time was to get up early on Sunday morning, catch the bus to downtown Columbus and walk to the Ralston Hotel. There, in a high-ceilinged dining room, I would have breakfast on a white linen tablecloth: toast, two eggs sunny-side up, sausage, grits, kadota figs in heavy cream and coffee—all the great southern comfort food, topped by reading the Sunday edition of the *Atlanta Constitution*. I had had all the extroversion I could stand for six days a week, and Sunday was for feeding the introvert.

Jump school and Ranger training were like Bad Tolz on steroids—a feast for me, by which I do not mean to imply they were a piece of cake. Each day there was something hard for me to do, that I might not be able to do, but had to succeed at. I loved the exertion this training demanded. Conclude what you may, but the harder something is for me to do, the better I like it. And, I was not going to my first and only duty station, Fort Bragg, without passing these tests. I had a great Ranger buddy from the OCS 4th platoon who made it all possible. It was one of the best times of my life, and it was hard to see my Fort Benning year come to an end: October 1961–July 1962.

Somehow, I had managed to get an assignment to the 82nd Airborne. I was shocked. I suspected strings were pulled by my family, and made inquiries. No, I was told, it didn't happen that way. Odd, that of all the assignments I might have chosen, if it hadn't been the 101st, I would have chosen the 82nd, and would have felt—even had I been able to choose—exactly the same as I did on the day of the announcement: Do I really deserve this, and will I be able to make the grade? I had finished OCS some distance from the distinguished graduate category, and I had no infantry experience. I left Fort Benning for Fort Bragg, uncertain.

82nd Airborne Division

I reported to my battle group in July 1962. The Sergeant Major of the 325th had landed with the 82nd in Normandy in a glider. He had a hard time saluting me. It seemed there was always some question, for him and for me, as to whether it was going to happen whenever we crossed paths. I think he rather felt as though I should be carrying his briefcase and walking on his left and a half step off his shoulder. I can't say that I blamed him. Thanks to my mother's genetics, I have always looked ten years younger than I am, and I looked like a teenager. He probably suspected there was a chance I would be acting like one. If that is what he thought, he didn't miss the mark by much over the next six months.

I struggled. To this day, I am not certain why. Some of it had to do with awe. Some of it had to do with garrison soldiering. Some of it had to do with not being in it for a career. Some of it had to do with my chronic dreaminess. Some of it had to do with, "Is that all there is?", a sort of letdown after the intensity of three years striving to reach this sweet spot. I am still embarrassed to recall some of the things I did and didn't do the first six months. But, as with almost every teacher I have had over my whole life, it was not for want of my leaders in the 82nd trying to help me. They were very patient.

A strange thing happened two years later when I was a month or so from leaving active duty. I had earned the respect of my leaders and peers. I could finally hold my head up and there was talk of assignments

I was being considered for, which were not to be, when one day passing a young second lieutenant on the battalion grounds (we were no longer a battle group) he stopped me. I cannot remember exactly what he said or how I tried to respond to him, but the heart of the matter was that he was floundering, just as I had been, and which perhaps he had heard about. He was a West Point graduate, and there was no more "long, gray line." There were only long hours of garrison soldiering away from his young spouse. I understood, and I think I was able to convey my understanding. I don't believe we ever spoke again, and I don't know what happened to him, but I still remember his name.

In August 1962 the division and other units were involved in Swift Strike, a large scale jump and field exercise in South Carolina. In September, I was called into the S-1's office. The S-1 was one of the captains who graduated with me from the Ranger course and later became a Company Commander in the battle group. A levy had come down the chain requiring the 82nd and other units to provide junior officers for a temporary assignment in California where he knew I had family. He asked if I was interested. We talked about it not being the best way for me to sink my teeth into being a platoon leader in Bravo Company. It would truncate the process. But I had no momentum going for me at Fort Bragg, and my family was in another tight spot. I took the assignment and was gone for most of October and November—missing the tension of the Cuban missile crisis—back at Camp Hunter Liggett working for CDEC. The day I returned to Fort Bragg, the 325th was on stand-by and was alerted to muster that night. In my absence, new web gear had been issued, but not to me or on my behalf. I was the only member of the battle group at the muster carrying a horseshoe-roll pack.

I am not sure whether this was the nadir for me or not, but at some point that winter, I said to myself something like, "Look! This is what you wanted to be. Right? So, be it!" Yet, even this misrepresents the consciousness of the reversal. I had taken careful note of what was going on around me, and then one day, unnoticed by myself, enough had become enough. And, I accelerated, powered by my disgust with my past performance: "Okay. My turn!"

I got the chance to be the Bravo Company Executive Officer. Then there was an opening at battle group headquarters. They needed a new

S & T platoon leader, and, of course, no one wanted it: Supply and Transportation; S-4; logistics? But an interesting thing happened. I was talked to by the outgoing S & T Platoon Leader who happened to be Al Gross. Al had been a distinguished graduate of OCS 1-62, the class just ahead of ours. I remembered our class marching or riding past the parade grounds where the 1-62 distinguished graduates were rehearsing for their graduation ceremony. There was Al, back to us, ramrod straight, standing at attention for what seemed forever. Al had ended up in the 325th, but we had never spoken about anything of consequence. Everyone knew he had taken over an S & T platoon in disarray and turned it into a showcase. I was offered the job and took it. I saw up close what Al had done and could do, and I followed in his footsteps, maintaining what I had inherited from him and trying to improve upon it where I could. He was a mentor and a friend. I enjoyed the assignment and did well. It seemed to me to be all about imaginative anticipation and diligent fulfillment of the battle group's logistical needs. It was "a pitch in my wheelhouse," and I "turned on it." The Army reorganized its divisions and the battle group was split up into battalions. I became a battalion S-4, and in 1964, I left the Army in that capacity as a first lieutenant. (I read with interest the account of the actions of a battalion S-4 at Ia Drang in *We Were Soldiers Once... And Young*.)

Going To School For Good

My time in Sparta could have been better, if only I had made it so. Nevertheless, I walked away from Fort Bragg feeling very good about what I had done there. I had been on the brink of letting down a lot of people and an organization I felt honored to join, and I ended by not having to lug around the baggage of that sort of disappointment for the rest of my life.

Now it was time to move to Athens. I traded the dogwood blossoms of a North Carolina spring, floating among the pines, and the scent of dropped pine needles on a hot summer day in the woods, for another state famous for its woods and pine, Maine, where I earned a bachelor's degree reading history and literature and philosophy.

However, once again, in October 1964, I came close to bolting from academia for a third time. It just didn't agree with me. What I needed was a skill, a trade or a craft to live on and to support my addiction to speculation, imagination and meditation. I had heard of Baruch Spinoza and Eric Hoffer. They were the models, but I still hadn't understood what they were signaling. My post-high school work in a cabinet shop had been my first failed attempt to locate myself and understand my genealogy: a journeyman dreamer, who badly needed to work with his hands while engaged in the solitary inclinations that appealed to his temperament.

It was a Friday in October 1964, end of the college week. I was in class. My advisor was teaching. Class over, we walked out of the building together along the basement corridor. It was a crushingly beautiful autumn afternoon. Heartbreaking. I said some things to him. He took me by the arm and to supper with his wife and children. It was the end of my bridling over the academic bit in my mouth. I soon found my community-within-the-community. It included other faculty and a few students, foremost among them the woman I would marry, and to whom I am still married; and two men who, in different ways, didn't survive the Vietnam War Era. I studied as hard as I could, but I was a middling student. It was a hard place for me to go to college. I managed to graduate: a crucial experience and one I cannot imagine—like my experiences at Fort Benning and Fort Bragg—having lived the life I have, missing that unique time and place.

As college was ending, a storm was forming within my family that would permanently alter or affect, in one way or another and for the rest of my life, every relationship I had and was to have. It concerned Vietnam, but not the issue of whether our country should be in a war there, about which at the time I had no opinion. Instead, it had to do with the circumstances surrounding the decision of one of those two men to whom I was closest, to leave college and enlist in the Marines. He had been counseled to consider doing so by me and the same relative who had suggested the military option to me in 1959. The difference, of course, was this: a war was raging.

The storm didn't hit until we had buried my friend in Arlington: a Second Lieutenant who did not survive the Tet offensive. The foul weather in my family specifically involved a written exchange between me and my relative. I fired the first shot in the exchange. As in a duel, my shot was grazing. The return shot was nuclear. Though it is far from perfectly analogous, I sometimes think of that duel as I do Alec Guiness' performance in *Tunes of Glory*, which I understand was his favorite movie role. Along with *Breaker Morant*, it is my favorite movie about soldiering. It was imperative for Guiness' character, and absolutely necessary for those dependent upon his character, that he expose the leader of his unit. This required him to act in a deeply conflicted way. Was his behavior selfish or selfless or indistinguishably both? His action destroyed the credibility of the leader, which, arguably, should have been destroyed, for the leader was not what he appeared to others to be, and the risk posed to others by his fraudulence was truly a matter of life and death. As a consequence, the leader took his own life. The consequences of the deed for the Guiness character, the psychic collateral damage he sustained, marked him, but he assumed the leadership role of his deceased superior. His conflicted behavior was messy. It was not selfish. It was not selfless. It was both, flashing between these poles like an electrical charge, indistinguishably lighting up both at once and grounding itself with roots like cancer extending throughout the body in directions one cannot imagine and doesn't want to know, unfailingly seeking out and finding the fraudulence in another and in one's self. It was the lesson of a lifetime, which I am still learning. Sometimes books like *Tunes of Glory* make better movies. This may be the case for *Breaker Morant* as well.

I was eight months out of college when the Tet offensive commenced on January 30, 1968. Things got worse. Everyone knows the story: King and Kennedy assassinated; President Johnson refusing both to help win the war or get us out and telling us he would not seek, nor would he accept a nomination for a second full term as President. For the first and only time in my life, I had to resist throwing a hard object at the tube's image of my President. "Don't run away from this, LBJ. Give Westmoreland what he needs or get us out. Either alternative necessitates your continuing as President." I was outraged by LBJ's behavior.

After graduation from college in June 1967, I took a job as a laborer in a paper mill and walked off the job at the end of the summer because in every respect I was unable to perform. It was the only time I ever walked off a job, and I still regret it. In the fall of 1967, I worked as a laborer rebuilding a generator on one of Maine's dams. Then, until

Tet, I did nothing except read and fiddle around with narrative. After Tet, I did nothing except bury my friend and be angry and grieve. My wife supported us teaching school. Following her lead, I took a job in September 1968 at a different school teaching the same grade level.

In December 1968, the return shot from my relative arrived by what we now call snail mail: 40 pages, typed, single-spaced. It was a breathtaking misuse of confidences and my personal history, betrayal of trust and revelation of character by a person whose mellifluous verbal sadism, rigorously disciplined and masked, tinged with necrophilia and weaponized by a formidable intellect I was just beginning to understand after a lifetime of very close family contact. As we know now, all too well, the family is the preferred hunting ground of the abuser. I believed I had offered this person an opportunity for painful and intimate dialogue concerning the death of my friend, but what occurred was the breaching of "the citadel of my integrity," as one of the author's experiences in *Seven Pillars of Wisdom* is summarized. The hue of the lens with which I looked back at my experience as a soldier had been stained.

I could not continue teaching. The kids and teachers were great, but it was the hardest work I had ever tried and sadly underappreciated and unrewarded by our culture. It seems to me it is becoming more obviously visible that we have a national tragedy in our collective failure to nurture our form of governance by means of the education of our people.

In the spring of 1969, I responded to an ad on the front page of the local paper: Welding lessons; $5 an hour. I had never seen my father pick up a tool, but on my mother's side there was a blacksmith from Glasgow. After 20 hours of lessons, I took and passed the State of Maine test for "Metal-Arc Welder." I still carry that certification card. It was another example of my good fortune with teachers: Earl Bacon, Steamfitter.

And so was birthed and begun in earnest, and for the first time with some clarity, a 15-year period of supporting my addiction to dreaming-my-way-through-life, working as a welder in factories, foundries and machine shops in Maine, California, Oregon and Minnesota. Even more than my time in the Army, these were my "years before the mast." They were mine, not by default. This was the work and the time of my life that best fit me. During this period I also earned several graduate degrees and various certifications, always keeping my hands on a tool, always returning to the shop. After class one night in the spring of 1974, I was walking back to my office across campus with one of my students (I was a graduate teaching assistant being paid by the university, while working full-time in a factory and taking the G.I. Bill for my years of military service) when she asked me if I was going to teach after graduation. I think I was more surprised than she when I said no, I was going to stay in the factory.

I had, and still have, never been able to grasp the notion of a career, in any context. What I understood, wanted and found was work: essentially, a series of odd jobs which challenged and interested me, beginning with my two years at Fort Bragg, which was my first good job and one of the three best of my life. Indeed, I could conveniently divide my life into two periods of odd jobs: before Fort Bragg and Fort Bragg, and after. The difference between the two is that the odd jobs before tended to be of shorter duration and much less interesting.

This 15-year period ended only because of the effects of the physical labor on the good body I had been born with. Before it ended, I was also able to do the other thing in my life which, aside from supporting my addiction, I most wanted to do: found a family. We have two children, both of them educators.

During this 15-year period, and subsequently, I paid serious attention to my love of narrative, understanding that term in the broadest possible sense, and to a concern I will mention as expressed in *Man's Search for Meaning*. Certain other narratives, too, were like buoys on the voyage, and since my life has been very much about books, a few, arguably the most influential, are important for me to mention, for, along with what I have said here about my parents, their authors and my wife have been my best friends, and they, better than anything, tell the story of what I have been about: *Under the Volcano; Living; The Diary of a Country Priest; The Idiot; Waiting for Godot; Call It Sleep; The Iliad or The Poem of Force; Gravity and Grace; Interpretation Theory: Discourse and The Surplus of Meaning; Process and Reality; The Book of Privy Counseling*.

My graduate school years were blessed with good teaching which enabled me to write and think about narrative in a far better way than I would have been able to do without these experiences. My academic concentration was on the fabrication and interpretation of narrative. As one of our children, whose primary interest is in studio art, remarked at a tender age, "If you don't have composition, you don't have anything." I have been interested in many things, but graduate school met, head on, my tendency to be too diffuse, and it focused my interest: to clarify, in a personally meaningful form, the expression of our blind, groping, forward-moving direction as a community. My father's fact-orientation had come forward to balance my mother's intuition, which was like a cat's Jacobson's organ, a sixth sense.

After 15 years of directed drift—far better focused than during my pre-Fort Bragg life and significantly enhanced by my years at Fort Benning and Fort Bragg—I was almost done with the education I thought I needed, and my body was beginning to be done with long hours of heavy lifting. I said goodbye to that sort of labor and to my mentors and bosses, Bill Angleton and Dick Hill, both among the four or five best bosses I ever had, and I took up "the family business."

One of my brothers was practicing law at the time. I had never seriously considered the law as a profession, and I wouldn't for a few more years, when I then did realize this was probably another "coulda," but one for which I no longer had time. I needed an alternative to fabrication welding, fast! I went to school, again, to obtain certification as a legal paraprofessional, and I worked in this capacity for 28 years in the corporate law departments of Prudential and American Express. These were experiences rich beyond anything I could have imagined. Among other things, a strong residue of these 28 years is my respect and admiration, in spite of all the lawyer jokes, for what had been my father's profession. If I had to choose between a doctor who could keep me alive, though I lived under tyranny, and a lawyer who could keep me free, though I lived with sickness, I would choose the lawyer. Better to be free and sick than healthy and tyrannized. Or, as they like to say in New Hampshire, "Live free or die!" A half step behind that rallying cry is the one of the Queen of Battle, "Follow Me!"

Epilogue

I was on active duty far longer than I expected to be. The CDEC battery clerk dramatically changed the course of my life. I have some regrets about not having stayed in the Army for 20 years or more, but to express what I mean when I say that would require a perspective closer to the ground than I can offer in this high-altitude overview of my life. After I left Fort Bragg, I never again sought a leadership role. The reason for this was not that I didn't enjoy it or believed I wasn't good at it. I enjoyed other things more, and wanted to become as good at doing them as my capacities would allow. I have always been, and always will be proud of having been a soldier, and honored to have been associated with those of my OCS classmates who were born to the warrior class and for much of their life bore the risks of soldiering.

As for my life, on balance it has been good and the right kind for me: quiet, more often than not, and about as reflective as I could tolerate. To quote Breaker Morant, "I've seen [the world]. I've had a good run." I hope to die with a book or pencil in my hand having just glanced up to look out the window a last time.

With regard to what it all means, from my vantage point in St. Paul, Minnesota in early December 2012, I do indeed wonder, vaguely aware of a fleeting sense it is presumptuous of me to wonder, even as it delights me. We are at the mercy of a process we struggle to understand on an azimuth that includes arbitrary death. The fact that "meaning" does not appear susceptible to a satisfying finality of expression underscores our vulnerability to change, and agitates us, compels us to wonder and convinces us to ask. But, is it possible to ask about or for anything, and actually believe the gesture is made in a vacuum; believe that the act does not occur in a context, a conversation, a relationship and, in particular, that reciprocity is not fundamental to asking? I believe the author of *Man's Search for Meaning* has set foot on the path of the better fork in the road when he says, "What was really needed was a fundamental change in our attitude toward life. We had to learn ourselves and, furthermore, we had to teach the despairing men, that *it did not really matter what we expected from life, but rather what life expected from us.* We needed to stop asking about the meaning of life, and instead to think of ourselves as those who were being questioned by life—daily and hourly." (Italics are the author's.)

As all of our parents said to us, at one time or another, "You've got a bad attitude!" And, it is very likely they followed up that assessment with the injunction, "You better straighten up and fly right!"

"When true simplicity is gain'd,

To bow and to bend we shan't be asham'd,
To turn, turn will be our delight,
'Til by turning, turning we come 'round right."

These words of the author of the famous Shaker hymn and those of the author of *Man's Search for Meaning* seem to me to suggest that posture shapes the reciprocity fundamental to asking. Posture: hardly something to lure one, overwhelmed as we are in our culture with distractions intended to satisfy our vast and complex appetite for distraction. Or, to cast the same sentiment in the form of a sardonic aphorism, borrowing the style of the author of *Mystery and Manners*, if you can only learn how to distract people from the sense of their own fraudulence, you can make a lot of money, and additionally, they will be grateful to you, if not eternally—for as long as they have to live.

Authenticity eludes us, "'Til by turning, turning we come 'round right."

Terry Vestermark, wife Paula, daughter Leah on her
wedding day, and son Jesse, June 15, 2012.

First Lieutenant (later Lieutenant Colonel) Ken Weitzel, Korea, 1963.

I am 72 and I don't know how I got here.

The Early Days

I grew up in Berea, Ohio. The city was home to a small college that influenced the quality of education in the community. It was not a perfect environment, but it would have made Norman Rockwell proud. While I have fond memories of Berea, I lived on the wrong side of the tracks in a post-WWII public housing project built to accommodate returning veterans. Most of my childhood years were spent in old Army barracks that were disassembled on some distant Army installation and reassembled outside of Berea. A standard wooden barracks was subdivided into four family units. About half of the families were on welfare, had six or more children, and only one parent. I was lucky. I had two loving parents and three siblings who were less loving. We were poor, but I never knew it.

The town fought the development, and never accepted the presence of the people who lived there. I never felt like I lived in Berea. I felt like I was viewing the city through a window in my project home. I was driven to be "normal," which meant to move from the projects and live in a real house. I recall waking up my first morning in Basic Training and thinking, "Oh Christ! I am back in the projects again."

My formal schooling started at the local Catholic elementary school. I was an outstanding student, an altar boy at Mass and a crossing guard. I was the complete package. Hell, I even sang in the choir. The traveling priest recruiter honed in on me and I was subjected to quarterly meetings with him for over four years. Little did he know there were two sides to me and the one he didn't know was an absolute terror. I was always in trouble for what were really only small transgressions against humanity.

My father wanted me to attend an all boys' high school, but I decided that I was already Catholic enough and I did not think I was lacking in boy skills. So, I was off to Berea High and a mixed gender candy shop. Public high school was not a continuation of splendid academic excellence for me. I flunked my freshman year, which I didn't mind at all because I was able to set a record as the only student who played point guard on the freshman basketball team for two years. The pattern of my first year, being the "smart aleck" and taking nothing seriously, continued through the rest of my high school years. I was, however, able to take summer courses and graduate on time. My class standing even improved to 285 out of 286. I often wonder whatever became of 286. I don't recall his full name but we called him Barry or Barack.

Although it seemed unlikely, I was determined to go to college. No one in my extended family had ever gone to college. My father wanted me to work for him in his homebuilding business, but my mother convinced him to give me a shot at college.

Lacking money for college, I read college catalogues in the school library with one screen: Was it cheap? I settled on Kentucky State College and made application. My high school yearbook for 1958 had a notation that I would continue my academic pursuits at Kentucky State College. A rejection letter arrived soon after my application was received. It seemed that I was ahead of the civil rights movement and the all-black college was not ready to integrate by accepting its first white student. Over the years I have fantasized about liberal members of my class who must have been so proud that I was one of the leaders of the civil rights movement. Ultimately, I settled on nearby Kent State

University. The tuition was inexpensive; I could come home every weekend; and it was known for its relatively low academic standards—a perfect fit for me.

My parents struggled to scrape up the money for college but resources were short. After two quarters where I mostly played, the money ran out and I could not return to Kent State. As I explored my options, I feared that if I took a job with a goal of returning to college, I would not make enough to cover living expenses and also save for college. I would fall into the same rut with everyone else in my family, and never get a college education. I never wanted to be in the military, but while at Kent State, I met Korean War vets who were using the GI Bill to pay for their educations. They always appeared to have money to spend. I determined their financial condition by the fact they were always drinking beer when I went to my favorite spot. The GI Bill had expired, but there was active legislation pending to reinstate the program. Out of all other options I joined the Army for three years, confident that the GI Bill would get passed in time for me to return to college after I finished my enlistment.

Army Life

My goals were to get the Army out of the way, qualify for the GI Bill, and return to Kent State for my degree. Three years in the Army turned into twenty-one. I never used the GI Bill benefits, but I did return to Kent State.

Basic training at Fort Knox confirmed my beliefs that I never wanted to be in the military. I adjusted to the new life only because there was no other option. My survival instincts kicked in, driven by fear of what I thought at the time to be demented drill sergeants. The eight weeks of Basic passed quickly and the desired transformation from civilian to soldier was completed.

As I look back on those eight weeks and the following twenty-one years, I view the military as a largely under-appreciated player in the civil rights movement. The Army, principally through the draft, brought together people from all segments of American society. The rich met the poor. The white met the black, brown and yellow. The highly educated met the undereducated. The rural met the urban. The military was a great mixing bowl with but one goal, to provide for the National Defense. The unintended additional benefit of this mixing effect was the role it played in reducing the strain on a society seeking to move toward equality.

My first assignment after Basic was to the 24th Air Defense Artillery in Philadelphia. Most people under 50 are probably not aware that missile sites designed to provide air defense against Russian attack once ringed major cities in America. I played a "critical role" in the functioning of the unit. Without my skills as a clerk typist, no one would have been able to get a new military ID card. I seemed destined to type ID cards until my enlistment was up, which would prepare me for a career at a drivers license bureau.

As I look back at major turning points in my life, there was always someone who played a pivotal role. In this case, it was my unit commander, Captain Edward Zabarowski, who changed my direction. He encouraged me to take the competitive exam to attend the United States Military Academy Prep School. Slots at West Point were reserved each year for active duty enlisted personnel. Selections were made from the ranks of those who completed the nine-month Prep program. I never expected to be selected to attend, but I scored well on the test and received orders to report to the school.

The primary goal of the Prep School was to prepare students to take the College Boards and to score high enough to qualify for the Academy. For most of the candidates, the academics were a refresher. For me they were base subjects I had not previously mastered. The academics were brutal, and the prize at the end stimulated us. For me, Prep School provided the ideal environment for learning. I was taught how to learn, how to speed read, how to retain information, how to study and much more. Our academic day was structured as six core courses and four hours of study. We were tested in all subjects every three weeks. You were on probation if you flunked any of these tests and booted out if you flunked a second test. This combination of structure, discipline, focus and consequence was exactly what I lacked in the past. I finished the program, but did not score high enough on the College Boards to be selected. The experience was not wasted. The Prep School was the impetus for my desire to become an officer.

Dick White, Bill O'Neill (nephew of the to-be-Speaker of the

House) and I were the closest of friends. All three of us were transferred to Fort Myer after Prep School. To his credit, Dick ended up as a guard on the Tomb of the Unknown Soldier.

Dick and I decided to apply for OCS, but I had a problem that I was sure would disqualify me. In the closing weeks of school, Speaker O'Neill offered Bill an opening to the Merchant Marine Academy that was available from a North Dakota congressman. Bill was not interested, so Speaker O'Neill made the offer to me contingent on interviewing with the congressman the next day. I signed out for sick call and went to the interview. When I returned, I turned myself in for an honor violation and I was demoted to E-2. Dick was there at my turning point. He urged me to apply for OCS and take my chances in front of the board. If not for him, I probably would have finished out my enlistment and returned home. To this day, I cannot fathom how a board of officers could look at my record of service and select someone who was recently reduced in rank to private. I can only assume that attendance at the USMA Prep School weighed heavily in their decision.

Officer Candidate School

I entered OCS probably as the lowest ranking person in our class. Besides the Prep School, my military experience was nine months of typing ID cards. I was never in charge of anything, never gave an order to anyone, never marched troops or knew the commands to do so. Dick White was in a similar boat. What are the chances that we could compete with the experience levels of folks who had been platoon sergeants, squad leaders, Ranger and Airborne graduates? Dick was selected as the first platoon leader as OCS began and I was the second. We were dismal failures. The first peer reviews ripped the two of us up. The only saving grace for us was the personal responsibility fellow candidate Thomas B. Vaughn took to mentor us. I appreciate the greatness of this man more today than ever. While others saw us as road kill, Tom saw potential. We made it because of him and later because of Lieutenant Powell Moore as our Tactical Officer. I am forever grateful to both of them.

OCS actually was not that demanding if you already knew the roles and responsibilities of leaders of squads and platoons. OCS built on that foundation and transitioned NCOs to the mindset expected of an officer. Dick and I were learning in reverse. Prep School focused us on the mindset of an officer, but little on small unit leadership. A seminal event for me was being assigned to the Bivouac Chain of Command as the Transportation Officer. Up to that point, OCS was an exercise of the leader leading the willing. As Transportation Officer, I had to lead the unwilling at a time I knew failure meant elimination for me. The supporting troops from the Transportation Company quickly tried to establish that this was a game for them and they were not interested in following a toy soldier. Suffice it to say, I rose to the occasion, but this event solidified my love for the challenge of leadership and the feeling of success.

Graduation day remains one of the fondest memories of my life. My loving parents and my aunt traveled from Berea, Ohio to be there and to pin on the gold bars. No one in my family had ever earned such an honor. Between the USMA Prep School and Infantry OCS, a wandering dolt had been transformed. Success breeds success, or at least it did with me. For the first time in my life, I was dedicated to something greater than me. For the first time, my performance equaled my potential. I cannot recall a moment following that when I didn't give my absolute best. Others might outperform me, but no one would try harder. I never competed with others, I competed with myself and I seldom won. I built two careers on the basis of these two schools, and I had a hell of a good time along the way.

My Commissioned Career

Following completion of OCS, I attended helicopter flight school. Learning to fly certainly had its challenges. The helicopter seemed to have a mind of its own. You have to understand its propensities and be ahead of it at all times. By the time I finished flight school, I had reached the point where I would win on some days and the helicopter would win on others. Over the years I won most of the time, but I never lost respect for the potential of the helicopter winning at a critical moment.

The last weeks at flight school at Fort Rucker were interesting. The Cuban Missile Crisis was underway and the aviation assets at Fort Rucker were put on alert to reposition to Homestead Air Base in South Florida to support a potential US invasion of Cuba. We were the most advanced flight students at Fort Rucker, so each of us was paired with an experienced aviator to fly combat missions in support of any invasion. The seriousness of an all-out war certainly grabbed our attention for a week or so.

In those days there was no Aviation Branch. If there had been an Aviation Branch, I would never have gone to flight school. I was an Infantry Officer and damned proud of it. I was perfectly aligned to the doctrine of the time: you were Infantry first and Aviation was just a skill. I actively sought ground assignments, not for promotional benefit, but to be where I thought I belonged. If I did fly, I wanted to be as close to the troops as possible. I flew slicks instead of gunships or cargo choppers because I wanted to be with troops during assaults, extractions, or medical evacuations. If the skids didn't touch the ground in combat, I wanted nothing to do with it.

My first flight assignment was in South Korea in 1963. I was assigned to the 1st Cavalry Division aviation company as the leader of an infantry brigade aviation section. It was an example of my benefiting from taking on a job others didn't want. This job required me to move up near the DMZ and live with the brigade instead of the cozier quarters at the division airfield. No one else wanted to be there, and I wanted the freedom to operate without the interference of supervision. I jumped at the chance. I spent hours with the Brigade Commander every day, and worked with the S-3 Air when I was not flying. The division was in the early stages of spending millions of dollars to harden the defensive positions south of the DMZ. Each brigade had to complete detailed defensive plans before construction would begin. The Brigade Commander spent weeks walking every inch of the front. I listened and learned. When others were not around, he would drill me on my thoughts and make me justify my rationale. What a great learning environment!

One additional anecdote—When news of the assassination of President Kennedy came down, the Division went on full alert. No one knew if this was part of a larger attack. It was the second time in months that the specter of a world war reared its ugly head. It was estimated that we would be in retrograde operations in short order if the North launched an all out attack. It was a sobering time for all of us. At the end of my tour in Korea, I received a performance review where the endorser, the Aviation Unit Commander, stated that I had the potential to be a general officer. I was a first lieutenant and it was a preposterous, unfounded comment. But I took it seriously, and it positively impacted my future performance. I wish the endorser had been correct.

I returned to Fort Rucker and joined the 31st Infantry Battalion, which was a composite support battalion consisting of a rifle company, artillery battery, aviation company and headquarters company. Command time was so cherished for career development that every fair-haired captain on post stood in line for the jobs. I was assigned as a pilot in the aviation company, but I volunteered for the full-time position of Battalion Maintenance Officer. I knew nothing about vehicle maintenance, but it beat sitting around the dayroom of the aviation company. My performance gained me command of the Headquarters Company as a first lieutenant. After exactly two weeks in command, I received orders to join the 229th Assault Helicopter Battalion, 1st Air Cavalry Division at Fort Benning, Georgia. I assumed the short notice was because of impending deployment, but that information was highly classified. When I arrived two weeks later and reported in at my unit, all unit equipment was packed, and daily convoys were leaving for ports in the Gulf and along the Eastern Seaboard. The night we boarded the troop transport ship, President Johnson addressed the Nation and announced he had ordered deployment of the 1st Air Cavalry Division to Vietnam.

The troop transport moved from the dock in Charleston in the dead of the night. A band played Auld Lang Syne as we drifted away. I thought of World War II with the screaming crowds. This was different. We left without fanfare, and as we all know, we returned the same way. After 17 days of sailing, we anchored off the coast of Vietnam. I stood on deck and wondered what this country had in store for me. After all these years of training how would I perform? Would I lead in time of adversity? Would I make it back? I had no doubts, but I had more questions than answers. By the end of this tour I would have the answers. The next day we moved by convoy and air to our base camp in the Central Highlands.

During my tour, I had two jobs. I flew missions for my aviation company and, whenever the 2nd Battalion, 7th Cavalry Regiment went on operations, I accompanied them and basically functioned as the S-3 Air. I was responsible for coordination and planning of all airmobile operations and support. Again, I benefited because no other aviator wanted to be on the ground for combat operations. Thirty years later I met my Aviation Commander, and he thought I had ill feelings because he assigned me to the dual role. He was relieved that I would not have had it any other way.

In late November 1965, our brigade engaged a multiple division enemy force in what has since been named the Battle of Ia Drang Valley. The 1st Battalion, 7th Cavalry Regiment, led by LTC Hal Moore, assaulted into LZ X-Ray and fought a pitched battle for three days. My unit, the 2nd Battalion, 7th Cavalry, secured a two-battery firebase with primary fire to Moore's battalion. We then performed a night linkup to reinforce Moore. When the 1/7th Battalion returned to brigade reserve, we took control of the landing zone.

The following day, a B-52 strike was scheduled on the mountain that overlooked the valley. To deceive the enemy and hold them in place, we were ordered to move to LZ Albany on foot, a four-hour march through the jungle. A no-fly zone was established prior to the scheduled time for the B-52 strike. This deprived the battalion of scout ships to work our flanks and our route of advance. Normally, we walked artillery fire along the route of advance and had TAC air on cap. All of our normal security measures were compromised to facilitate the B-52 strike. (This was to be the first time a B-52 strike was used in direct support of a ground unit.)

En route, a force estimated at over 900 men ambushed us. Within minutes we were in a pitched battle for our lives. It was a horrendous battle, well-documented in the book *We Were Soldiers Once...and Young*. The result of the compromises in security was that 151 of our troops were killed and 121 wounded out of about 400 on the march. It was to be the highest casualty rate of the entire war in a single battle. Every platoon leader that walked into battle that day was carried out. Most died.

Within 15 minutes, unit integrity was lost and we were engaged in a vicious hand-to-hand battle. I was with the Operations Group; past the kill zone of the ambush. There were ten of us isolated from the main body of the battalion. Within minutes, we were under withering fire from all directions. Our position was not tenable. As we started to withdraw, the firing intensified. Seven soldiers were killed instantly and two were wounded. I moved south with the two wounded until I saw the Recon Platoon trying to set up a defensive position in a tree line. We joined them and took up the fight to hold our position.

The Command Group joined us to bring us to about 40 men. We were unable to employ air or artillery because we feared hitting our own who were now scattered over a large area. Our radios were jammed so there was no radio contact. We had lost command and control of the battalion. We assumed we were the only organized defense. We had been in small battles the first three months in country, but I never fired my rifle in any of them. Now, in five minutes, I went from a walk in the sun to a walk in hell. No firing range could have prepared me for the chaos of exchanging fire at close range. No time to aim; no time to squeeze the round off. This was running and firing. This was more like being the pop up target at the range at Fort Benning versus the person firing at the targets.

We repulsed wave after wave of assaults that night. When there was a lull while the enemy regrouped, we could hear our soldiers still fighting, screaming and dying. We were helpless to come to their aid. The pain was unbearable, and it is still buried deep in me. To a man, we did not expect to make it through the night.

The enemy broke through our lines repeatedly, and ran into the center of the perimeter. We repulsed them, mostly by hand-to-hand combat. We were able to extract our wounded by what amounted to a suicide medevac flight. What is it that takes men who are convinced they will not last the night, and motivates them to get the wounded out at any cost? It takes loyalty and commitment only grunts can understand. Later in the night, we were reinforced by a platoon of 29 men. By the next day the enemy withdrew. For three days, we went through the carnage of the battlefield to recover our wounded and dead.

One of many heroes of this battle was Battalion Surgeon, Captain William Shucart. During the fighting, Captain Shucart gathered the wounded around a large tree and set up a defensive perimeter, manned by the least wounded. He directed the defense and actively engaged in the fighting. During lulls later in the night, he crawled out and brought other wounded to his position, saving them from roaming enemy troops who were executing our wounded as they lay on the battlefield. For his actions, Captain Shucart was awarded the Silver Star.

This battle answered the questions I had about how I would react to combat. I had misjudged the fog and chaos of battle. Everything was turned upside down. I also learned the power of the will to survive. After the battle many of us received medals of various levels handed out by General Westmoreland. It was no honor to stand there and have a ribbon pinned on when I knew 151 families had just had their lives crushed.

I continued to fly whenever I was not out on a ground operation. It was a relief, but I never got the rest the Infantry did, and I was always tired. Funny thing, even after all I had been through in Ia Drang, I found combat assaults as a helicopter pilot to be more emotionally draining. In ground operations, you walked for days without contact, then got into a battle. The battle ends, the adrenaline subsides and peace returns. In combat assaults, you flew into hell, flew out, went back for more troops and went back in again, over and over. The adrenaline was up and down in short bursts. My experiences flying were typical for those of a combat assault pilot. Some times were quiet and other times we lost crews. One day we had a 56-ship combat assault. I took around 20 hits on short final, but no one was hit and the aircraft was operating normally. At 600 feet after takeoff, the engine quit and we ended up in a rice paddy. We were receiving heavy fire from a tree line and took cover behind the paddy dikes. We had to lie there for an hour and watch jets soften things up before a rescue slick came in. Our crew drank a lot of free beer that night.

Toward the end of my tour, the Battalion Commander of 2nd Battalion, 7th Regiment offered me a company command if I extended my tour. I jumped at it, but the Brigade Commander turned it down because I had never served in an Infantry company at any level. I was disappointed, but proud to have been considered.

During the next two years, I attended the Infantry Career Course, commanded a Basic Training Company, was Chief G-3 Training, and completed a second Vietnam tour with an aviation company. The second tour was straight flying, and I hated it because it was flying ARVN units that were not interested in finding, fighting and finishing the enemy. I did have a serious accident when I lost the tail rotor drive shaft while hovering into a parking stall constructed of 55-gallon drums. In a split second the chopper flipped upside down and sent rotor blades and the tail rotor everywhere. Everyone got away uninjured. We were pretty lucky. Pilots will tell you that if you lose the tail rotor in flight, you will probably buy the farm.

I served a short tour at Hunter Army Airfield as Company Commander of a Warrant Officer Candidate Company. Hazing had been going on and I pissed off the Battalion Commander when I quickly put a halt to it, and he had to explain his policies to the Brigade Commander. I left several weeks later with my refusing a review from him and his refusing to write one. I wanted to go to war with him, and he wanted to end his career on an up note. We agreed to a stalemate. I was glad to depart for nine months at the University of Omaha for degree completion. (I finally got my college degree.)

The next three years at Fort Riley, Kansas were the most rewarding of my career. I had the honor to serve in a brigade commanded by the greatest leader I knew in my career–Colonel Richard Cavazos. What a soldier!! He earned the Distinguished Service Cross in Korea and again in Vietnam while commanding 1st Battalion, 18th Infantry. Cavazos later retired as the first Mexican American to attain the rank of four-star general.

I was assigned as the S-3 of the same 1st Battalion, 18th Infantry under LTC James Tucker, who had been the S-3 for Cavazos in Vietnam. Tucker was bigger than life! He was a warrior. He had just left command of the Florida Ranger Camp, and was driven to make his battalion the most combat ready in the Army. The atmosphere was dynamic. Everything flowed through the S-3 and I loved it. It just didn't get any better than working with him. I maxed out on my review like most of us did at that time in the Army, but my endorser, Colonel Cavazos went a step further with my second comment about being a general officer. Again, I was smart enough to know that was not possible, but it is a compliment I have cherished since then. It was a step below God telling me I was a good Christian.

After a year and a half as S-3, I took over as Chief of the G-3 Operations for the Big Red One. During my tenure, the Division trained for and deployed to Germany, where we drew mothballed equipment, conducted a graded Corps field training exercise, qualified in all weapons and redeployed back to Fort Riley. That was a real test for G-3 Operations and G-3 Plans. We did well.

The Division also had responsibility for execution of the State funeral for former President Harry Truman. It was an elaborate plan, with several thousand pages covering everything imaginable. I was the owner of the plan and the person who would execute it if President Truman died. All of my predecessors for two decades hoped they were gone when it had to be executed. It was complex to say the least. Periodically, we visited with President Truman to review the plan that he had signed off on. I had the privilege of attending a coordination meeting with President Truman in his library. Six months later we had a division commander change of command. Three days thereafter, word came that President Truman had been hospitalized in critical condition. The new CG came into my office to see the plan. He took one look at the volume of the book, handed it back to me and said, "My career is in your hands. Execute the plan and let me know if you need anything." Fortunately, Margaret Truman, the President's daughter, interceded and decided to have a private family funeral. Department of State lobbied for a State funeral because of President Truman's impact on post-World War II recovery. She wavered some, but after years of planning we had nothing to execute.

Command & General Staff College was bittersweet. I enjoyed the experience, but left a marriage behind in the middle of the program. My career was still on course. Tom Vaughn was an Infantry Branch Assignments Officer while I was in school. I am sure he influenced my being offered assignment to Infantry Branch in Washington. I was on a cloud for about a month until General Abrams ordered a reduction of forces in Washington. Vacancies were to be filled from within. Tom called me with the news. By now my classmates had filled the attractive jobs, and I was offered reserve component duty, Infantry instruction at any career course, recruiting command in Cincinnati, or ROTC. I ended up at Kent State ROTC four years after the four students were killed and the ROTC building was burned down, events which shocked the nation. I was coming off a high at Fort Riley and this was going in the wrong direction.

Early in my career I had decided I would stay in the Army until I was no longer in the mainstream. I had seen too many full Colonels sitting at the Officers Club drinking on a Saturday afternoon, and I was never going to be one of them. I had a career until I got the ROTC assignment, and now I just had a job.

So, the circle was complete. I started at Kent State and now I would end my career there. I was upset, but not as much as the Colonel also assigned there. He had stars in his eyes, and had just finished with the War College. He retired in two years, and I took over the program. The challenge at Kent State was rejuvenating ROTC after the events of 1970. The year before we got there, the program only commissioned three officers. By the time I left, we had 500 students in the program and we were commissioning over 25 each year. Toward the end of my career, I was in a contest with my branch officer who sent me orders to Germany. I won the battle and retired in May 1980 with 21 years.

I was offered a retirement ceremony as part of the Fort Knox monthly ceremony. I had not served there, knew no one there, and had no desire to be the unknown retiree. I drove from Kent to Fort Knox and went through out-processing. A sergeant walked me through the paperwork, completed a new ID and said, "Goodbye." Before getting into my car, I removed all insignia, medals and the nametag from my uniform, and tossed the top into the trash. I didn't do that out of disrespect; it was just a rite of passage, a statement that part of my life was over.

I pulled my shirt out of my trousers, and settled into my car for the journey home. I was on the Interstate for a brief time when a State Trooper lit me up for going over 90 in a 65 zone. As I pulled over my mind raced for a great story. I got out of my car and walked back toward the cruiser. (You couldn't do that today.) State Troopers around Fort Knox are used to dealing with offenders from Post, and are keenly aware of appearance standards. He approached me with the statement, "Little out of uniform, soldier." I informed him that 21 years ago I arrived by bus at Fort Knox to begin Basic Training. I went through OCS and today I finished my career and was heading home. He asked if I had served in Vietnam, and I told him two tours. He said, "After everything you have been through, don't you deserve to arrive home alive?" He handed my license back, gave me a little salute and said, "Thanks for your service, Sir." Alongside the Interstate I had just had my retirement ceremony!

Would you like fries with that?

Immediately after retirement I took a position with a small, seven-branch bank in Kent, Ohio. The bank president was the sole owner of the bank and I was hired as VP of Operations and Commercial Loans. It was a great title, but you don't make money in banking unless you have an ownership position.

I was concerned about not relocating to Atlanta to be near my three beautiful children by taking this position. I sent out resumes to every conceivable entity in Atlanta, and only the regional office for McDonald's interviewed me. They offered me their version of a fast track program into middle management. They were impressed with my background, but also concerned that I might not be successful unless I could lose my military leadership style. I was seeking an operations position, and NO ONE moves to middle management operations in McDonald's without working their way through the restaurants and out-performing everyone else. I accepted the position with the thought that once I got to Atlanta, I would aggressively pursue employment more in line with my qualifications. There was no way I was going to go from being a lieutenant colonel to running the fry station at a McDonald's.

I started out as a manager trainee, worked 14 hours a day and had my first day off after 37 days. My job search was on hold, as I was kept too busy to do anything except work and sleep. I threw myself into learning. I read manuals on the drive down the interstate to my restaurant. After work ended, I went to another restaurant so I would be left alone to study more or to perfect some aspect of operations. After nine months I was promoted to Manager of my own restaurant. Running a restaurant is close to combat. The unexpected always happens, and emergencies are the normal. Nothing gets fixed and stays fixed. Your plan for the day is valid for a very short time before the operation turns you in different directions. You fight to stay above the battle and anticipate versus reacting. I found myself loving the chaos, and I found out that no change in leadership style was needed. My little secret I never shared was that my past culture was the same as the corporate culture of McDonald's. Two years after joining the company, I was promoted to middle management and given responsibility for five restaurants. I also was awarded the

President's Award, which was like a Legion of Merit with $25,000 dollars thrown in. My financial goal was to be earning more than I had when I retired. I reached that goal with the promotion to middle management. I also had committed to McDonald's as a second career.

In ten years, I was promoted to Regional Manager. McDonald's is a highly decentralized corporation. Regional Managers present an annual plan for people, profit, sales, and development of new restaurants. Once approved by top management, they are left alone to execute and achieve the results promised. My region covered two states and over 450 restaurants.

Later, I was promoted to the corporate headquarters outside of Chicago. The experience was similar to promotion to the Pentagon. People with broad knowledge were pigeonholed into a narrow responsibility. Along with four others, I was responsible for operations development for the domestic market. We were the functional experts for the system, and had total freedom to be creative. An example would be doing in-depth on-site studies of the best restaurants in the country in order to create a *Best Practices Road Map* for other restaurants to follow. Because Australia was considered to run the best operations in the world, we expanded the study and took our team there to do a parallel study. We combined the two studies and delivered the *Best Practices Road Map* to 25,000 restaurants. I enjoyed the opportunity to improve the McDonald's brand.

McDonald's was changing during this time and we were shifting from the concept of a dynamic leader moving the ball down the field to a consensus team approach where everyone was equal and limited to his or her specialty. The meetings drove me crazy and the results were never the best, only a compromise result. The fun had gone out of the balloon and I chose to retire at age 59.

Prep School gave me the base to qualify for OCS. OCS prepared me to gain leadership and management experience in the Army. The Army gave me the experience to excel at McDonald's. McDonald's was a great second career and made me financially secure for life. My careers are neatly tied together.

I have been retired since 1999 and I long to saddle up one more time and take on a challenge. The best recent offer has been as a Walmart Greeter.

Isn't this a unique country? God Bless America!

Lieutenant Colonel (Retired) Ken Weitzel and Companion Cocobama, September 2010, Jacksonville, FL. "Life doesn't get any better!"

Captain (later Lieutenant Colonel) Dick White receiving Silver Star,
Bronze Star for Valor, Vietnamese Cross of Gallantry, and Staff
Honor Medal from Major General Pepke, 4th Infantry Division
Commanding General, upon his departure from Vietnam.

The Early Days

It was a mere oversight on the part of my father, a lieutenant colonel on
the faculty and staff at West Point, that I came to be born in Orange,
New Jersey on February 17, 1942, rather than the more-prestigious,
much-thought-out and pre-planned locale of choice, West Point. By
oversight, I mean the snowstorm and cocktail party that night clearly
provided a legitimate excuse for not racing home to pick up my mother
in Maplewood, New Jersey once he got "the call." However, I was
baptized at the Cadet Chapel at West Point, and we lived in quarters at
the academy during World War II.

A West Point graduate, yet not commissioned by the Army after
an injury due to a fall from a horse, my father was given a disability
discharge. He entered the New York National Guard and was shortly

thereafter recruited by the President of General Motors, whom he had met at a classmate's wedding. When World War II broke out, he was recalled to active duty on the staff and faculty at West Point as a lieutenant colonel, US Army Reserve. Once the war ended, his contacts at GM were gone and jobs were scarce, but the Army offered him a Regular Army commission as a major in the Quartermaster Corps, where his disability wouldn't have an impact on assignments. A brutal aside is that all of his classmates who were commissioned as artillery officers, as he would have been, wound up on the Bataan Death March.

Being an Army brat, an education in itself, my early school years were, in retrospect, a colorful escapade of travel and adventure, with an appropriate amount of mischief sprinkled throughout. I spent first and second grades in Giessen, Germany, where my father was stationed immediately after the war. I became an accomplished horseman under the tutelage of Frau Fran Vogt, a pre-war European champion. From Germany, we were transferred to Fort Lee, VA. At Robert E. Lee Elementary in third grade, I was reprimanded and instructed to wear only long sleeves. Who knew ink tattoos drawn on me by my father would wreak such disapproval by the principal? On to Syracuse, New York where my father earned his MBA in the Army Comptroller Program and I attended sixth grade, learned to ice skate and played Little League baseball. Then we were stationed in Japan where my dad was a comptroller for Army Forces Far East Headquarters staff. That is where I began my junior high and high school years. We were stationed at Camp Zama and Camp Kobe from 1955 to 1957.

I can still hear the American rock 'n roll being belted out by the Japanese boys at The Gekko, a local club where they reveled in our applause not only as enjoyment, but as approval as they mimicked everyone from Bill Haley and the Comets to Elvis Presley, without skipping a beat or a lyric, even with the language barrier. I recall a night where the sign read "Pot Boone Style Music," and unfortunate misspelling aside, they nailed that too as we cheered them on, twisting and shouting. There was my steady girl and prom date from the Canadian Academy, a German gal called Skeeter, and my Turkish pal and partner in crime, Rhoul. We rode in chauffeured cars to school dances or cheap cab rides downtown if we couldn't get a ride from an enlisted soldier or airman.

I finished seventh grade there at Zama Junior High and during the summer worked as a lifeguard at the base pool. I also played and lettered in basketball and played on the Pony League baseball team for the Yokohama Engineering Depot Yankees, where we won the Japan World Series. Zama being the Army Forces Far East HQ, we had great sports teams because of the draft. The post commander ensured that all incoming personnel to the Far East were screened for athletic ability. Consequently, we had on our football team seven All-Americans, including All-Pro Art Hunter, and on our basketball team, Ralph Beard, a three-time Kentucky All-American and Olympic team member who went on to consecutively make the "Best Ever" teams. Ralph presented me with my Zama Junior High letter.

My freshman year at Yokohama High, I played junior varsity basketball, and was president of my freshman class. Later, Dad got orders to Kobe, Japan where I would attend Kyoto American High School. I was immediately recruited to varsity basketball on an inflated description of my ability from my former coach. I was 6'3" by then, and we only had nine guys! I thought I had the good fortune of not having to take Latin class, as it wasn't offered there, but no such luck. The principal happened to love it and insisted we meet an hour each day in her office for instruction. Fortunately she was very nice and good looking to boot, and my college board exams benefited from her personal instruction.

In 1957, we returned to the 'States and lived at Fort Lee, Virginia in just-completed quarters. I attended Prince George High School my sophomore and junior years. It was a county school with students from Fort Lee and Prince George farm kids. I was elected vice-president of the school and lettered in football, basketball, and track. Summers, I was a lifeguard at the Fort Lee Officers' Club. The other lifeguards were college athletes, and the recently graduated lieutenants included us in their parties on the grass terrace of the club. Many of the local college girls and town girls came to the parties. Life was good there.

The beginning of my senior year, my dad was transferred to Fort Ord, where I attended Monterey High School. Because it was late in the football season and I had low grades after transferring, I was kept out of sports, so I could concentrate on my grades and my dream of going to West Point. It was tempting to stay on the Monterey peninsula and attend college there, but my dad had other plans. He took me to the Oakland recruiting station and swore me in. I immediately went back to Fort Ord for basic training, where I completed five weeks, to include weapons qualification. I was pulled out of basic and sent to the USMA Preparatory School at Fort Belvoir, VA. There, we were taught math and English by Ph.D. civilians in preparation for college board exams. Although I scored high enough on the college boards, I was not accepted at West Point. Classmates of my father on the academic board said that my low high school grades overrode my college board scores for acceptance.

I was immediately sent to the post replacement company and then given orders to the 3rd Infantry (the Old Guard) at Fort Meyer. After being interviewed by the Honor Guard Commander and expressing my desire to go to OCS, I was sent to A Company, 3rd Infantry at Fort McNair. Upon arrival there, A Company First Sergeant Darling handed me the application for OCS and told me to fill it out. A Company's duties included retirement parades, airport and street cordons for President Kennedy, and covering special events and ceremonies in the Washington, DC area.

First Sergeant Darling was promoted to sergeant major, and became the Sergeant Major of Fort Meyer, with prep school classmate, Ken Weitzel as his company clerk. One of the Sergeant Major's first orders to Ken was to write up orders for an OCS Board, before which we would both appear. We were selected to attend infantry OCS starting in October 1961.

After I was selected, the Company Commander called me in and said that he had a requirement for a lifeguard at the post, and since I was lifeguard qualified I could have the job, if I could assure him that I could stay away from the under eighteen-year-old girls. I said, "I can do it, Sir!" It was a great job and a nice break before starting OCS.

Once I got to Fort Benning and started OCS, I realized I was great at the drill and ceremonies but sadly lacking when it came to tactics. But many of my classmates, particularly Tom Vaughn, were able to bring me up to speed on tactics and leadership techniques. Tom adopted Ken Weitzel and me, and helped us through the initial tough weeks. Because of my Old Guard experience, I was selected as the Blue Day Company Guidon Bearer. Our class was a balanced mix of experienced sergeants, college graduates, and a couple of young soldiers like me. We quickly came together as a high-performing team and earned our gold bars. My dad was able to attend our graduation. The Major General who spoke at graduation and presented our gold bars was a classmate of my dad's at West Point. After graduation, my dad took me straight to the Fort Benning Officers' Club to celebrate.

I went straight to Airborne School and Ranger School. I was the outstanding Ranger student in the Benning phase of Ranger School. I also thought I was going to be recycled because of an ankle injury on the final obstacle course, but was saved by a new technique involving an ace bandage and calamine lotion, which immobilized my ankle but still allowed me to wear boots and continue my training in the mountains and the swamps. After graduation I headed for leave in California; then on to Korea.

In Korea, I was assigned to the 1st Battle Group, 31st Infantry, 7th Infantry Division. The current members of the unit were part of a special unit from Fort Riley, KS, and were due to depart within thirty days of each other. Captain Bob Meese, a Ranger School buddy, was the new S-3 and he recommended me as a company commander. I was given A Company. Fortunately my First Sergeant and Platoon Sergeants were experienced war veterans and supported their brand-spanking new Second Lieutenant. A couple of months later, I was replaced by a senior captain and became the unit S-2. During my time there I also served as Recon Platoon Leader and was selected as an instructor in the Division Counterguerilla Warfare School because of my Ranger qualifications. There were many exciting situations since all of our demolitions were live and once they were placed, I had to move them so that they didn't blow up the actual targets (e.g. railroad tracks). I carried live ammo as there were instances of North Koreans infiltrating the area. Fortunately, the need for that never occurred.

After completing my tour in Korea, I was assigned to the 101st

Airborne Division, in the 1st Battle Group of the 327th Infantry, where I was the Recon Platoon Leader and later the Headquarters Company XO. When we reorganized, I was the S-2 of the 2nd Battalion/327th Infantry. Major exercises included jumping into Iran as a show of force to the USSR, and Desert Strike, the largest peacetime exercise since WWII. I was air landed into an unimproved airstrip in the California desert, where I was responsible for all the Davy Crockett equipment and documents.

Two months later, I processed out of the Army to attend UCLA, where I majored in political science and international relations. For income, I was a coach at the Psychology Clinic School, gave swimming lessons on the side, worked as a part-time bartender in the beach town of Playa del Ray, and worked as an extra in the movies because my stepfather was able to get me into the Screen Extras Guild. I was a regular on the TV show *Hogan's Heroes*, and worked on *Batman*, *McHale's Navy*, and *Blue Light*, and appeared as an extra in many movies. The ones that stand out in my memory are *Tobruk, Beau Geste, Happiest Millionaire* and *First to Fight*. Some of the stars I worked with were Natalie Wood, Adam West, Peter Falk, and Geraldine Page. It was an exciting time in Los Angeles, and I enjoyed being in the thick of things, the buzz and drama of casting calls and after-theatre parties. During this time I was also in the Reserves where I was XO, HHC , 311th Logistics Command.

In 1967 the Reserve Senior Advisor said, "The Army is looking for you as a Vietnam volunteer." He was an infantry officer and I was the only Airborne Ranger in the command. It didn't take me long to decide that that was where I needed to be.

Soon after volunteering for Vietnam, I commanded a basic training company at Fort Polk, LA in order to get a sense of the current soldiers and to qualify personally on all of the new weapons; M16, etc. that had changed in the three years I had been in the Reserves. I then went on my pre-deployment leave during which my older daughter, Doree, was born at UCLA Hospital. (She is now a sergeant with the Los Angeles Sheriffs Department.) After leave, I departed for Vietnam from Travis AFB on a Continental 707. During a short stopover in Hawaii, my father, now an Army colonel serving as CINCPAC Comptroller, met me with friends and drinks to wish me good luck and a safe return.

My first view of Vietnam was from a dive of 30,000 feet into the Saigon airport, since Tet '68, was in full swing. After being issued basic combat gear, I left immediately for Pleiku and the 4th Division. I spent a day getting assigned to the 1/22nd Infantry, and being issued my combat gear and weapon. I received no orientation or acclimation before going to my unit because of the Tet situation. The Battalion Commander welcomed me and handed me a drink, just before bestowing upon me command of Charlie Company, which had just lost its company commander in battle. I realized he had jumped me ahead of three captains who were waiting for a company command. I was sort of flattered, I guess. I asked him if they would be disappointed, and he put his arm around me rubbing my Ranger Tab, and said he didn't give a shit. I was his man for the job! I thanked him and had another drink.

The next morning, I left by chopper to meet my new company at Kontum airfield. The pilots wished me good luck. After a thirty-minute wait alone, my company arrived by helicopter from the nearby mountains where they had been fighting. A very ragged but happy lieutenant greeted me with a salute, a handshake and said, "She's all yours, sir." We then secured some old French bombed-out buildings for an overnight stay, providing some security for the airfield.

The next day we moved to a blocking position to provide security for an artillery battery on a Vietnamese firing range where I got to know my men. They were combat-hardened and happy to have survived Tet. I was blessed with good platoon leaders and NCOs including First Sergeant "Pappy" Ledford, World War II vet and Ranger Mountain Camp instructor. From then on, no matter how intense the combat situation, he always had coffee made and moved amongst our positions checking and encouraging the men. After one particular battle, I put him in for a Bronze Star Medal for Valor, which the CG presented to him. He came to me with tears in his eyes and thanked me, saying that he had been put in for two Silver Stars during WWII and didn't get them because the Company Commander was killed and the paperwork lost. He was always an inspiration to the men and to me. After Tet, throughout my six-month command, we were given special missions, assisting Special Forces, leading Montagnard units and reinforcing other 4th Division units under siege in the Central Highlands and in the tri-border area.

On one mission to seize and destroy an NVA artillery unit, Sean Flynn, a TV news journalist and son of actor Errol Flynn, accompanied us. I knew this meant that higher headquarters thought the intelligence was valid, and Flynn thought the action would get national TV attention. He was as good-looking as his famous father, and had custom-made jungle fatigues and equipment. The first night I had to admonish him for smoking a joint, but other than that he was savvy about military discipline. He demonstrated his experience the next morning when he pointed out bark rubbings on some of the trees that came from elephants. A little further on, he verified it by pointing out a pile of elephant turds. I told him I was relieved by his knowledge, since if the turds had been human, I would have asked for reinforcements because it would have meant giant NVA. Sadly, a month later, he was last seen going into Laos in a jeep. Just last year his body was found. He had been killed by the enemy.

After my six months company command time, I was slated to take over the Division Long Range Recon Patrol. However, a radio message for me at battalion asked if I wanted to be the Commanding General's Senior Aide de Camp. My response was that I did want to be considered. I was then told that was not the question; it was, "Will you take the job?" For the remainder of my tour I served as the Aide de Camp to General. Charles P. Stone, and then General Don Pepke. Both had received Regular Army commissions from ROTC, and came out of WWII as Colonels. General Stone completed WWII as the Chief of Staff for the 1st Infantry Division, and General Pepke was the youngest Regimental Commander in the Pacific. Both were outstanding commanders and were respected by the men of the 4th Infantry Division.

In spite of the dangers and seriousness of the war, there were some fun moments. I escorted Tippi Hedren and Joey Bishop on a wild helicopter ride low-level flying over old enemy bunkers when they came to visit the troops. When I was sent to escort Gypsy Rose Lee to the General's office, she invited me into her guest trailer, partially dressed. Comedian Martha Raye came to visit, escorted by Special Forces personnel. You could tell that she was enamored by her escorts, as she wore a green beret and a full Special Forces uniform, and referred to the 4th as "legs."

As the Aide, I met and sat in on discussions with many interesting, high-level people, including the CINCPAC, Admiral McCain; General Abrams; South Vietnam President Theiu and Vice-President Ky; and numerous high-level officers from allied countries serving in Vietnam. Other highlights were visiting the Vietnamese Military Academy, having lunch with the Captain of the Battleship New Jersey, and being made a member of the Pleiku Elephant Riding Society. Upon departure, I was awarded the Silver Star, Bronze Star with V for Valor and Oak Leaf Cluster, four Air Medals, the Army Commendation Medal for Valor, Vietnamese Gallantry Cross, and Staff Honor Medal.

Following Vietnam, I was Chief Instructor at the Florida Ranger Camp, Eglin AFB, where my second daughter, Toby, was born in 1970. (She is now a published writer living in Valencia, CA.) I had ten gung ho captains and ten senior NCOs, all combat veterans. In 1972 I was selected to attend the Infantry Officer Advanced Course at Fort Benning. Near graduation, we received our next orders; the 25th Infantry Division, Hawaii.

In Hawaii, my assignments included C Company Commander, 1st Battalion/5th Infantry, S-3 Operations and Training Officer, 1stBattalion/ 5th Infantry, and Assistant G-3 (General Staff Operations and Training). I completed my B.S. from Chaminade University, while we raised two beach babies who enjoyed island living, including pool and family time with my father and stepmom, who by then lived in nearby Kailua.

About the time I was due orders, OCS classmate Major Richards, Assistant G-1, asked me if I would like to stay in Hawaii for another assignment. Who wouldn't? "What is it?" I asked. He responded, "I can see that you get nominated for the Assistant IG position at HQ, US Army, Hawaii, at Fort Shafter." I got to travel around to all the bases in the Pacific under the Army command. Those were great years! On my departure, I was awarded the Meritorious Service Medal and had completed my M.B.A at Pepperdine University.

From there, I went to the Command and General Staff College at Fort Leavenworth, KS. While there, I was nominated to attend the US Army Organizational Effectiveness School at Fort Ord, California, where I was to remain on the staff and faculty. My primary responsibilities were working with battle staffs to improve their combat effectiveness and to teach those techniques to Organizational Effectiveness students going through the school. I also did consulting with battalion staffs at the Combined Arms Tactical Training Simulation Center at Fort Leavenworth, KS.

From 1980 to 1984, I enjoyed living on the base at the prestigious, picturesque, and historic Presidio, in the heart of San Francisco, as a Deputy Senior Advisor to the 91st Training Division, and Chief, Combat Arms Group. There, I got involved with the Big Sisters program, throwing one of their biggest events in history (for which I took sole credit, even though 90% was most likely due to the fact that the Presidio was the only venue in town that had sufficient parking). I thoroughly enjoyed life in "the city," with its cultural diversity and many activities. I spent quality time with my two daughters, and enjoyed all of the great food and even better nightlife. During this time, I was an avid runner and recruited anyone with Nikes and an adventurous streak to join me in the now infamous Bay to Breakers race.

Civilian Life

I retired in April 1984 as a lieutenant colonel, after being recruited by Lockheed Aeronautical Systems in Burbank, California. I worked there until 1989, while I completed course work for my Ph.D. at Golden Gate University. My time at Lockheed not only broadened my scope of experience, but narrowed my focus back onto matters of the heart, as it brought me to my lovely wife, Cheryl.

In 1989, we relocated to Merritt Island, Florida where I launched my consulting firm, R.A. White & Associates, providing strategic application of business planning, proposal development, and management training for clients, including McDonnell Douglas, Rockwell International and the City of Melbourne. In addition, I managed a Small Business Innovation Research grant for the US Army Research Institute of the Behavioral and Social Sciences, examining the identification and prediction of performance measurement traits in combat personnel. My interviews included Iraq war veterans at Fort Stewart, Fort Benning and Kuwait. I found this work rewarding in that it combined both my military and management expertise.

Today, we share a quiet, yet abundant life in beautiful Marietta, Georgia. Our family includes our four daughters (we have two each), and eight grandchildren living in Georgia and California. We also have a golden retriever and a yellow lab that provide constant entertainment and companionship. We enjoy attending, volunteering and sharing good times with our extended family at St. James Episcopal Church; community arts and events; and entertaining friends and family.

I am proud to be a "Boy of Benning" and to have this rare opportunity to revisit as well as share slices of my life, most of which were shaped by my experiences serving my country with the men with whom I went into battle, answered to, wept for, stood by, commanded, and consoled.

Lieutenant Colonel (retired) Dick White with wife Cheryl, daughter Toby, and grandson Dane in Marietta, GA, November 2012.

Epilogue

My wife Zia (Lieutenant Colonel, USAR, retired) and I have had the honor of serving as co-editors for the foregoing chapters. In fulfilling our editorial responsibilities, we have tried to limit our editing to spelling, punctuation and grammar, leaving the various writing styles and prose intact insofar as practical. Along the way, we have encountered commonalities and life lessons in the stories of my classmates.

First and foremost, there is a common thread of advancement above beginnings; if not from rags to riches, at least from what would be considered below "poverty level" today to very successful lives. The epitome of this concept may be found in the story of Rudy Baker, the first of our graduates' chapters. Rudy began life in a one-room wooden sharecropper's shack, with no glass windows, running water or indoor toilet. The first shower he ever had was in Army Basic Training. He had a high school education from what was essentially a country school. Rudy finished his military career as a Regular Army full colonel with a master's degree, and followed that with a successful career in banking, rising from management trainee to senior bank executive and chairmanship on a number of important boards.

Another good example may be found in Ken Weitzel's story, the next-to-last of our graduates' chapters. Following a very successful military career, Ken took a job as a management trainee with McDonald's, flipping burgers along with all the new employees. From lieutenant colonel to burger cook, it was not a job he wanted. He took it because it was the only thing available near his children. From flipping burgers,

Ken went on to become a McDonald's Regional Manager with authority over 450 restaurants and eventual promotion to corporate executive.

There is a lesson here for many today who bemoan the lack of appropriate jobs befitting their educations and intellects. Every manager at any level in McDonald's starts out flipping burgers.

A second common thread is patriotism; not flag waving, but dedication to duty, honor, and country. All but two of our authors served in Vietnam, most having multiple tours. Many were wounded, some several times, and then went back for more. I don't know anyone who served in time of war because of a love of battle. They served because their country called upon them to do so. Every one of our graduates had the opportunity to avoid further combat by leaving the service when his obligation was met. Most stayed in through repetitive combat assignments, many of which were voluntary.

A third common element in these stories is gratitude. Not one of our authors expected or asked for the gratitude of his countrymen who stayed safely at home when these men went to war. Instead, they expressed gratitude for the opportunities to serve their country, and for the successful lives that followed.

That includes gratitude that we were born in a country that rewards effort and service. The United States does not demand service, though I believe it should, but it recognizes and rewards service. Far fewer young people today would be concerned about lack of opportunities for advancement, if they were not blind to the opportunities for service. For all its faults, the United States still offers the best opportunity for advancement through service of any country in the world. I thank God we were born in the United States. That was a stroke of luck for which we cannot take any credit. Having had the good fortune to be born in the best country in the world, we did not need any additional advantage. After that, even for a poorly educated Mississippi country boy, or a North Carolina share cropper, everything else was possible.

It has been a pleasure to work with my fellow graduates on these, their life stories. It was a privilege to be one of their number.

WILLIAM D. (DAN) TELFAIR
LIEUTENANT COLONEL, US ARMY (RETIRED)
CO-EDITOR
THE BOYS OF BENNING

About the Editors

Dan Telfair spent twenty-four years on active duty in the Army, three years of which were in South East Asia, and retired as a lieutenant colonel, Regular Army. Zia Telfair spent eight years on active duty in the Army, and retired from the Army Reserve as a lieutenant colonel. Dan and Zia are spending their retirement years in Albuquerque, New Mexico, where they are both very active in volunteer and charitable organizations.

Thomas B. Vaughn spent over thirty years on active duty, including two tours in Vietnam and one in the Pentagon. He retired as a Regular Army colonel at Fort Campbell, KY in 1988. Since then he has been a radio personality, college teacher, newspaper columnist, political consultant, public speaker, songwriter, and music publisher. Tom and wife Betty now live near Rock Island, Tennessee, where they enjoy their family, friends, and volunteer work with the Tennessee Fisher House Foundation.

58163103R00171

Made in the USA
Lexington, KY
04 December 2016